Regulating Risk

When governments impose stringent regulations that impede domestic competition and international trade, should we conclude that this is a deliberate attempt to protect industry or an honest effort to protect the population? *Regulating Risk* offers a third possibility: that these regulations reflect producers' ability to exploit private information. Combining extensive data and qualitative evidence from the pesticide, pharmaceutical, and chemical sectors, the book demonstrates how companies have leveraged product safety information to win stricter standards on less profitable products for which they offer a more profitable alternative. Companies have additionally supported regulatory institutions that, while intended to protect the public, also help companies use information to eliminate less profitable products more systematically, creating barriers to commerce that disproportionally disadvantage developing countries. These dynamics play out not only domestically but also internationally, under organizations charged with providing objective regulatory recommendations. The result has been the global legitimization of biased regulatory rules.

Rebecca L. Perlman is an assistant professor of politics and international affairs at Princeton University. Her research has been published in the *American Journal of Political Science*, *Science Advances*, *Comparative Political Studies*, *International Studies Quarterly*, and the *Journal of Legal Analysis*. She has a Ph.D. from Stanford and a master's from the Fletcher School at Tufts. Her undergraduate degree is from Princeton, where she graduated summa cum laude and phi beta kappa.

Regulating Risk

How Private Information Shapes Global Safety Standards

REBECCA L. PERLMAN

Princeton University

CAMBRIDGE
UNIVERSITY PRESS

CAMBRIDGE
UNIVERSITY PRESS

Shaftesbury Road, Cambridge CB2 8EA, United Kingdom

One Liberty Plaza, 20th Floor, New York, NY 10006, USA

477 Williamstown Road, Port Melbourne, VIC 3207, Australia

314–321, 3rd Floor, Plot 3, Splendor Forum, Jasola District Centre, New Delhi – 110025, India

103 Penang Road, #05–06/07, Visioncrest Commercial, Singapore 238467

Cambridge University Press is part of Cambridge University Press & Assessment, a department of the University of Cambridge.

We share the University's mission to contribute to society through the pursuit of education, learning and research at the highest international levels of excellence.

www.cambridge.org
Information on this title: www.cambridge.org/9781009291927

DOI: 10.1017/9781009291880

First published 2023

A catalogue record for this publication is available from the British Library

A Cataloging-in-Publication data record for this book is available from the Library of Congress

ISBN 978-1-009-29192-7 Hardback

Contents

Figures

Tables

Acknowledgments

I first began work on this project during the third year of my graduate studies at Stanford University. At the time, I could hardly conceive of turning the project into a completed dissertation, let alone successfully publishing it. As I developed the project from a half-formed idea into a paper, a dissertation, and now a book, I benefited immensely from the help of many along the way.

My dissertation chair, Judy Goldstein, dedicated untold hours to talking through ideas, reading drafts, and providing comments. She helped me focus on the bigger picture, and she never hesitated to provide the honest feedback that was necessary to take the work to the next level. I can only aspire to become the sort of mentor to my own students that Judy has been to me. The other members of my committee similarly played key roles in helping me make the project what it is. Mike Tomz pushed me to always go one step further in my analysis, and he gave me the confidence to pursue a project that didn't necessarily fit neatly into a box. Terry Moe convinced me to seek out some of the qualitative evidence I otherwise might have ignored and that, in the end, proved to be a key piece of the story. Steve Haber not only assigned the paper that first inspired my interest in this topic, back in my first year of graduate studies, but he consistently challenged me to hold the project to the highest standard. Finally, my outside chair, Alan Sykes, provided my initial foray into the publication process, while also always offering a willing ear and supportive word as my own work evolved.

My fellow Stanford graduate students and friends – Kerry Persen, Jane Esberg, Alex Blackman, Dan Thompson, Elisabeth van Lieshout, Zuhad Hai, Sung Mi Kim, Julia Payson, and Eric Min – served as sounding boards, draft readers, and commiserators along the way, while Øystein Daljord convinced me over lunch one day to abandon my first idea for a dissertation and instead seek out a project that would truly bring me joy. I wish he were still here to see how his advice ignited the spark that resulted in this book. Also, to my friend and longtime mentor John Ruggie, who not only convinced me to pursue graduate studies in the first place but also offered guidance on this project throughout the years: I will miss our chats on your porch and over family dinners. Thank you for all you have done for me and all you did for the world.

I have also been lucky to receive exceptional advice and feedback from numerous scholars both at Stanford and elsewhere over the years. I am particularly grateful to Ken Scheve, Avi Acharya, Jim Fearon, Clayton Nall, Justin Grimmer, Ken Oye, Allison Carnegie, Amanda Kennard, and Bobby Gulotty for their time and helpful suggestions. In addition, the project owes a great deal to the workshop participants who, through their questions or comments, inspired me to seek out additional evidence or revisit the evidence I had. I am grateful to audiences at APSA, IPES, and MPSA as well as workshop participants at Stanford, CDDRL, Princeton, Columbia, CU Boulder, the University of Pittsburgh, MIT, Yale, UCLA, and Berkeley. I am also extremely appreciative of the financial support from Stanford's Graduate Research Opportunity Grant, Stanford's Europe Center Grant, and the Horowitz Foundation for Social Policy Grant, without which I could not have done this research. I am similarly grateful for Stanford's Political Science Graduate Student Fellowship, the IRiSS Dissertation Fellowship, the CDDRL Pre-doctoral Fellowship, and the W. Glenn Campbell and Rita Ricardo-Campbell National Fellowship, all of which gave me the resources to dedicate my full time and attention to this work.

Since starting my assistant professorship at Princeton, I have been particularly fortunate to be surrounded by invested colleagues, who have helped me see the book through its final stages. Jim Vreeland has been a steadfast supporter, not only contributing comments on chapters and proposals but also offering broader advice on the publication process. Helen Milner and Andy Moravcsik have similarly taken the time to give detailed suggestions, both on the content of the project and also on the presentation. Melissa Lee has patiently fielded question after question, day after day, offering insight into how to wade through the publication process and also how to navigate every other step along the way. Finally, while at Princeton, I was able to enlist the help of two fantastic research assistants: Sayumi Miyano saved me countless hours of work scraping data and doing a far better job at it than I ever could, while Elena Evnin gamely dove into the technical side of commercial aircraft regulations in order to provide background knowledge and regulatory documents.

Despite being in the midst of a global pandemic during the final years working on this project, I was very fortunate to still be able to hold a book workshop, albeit a remote one. The book benefited enormously from the feedback I received over our marathon January Zoom session. I am thankful to Judy Goldstein for keeping everyone on topic and on time and to Andy Moravcsik for his eagerness to join in and his ability to help summarize some of the big picture takeaways after the fact. Most of all, I am enormously grateful to Dan Drezner, Peter Rosendorff, Tim Büthe, Duncan Snidal, and Dan Carpenter for engaging with their chapters so thoroughly and for offering additional feedback throughout the day of the workshop. The feedback they gave allowed me to reconceptualize, broaden, and deepen the book in substantial ways, and I only hope that I have done justice to their truly fantastic suggestions.

I would also like to thank the many individuals in government, international organizations, agricultural organizations, and the private sector who have taken the time to provide information about some of the more esoteric details that were needed to undergird the project.

Thank you, as well, to my editor at Cambridge University Press, Robert Dreesen, for believing in the project and allowing me to turn my manuscript into a finished book. Thank you as well to my two Cambridge University Press reviewers not only for seeing the value in the work but also for engaging with it so deeply and providing such thorough and thoughtful comments.

Finally, I could not have done any of this without my family. To my mother, Jacqueline Wolf – you have been an inspiration to me throughout my life, convincing me it was possible to pursue an academic career at the highest level while also being a dedicated mother and partner. As I prepare to welcome my own daughter into this world, I will strive to be the exemplar for her that you have been for me. To my father, David Perlman – you have been the number one believer in my potential throughout my life, envisioning possibilities for me that I never would have dreamed of envisioning for myself. Your enduring confidence in my future success helped me seek it out, even when my own confidence fell far short of yours. To my sister, Laura Perlman – I spent much of my life simply trying to match your accomplishments. Thank you for blazing the trail, and thank you for always being there on my days of doubt and uncertainty. Lastly, thank you to my husband, Max Child. You have been with me since the very first days of this project's conception. You patiently reassured me every day I had doubts, and despite not being an academic yourself, you always managed to provide insights that helped me make the work better. Thank you for putting up with me and holding my hand through it all.

1

The Informational Origins of Regulatory Barriers

In the summer of 2007, Argentina leveled an accusation against its wealthier trading partners, claiming they were unfairly impeding trade from poorer countries. Argentina's grievance, which was aired during a meeting of the World Trade Organization (WTO), centered on regulations restricting the amount of pesticide residue that could remain on agricultural imports. Argentina argued that because these restrictions often targeted older, cheaper pesticides, they "had a particularly negative impact on developing countries," which could not afford newer alternatives. A number of WTO members echoed Argentina's concern, with some suggesting that the regulations not only were unscientific but might represent a deliberate attempt to disadvantage less-developed nations.[1]

This complaint is one of hundreds of so-called "trade concerns" related to domestic regulatory practices registered during WTO meetings over the past two decades. It is also one of dozens about pesticide regulations, in particular, making agrochemical standards one of the most frequently contested regulatory issues at the WTO, a fact that reflects these standards' substantial potential to shape international trade.[2] The vast majority of complaints related to agrochemicals have been submitted by developing countries protesting the stricter standards of their wealthier

[1] World Trade Organization (2020*b*), G/SPS/R/45, para. 12–14.

[2] Chen, Yang and Findlay (2008) found, for example, that the strengthening of Japanese and EU pesticide standards in 2002 led to a $2.4 billion reduction in Chinese vegetable exports to those two markets in 2005 alone. Likewise, a study by Wilson and Otsuki (2004) concluded that a 1% increase in regulatory stringency among trade partners for a single agrochemical compound reduced Latin American banana exports by 1.63%.

trading partners. For example, in 2009, Brazil, China, and Ecuador all challenged Japan's strict limits on pesticide residues for imported agriculture, calling Japan's rules "arbitrary" and claiming they lacked any scientific justification, an accusation that Japan vigorously denied.[3] In 2010 India was joined by Argentina, Brazil, Pakistan, and Thailand in questioning the validity of the European Union's restrictive pesticide policies, with the complainants contending that "[n]o scientific evidence had been provided to justify" the stringent standards.[4] The complainants went on to raise the issue nine more times over the next several years, repeatedly expressing their frustration over the EU's barriers to agricultural shipments but appearing to make little progress. Likewise, in 2011, India raised a concern against the United States, noting that US limits on agrochemical residues had led to numerous rejected shipments of rice, one of India's primary exports. Over the course of several meetings, during which India reiterated its displeasure and emphasized the substantial costs it had incurred as a result of continued shipment rejections, the Indian representative alleged that the United States' restrictions were "contrary to the core principles" of the WTO agreement.[5]

It is easy to write off these disagreements as the inevitable result of diverging national risk preferences. After all, it seems reasonable that governments would seek to control the level of contaminants in their national food supply, and it is not surprising that developed and developing countries might differ in their perceptions of what level of risk is acceptable.[6] Indeed, those countries accused of overly stringent pesticide regulations regularly defend their policies by arguing that they are simply an implementation of the latest scientific evidence and necessary to protect their populations from harm.

At the same time, nations have a long history of seeking to advantage domestic producers through a variety of surreptitious measures, either in conjunction with or in place of taxes at the border. Considering that regulatory impediments are a well-understood method of such protectionism, it is perhaps not surprising that exporters impacted by these measures sometimes wonder whether governments' claims of necessity might be

[3] World Trade Organization (2020*b*), G/SPS/R/55, para. 37.
[4] Ibid., G/SPS/R/61, para. 17.
[5] Ibid., G/SPS/R/64, para. 47.
[6] Inglehart has traced how, as countries become wealthier, they experience a value shift, leading policymakers to prioritize "quality of life concerns such as environmental protection and lifestyle issues" (Inglehart (2000) p. 219).

overstated and whether these regulations are, if not a deliberate attempt to disadvantage foreign producers, at the very least an unnecessary and unscientific barrier to international commerce. But how do we determine whether a regulation is necessary or unnecessary, let alone whether it is scientific? Who provides the science upon which claims of necessity are based, and how might this bias both the regulatory outcomes themselves and subsequent determinations about their need?

Although there is often an implicit assumption that science reflects an objective, unbiased conclusion, this book will show that determinations about what regulations are and are not necessary to protect the population from harm are frequently a function of who has the relevant scientific information and what their incentives are to provide or withhold it. In particular, this book argues that a variety of regulatory barriers, including many of the agrochemical standards that have proven to be so contentious in the international arena, result from interest groups' ability to strategically leverage scientific information about the risks of their products in order to extract preferential policies that impede domestic competition and international trade. In addition, the book shows that when regulatory barriers stem from these dynamics, current international solutions for eliminating unnecessary barriers may end up legitimizing and even exacerbating them.

1.1 THE DEMAND FOR REGULATION

There are few responsibilities more central to the foundational purpose of government than the responsibility to protect the population from harm. Though the most obvious form of protection may be protection from external attack, protection from other forms of injury or death, including from unsafe products and technologies, is also a key function of governance. As such, all governments have an interest in implementing regulatory policies aimed at reducing risks to their population and the concomitant backlashes that can occur when governments fail to reduce these risks adequately. And there are backlashes. The 1999 discovery that Belgian regulators had declined to notify the public about the existence of toxic dioxins in the meat supply until months after they uncovered them led to the resignations of several high-level officials and the downfall of a Prime Minister.[7] Eight years later and several thousand

[7] James (1999).

miles away, the revelation that China's top food and drug regulator had been approving untested pharmaceuticals in exchange for bribes resulted in that official's execution.[8] Not long after, in a second scandal out of China that dominated international headlines, several officials were fired or forced to resign in the wake of realizations that multiple Chinese companies had intentionally added industrial chemicals to milk products used in infant formula. More recently, in the United States, the 2014 finding that the water supply in Flint, Michigan was heavily contaminated with lead resulted in manslaughter charges being brought against several local officials as well as a national reckoning over unequal access to clean water. Finally, the back-to-back crashes of two Boeing 737 MAX 8 aircraft in October 2018 and March 2019, as a result of a glitch in the flight control system, led to global scrutiny of how airplane regulators conduct oversight. This scrutiny has proved extremely damaging to the reputation of the US Federal Aviation Administration (FAA) and led to public pressure for an overhaul of how the regulatory agency operates.

While these are just a handful of examples, they illustrate the political consequences of failing to appropriately regulate the goods we all consume and depend upon in our daily lives. The potential for such political consequences has led some scholars to conclude that much of the temporal and cross-national variation that we see in regulatory stringency reflects the public pressures and political exigencies that come in the wake of prominent regulatory failures.[9] Certainly, it is not difficult to identify instances of regulations that seemingly stemmed from public crises. The 1906 US Pure Food and Drug Act followed immediately on the heels of Upton Sinclair's disturbing, albeit fictionalized, story describing conditions in US meatpacking factories. Likewise, a set of bans imposed by Europe on growth hormones in livestock during the 1980s can be traced back to an incident in Italy in which it was reported that infants were showing premature signs of puberty as a result of eating hormone-treated veal.[10] Finally, the 2008 Chinese milk contamination scandal that was mentioned previously spurred an attempt to restore confidence in the nation's food supply through several prominent revisions to China's food safety laws.

[8] Kahn (2007).

[9] See, e.g., Ansell and Vogel (2006); Bernauer and Caduff (2004); Bernauer and Meins (2003); Vogel (2012).

[10] Vogel (2012), ch. 3.

Nevertheless, while crises undoubtedly can help catalyze regulatory change, the precise shape that the change takes is less likely to respond to the public, whose lack of attention to or expertise in regulatory matters opens the door to those more informed and with stronger preferences.[11] More generally, even if large, structural changes sometimes occur, at least partially, in response to crises or public pressure, many of the regulations that become the subject of disagreements between nations in forums such as the WTO relate not to broad, structural legislation but rather to individual product or process standards. Such standards, in turn, are constantly evolving, entirely separate from any highly visible legislative change. Each month national regulators approve certain drug formulations, while others have their approvals withdrawn. Vehicle designs are accepted, rejected, and recalled on a rolling basis across different markets. And permissible contaminant levels are introduced, raised, or lowered as new evidence of benefits or dangers emerges. These product-level standards are usually determined by scientists or bureaucrats and largely go unnoticed by ordinary citizens. This suggests that the public is unlikely to be doing all or even most of the work when it comes to shaping the nuts and bolts of regulatory outcomes, raising the question of what else might be driving these policies. The answer, according to many, is special interests.

Specifically, a substantial body of scholarship, which traces its origins back to work by Bernstein (1955) and Huntington (1952), has posited that concentrated interest groups, frequently comprised of powerful industry members, tend to have an undue influence on regulatory policies. In his book, *Regulating Business by Independent Commission*, Bernstein argued that over the course of interactions between regulators and the regulated, it eventually becomes "unlikely that the commission ... will be able to extend regulation beyond the limits acceptable to the regulated groups."[12] Likewise, in his study of the Interstate Commerce Commission, Huntington described the relationship between the agency and the railroads as one of "benevolent paternalism."[13] A decade later, Olson helped lay the theoretical groundwork for explaining why industry tends to outmaneuver the public in the regulatory arena by focusing on the superior ability of business groups to mobilize.[14] Subsequently, in a

11 Moe (1989).
12 Bernstein (1955), p. 87.
13 Huntington (1952), p. 483.
14 See Olson (1965).

piece that effectively catalyzed what is often referred to as the "regulatory capture" literature, Stigler concluded that "as a rule, regulation is acquired by the industry and is designed and operated primarily for its benefit."[15]

As for what sorts of regulations industry sets out to acquire, Stigler (1971) and many of those writing after him argued that these actors will seek regulations that impose barriers to entry. Such regulations might include licensing requirements that dictate who can work in a profession, environmental emission standards limiting pollutants, or technical specifications restricting which variations of products can be sold. The common theme is that all of these rules make it more expensive for certain actors to operate, thereby reducing competition and increasing the profits of those that remain in the market.

The incentives of industry to acquire regulatory oversight provide an alternative explanation for why nations impose the sorts of stringent regulatory standards that can then create barriers to trade: These standards serve the interests of domestic groups. Thus we might observe that when the EU banned hormone-treated livestock, ostensibly in response to public concern over premature puberty in Italian infants, European cattle ranchers offered their wholehearted endorsement. Why did the European cattle ranchers support a measure that restricted how they could do business? The most obvious answer is that at the time of the regulation, these producers had already opted not to use the hormones in question, meaning their beef would not be impacted.[16] As a result, when American beef and veal producers went from selling hundreds of millions of dollars worth of meat to the EU annually to selling practically nothing after the ban went into effect,[17] European farmers stood ready to profit from the reduced competition.[18]

The anticompetitive nature of regulation means that governments have an incentive to use regulations as a form of disguised trade barrier, a

[15] Stigler (1971), p. 3. Later work has greatly expanded upon this insight, showing the many ways that regulations can benefit some firms over others. Posner (1974) and Peltzman (1976) provided some of the most notable theoretical expansions of Stigler's original conclusion, but there has been an enormous amount of work in this area. For a comprehensive review of the literature, see Dal Bó (2006).

[16] Johnson and Hanrahan (2010).

[17] WT/DS26/R/USA p. 17. (World Trade Organization [2020*a*]).

[18] It has similarly been noted that the US 1906 Pure Food and Drug Law, while undoubtedly helping to mollify consumers alarmed by Upton Sinclair's publication, also had support from members of industry, who saw in the law an opportunity for gaining competitive advantage (Wood (1985)).

strategy that may be particularly appealing to governments needing to feign an open trading posture.[19] Moreover, even in cases in which governments may not deliberately mean to block foreign products in favor of domestic ones, governments' tendencies to discount the interests of foreign producers can lead them to craft regulations in ways that are disadvantageous to foreign sellers, while perhaps containing more generous carveouts for producers at home.[20]

1.2 THE INTERNATIONAL SOLUTION

The potential for regulations to favor certain domestic sellers, often at the expense of foreign competitors, has led the international community to seek cooperative solutions so as to ensure that these behind-the-border measures do not simply replace tariffs as a less visible but no less damaging barrier to trade. In particular, under the WTO's Agreement on Sanitary and Phytosanitary Measures (SPS Agreement), as well as the WTO's Technical Barriers to Trade Agreement (TBT Agreement), nations are required to use relevant international standards as a basis for their domestic rules.[21] These international standards are developed by various international bodies in which technical experts and/or national representatives collaborate to arrive at non-binding yet highly influential recommendations. In addition to encouraging nations to base their regulations on international standards, the WTO agreements also specify that in instances in which governments decide to impose regulations that are more onerous than the international recommendation, they must be able to demonstrate, upon challenge, that their regulations are "based on scientific principles"[22] or are not "more trade restrictive than necessary to fulfill a legitimate objective," where determinations of legitimacy partially depend upon the consideration of "available scientific and technical information."[23]

19 Kono (2006), for example, notes how this tactic may be especially attractive to democracies.

20 Gulotty (2020) details these dynamics in his discussion of the EU's recent chemical safety legislation (REACH) and the United States' Food Safety Modernization Act.

21 Whereas the SPS Agreement lists three relevant international standard-setting bodies by name, the TBT Agreement leaves the interpretation of which standard-setting bodies are relevant more vague.

22 World Trade Organization (1995*b*), 2.2.

23 World Trade Organization (1995*a*), 2.2.

The WTO's strategy of championing international standards while requiring a scientific justification for regulations that go beyond the international recommendation raises an important question: Can international standard-setters actually provide a more objective guideline than national regulators? The international standard-setters themselves certainly make claims of this nature. For example, the International Organization for Standardization (ISO) asserts that its standards "level the playing field for developing countries and facilitate free and fair global trade."[24] Another international standard-setter, the Codex Alimentarius Commission, states that its standards are based on "sound science" and "contribute to the ... fairness of the international food trade."[25] Moreover, a large body of literature has long viewed delegation to international organizations as a way to help governments tie their own hands in order to avoid catering to a narrow set of private actors at the expense of the broader public good.[26] This suggests that greater delegation to international standard-setters under WTO law could reduce the ability of powerful interest groups to acquire regulations that harm foreign competitors. Along these lines, scholars have concluded that international decision-making bodies "should tend to ignore or discount demands made by interest groups in given member countries,"[27] which in turn ought to make international standards less biased toward these industry groups than their domestic counterparts.

Nevertheless, there are some reasons to be skeptical that international standards will offer greater objectivity than national regulations. First, several scholars have observed that international standard-setters have a tendency to cater to their most powerful national members[28] and to those countries whose domestic institutions allow them to gain first-mover advantage in the regulatory process.[29] As a result, we might expect that rather than simply bowing to science, these standard-setting organizations might instead bow to influential nations. Second, just because international standard-setters are more removed from the domestic political process does not mean that they are immune to it. Thus Mattli and Woods

24 International Organization for Standardization (2018).

25 Codex Alimentarius Commission (2016).

26 See, e.g., Grossman and Helpman (1994); Maggi and Rodriguez-Clare (2007); Bagwell and Staiger (2011).

27 Nielson and Tierney (2003), p. 250. Also see, e.g., Kapstein (1989); Keohane, Macedo and Moravcsik (2009).

28 See, e.g., Krasner (1991); Drezner (2004).

29 Mattli and Büthe (2003); Büthe and Mattli (2011).

(2009) contend that although international standard-setters *can* reduce interest group influence, this will only occur given that there is both a supply of good institutional conditions and a demand for outcomes that benefit the global good. Although these conditions may be met at times, in many areas of international standard-setting, such as the determination of global capital requirements for financial institutions, lack of public attention or understanding will likely undermine public oversight. It is, therefore, perhaps not surprising that numerous scholars have identified what appears to be capture in the creation of the second Basel Accord, a regulatory agreement intended to reduce systemic risk in banking.[30]

Taken together, the above discussion raises questions about whether international standard-setters will actually provide more objective outcomes than domestic regulators, particularly in cases in which powerful interests, be they private actors or sovereign nations, are best able to leverage their political influence to capture the standard-setting process. At the same time, the existing literature often presents a rather narrow view of what influence at international standard-setting organizations entails. By and large, influence is seen as a function of political might or, in the case of Büthe and Mattli (2003; 2011), of domestic institutions. Thus, private actors or specific nations win when they are able to leverage their economic, institutional, or military power, and standard-setters comply because they are, in some sense, captured by or beholden to the powerful. This conception of influence, in turn, generates specific predictions about who the winners will be, what strategies they will use, and under what conditions they will be more or less successful at imposing their preferences nationally versus internationally. This book, by contrast, shifts the emphasis from conventional power to instead focus squarely on scientific information about risk. In particular, this book highlights how information asymmetries about product risks between product producers, on the one hand, and national regulators, on the other, allow producers to impose regulatory barriers to competition and trade at the national level. In addition, the book demonstrates how these same information asymmetries are replicated internationally, thereby allowing producers to impose the same barriers at the international standard-setting level,

30 Underhill and Zhang (2008); Griffith-Jones and Persaud (2008); Lall (2009); Baker (2010).

under standard-setting organizations officially endorsed by the WTO and charged with leveling the global playing field and eliminating unnecessary impediments to international commerce.

1.3 THE ARGUMENT IN BRIEF

The book's argument builds off of two simple premises. The first is that those charged with setting regulatory rules need detailed, product-level information in order to do so. A regulator cannot know at what level a chemical is safe without knowledge of that chemical's toxic or carcinogenic potential. It is similarly impossible to predict if a plane is likely to crash or a crib to lead to an infant's death without information about the plane's aerodynamics or the crib's design. Information is the sine qua non of regulation.

The second premise is that producers frequently have a much greater ability to acquire information about the risks of their products than regulators, regardless of whether those regulators are domestic bureaucrats or international technocrats. This information asymmetry is often implicitly acknowledged during initial product approvals, when regulators typically rely on producers to conduct and share outcomes of clinical trials and safety tests. Yet this asymmetry is also present and may even become more pronounced over time, the longer a product is on the market. This is due to the fact that producers have the ability to accrue updated information about product risks to which regulators are not privy – information stemming from consumer complaints, in-house studies, and observations of worker exposure. Compounding the problem is the fact that scientific understanding and consumer acceptance of risk are constantly evolving, meaning prior regulations inevitably grow out of date, and unlike the producers of a given product, domestic regulators and international standard-setters generally lack the resources to continuously monitor all the products on the market to independently ensure that standards continue to meet modern criteria.

Taken together, these two premises suggest that producers will be uniquely positioned to influence product-level standards through the strategic provision and withholding of information about risks.

Notably, neither the idea that safety information is crucial to regulatory policymaking nor the observation that producers frequently enjoy an advantage over regulators in acquiring such information is novel. Various scholars, particularly those in the legal and science and technology studies disciplines, have made the role of information asymmetries in the regulation of risk central themes of their work.[31] Such scholars have observed that firms' superior knowledge of their products' qualities and hazards will lead them to avoid learning about dangers they are uniquely situated to uncover, to hide such dangers once they are discovered, and to suppress knowledge of any regulatory violations.[32] As a result, this literature concludes that one of the primary problems facing policymakers is determining how to incentivize producers to reveal product dangers so that regulators can then respond accordingly.

While it may seem intuitive that producers would try to suppress damaging information about their products if revealing such information would lead to product restrictions or bans, this book will show that, at times, restrictions or bans of their own products are precisely what producers want. Indeed, this book contends that whereas producers do have incentives to avoid stricter regulations on their most profitable products, the same is not always true of producers' less profitable products. Specifically, in those cases in which a producer makes two substitutable goods, one of which is less profitable than the other and is produced competitively by more than one firm – a situation that frequently arises in the context of patents – the dual-product producer may be able to increase profits by acquiring stricter standards on the less profitable (out-of-patent) good, thereby shifting demand toward the more profitable (patented) alternative.

Producers' incentives to acquire stricter regulations on their own out-of-patent products will not only lead producers to strategically reveal private information about product risks at convenient times, but these incentives will also encourage producers to support legal institutions ostensibly intended to reduce the very information asymmetry problems that give firms an advantage over regulators in the first place. The institutions in question are those that require all previously approved products to be reevaluated on a predetermined basis. During the reevaluations, producers must provide evidence that their products are safe or see those products removed from the market *automatically*. Such institutions thus impose a precautionary standard (no data, no market)

31 See, in particular, Coglianese, Zeckhauser and Parson (2004); Pelaez, da Silva and Araujo (2013); Jasanoff (2006); Collins (2010); Shavell (1984*a*,*b*); Viscusi (1989).

32 Asymmetric information problems between regulators and firms are also a common theme in the economics literature, much of which examines information asymmetries related to firms' costs. See, e.g., Baron and Myerson (1982); Baron and Besanko (1984); Besanko (1987); Laffont and Tirole (1986, 1991); Joskow and Schmalensee (1986).

retroactively to existing products, which is why this book refers to this type of institutional design as "retroactive precaution."

A sector-wide requirement of precautionary reevaluations seemingly helps solve the information problem that scholars have generally considered the primary concern in health and safety regulation: that those best situated to uncover product dangers (producers) will try to hide or avoid learning about them. It is, therefore, not surprising that in cases in which a lack of product safety information poses a particularly acute risk to consumers, public interest groups and politicians concerned about the potential for public backlash – particularly in wealthy countries, in which quality of life concerns tend to be foremost[33] – will seek out these legal institutions. What is more surprising, at least a priori, is that producers of potentially dangerous products will at times join forces with the public interest groups to support these precautionary rules. Of course, whereas the public seeks safety, producers seek profit. Specifically, producers that support retroactive precaution generally do so, at least in part, because they recognize that it can help shorten the product lifecycle of out-of-patent, competitively produced goods for which they have a more profitable, patented alternative. Moreover, retroactive precaution does this without forcing producers to harm their reputations by explicitly revealing damaging information about their own goods. Rather, producers can acquire stricter standards by simply not providing the information requested during reevaluations.

What this means in practice is that this type of precautionary regulatory institution will lead more affordable, out-of-patent products to be systematically regulated off the market for reasons that cannot be justified by science or safety alone. This, in turn, creates trade barriers that benefit larger, more innovative firms that tend to reside in developed countries, at the expense of their smaller, generic counterparts, which are more often located in the developing world. When the affected products are used as inputs into other traded goods, as is the case, for example, with agrochemicals, food additives, or veterinary drugs, the regulatory barriers become magnified, impacting not only the producers of the products being regulated but also those that utilize them.

Notably, both the implementation of retroactive precaution and the bias that results from it are a direct consequence of an information asymmetry problem. This differentiates the resulting regulatory barriers

33 Inglehart (2000).

from those that stem from political efforts to cater to domestic producers. The reason this matters is because the international standard-setters that have been tasked with eliminating arbitrary or otherwise unnecessary regulatory barriers suffer from the very same information asymmetry problems as their domestic counterparts. As a result, even those international standard-setting organizations that we might expect to be more insulated from the political pressures of domestic producers can still end up replicating the bias that stems from these actors' information advantages. Given that the resulting regulatory outcomes raise consumer costs and create barriers to trade for developing countries, in particular, this introduces fundamental questions about whether international standard-setting bodies can live up to their claims of providing scientifically objective rules that serve the interests of developed and developing countries alike.

1.4 CONTRIBUTIONS

In investigating how private actors benefit from and actively leverage information asymmetries to win regulatory barriers to competition domestically and internationally, this book makes several important contributions.

First, the book reveals an underexplored way in which regulatory barriers to trade develop and are sustained. Considering that regulatory standards have become an increasingly significant impediment to international commerce, there is a clear need for better scholarly understanding of how these barriers are formed and under what conditions they can be eliminated. Departing from the literature that focuses predominantly on interest group lobbying[34] or consumer preferences,[35] this book puts information front and center, focusing on who has it, how they seek to use it, and how regulatory institutions shape the resulting outcomes.

Second, the book speaks to the literature on how private actors "capture" the regulatory process, thereby adding to a rich body of work in economics and political economy. It is frequently asserted that regulations cater to industry, with the prevailing narrative one of bureaucratic complicity or, at the very least, undue sympathy toward the regulated. In other words, at least some members of the policy

34 E.g., Kono (2006); Gulotty (2020).

35 E.g., Bernauer and Meins (2003); Bernauer and Caduff (2004); Vogel (2012).

establishment are typically assumed to be culpable in setting suboptimal rules. This assumption not only pervades the earliest work on capture, in which influence occurs through votes, bribes, or promises of future employment, but it is also prevalent in much of the later and more sophisticated studies, including work that incorporates considerations of asymmetric information.[36] Although scholars have increasingly begun to conceptualize alternative avenues of influence,[37] while also questioning to what extent we can even conclude capture from pro-industry outcomes,[38] theorizing on nontransactional means of leverage – particularly outside the space of monopoly pricing, which has been a central focus for economists – remains underdeveloped. This book not only sharpens our understanding of how firms can capture the regulatory process without needing to capture the regulator himself, but it lays out concrete predictions for the precise ways in which this will systematically shape regulatory outcomes.

Third, the book provides evidence that certain producers will attempt to use health and safety standards as a means of eliminating products that they, themselves produce or develop. Scholars of regulation have shown how firm-level differences can lead some firms but not others to seek stricter regulations in their sector,[39] and trade scholars have highlighted the importance of intra-industry firm-level variation for understanding support for free trade,[40] with recent work additionally emphasizing the importance of product differentiation for facilitating political action.[41] Yet what has not received sustained attention is the idea that product differentiation might also lead firms to have divergent preferences across their own product lines, encouraging them to use regulations to undermine some of those products but not others. The finding that firms have incentives to acquire stricter regulations on some of their own goods means that, particularly under the types of institutions that require precautionary reevaluations, regulations may tend to become more stringent

36 See, e.g., Tirole (1986); Laffont and Tirole (1993), ch. 11.

37 See, e.g., Kwak (2014) discussion of cultural capture, McCarty (2017) on how regulatory complexity leads to more favorable outcomes for industry, Dedieu (2021) on the process of organized denial at regulatory agencies, or Bagley (2010), who argues that regulators frequently cater to industry even while acting in good faith.

38 See Carpenter (2004) and Carpenter and Moss (2014).

39 E.g., Grey (2018); Kennard (2020).

40 This is a central theme of the so-called new-new trade theory. See, e.g., Bernard et al. (2003); Melitz (2003).

41 Kim (2017); Osgood (2016).

on more affordable products, for reasons orthogonal to health and safety. Not only does this help explain some of the variation we see in regulatory standards across time and across countries, but it also provides insight into why similar products often receive dissimilar regulatory treatment.

Fourth, the book introduces a new consideration into the ongoing debate over whether international standards can provide a more objective alternative to domestic rules. The literature on this topic has tended to focus far too heavily on the question of lobbying and political might, framing the debate almost entirely around whether or not private actors wield more or less traditional influence at the international level. This has led a number of scholars to assume that international standards, at least under certain conditions, offer an improvement over their domestic counterparts,[42] a claim that has been promoted by the international standard-setters themselves. However, as this book demonstrates, solely focusing on lobbying or more conventional political strength misses an equally if not more important avenue of influence, the avenue of information.

Finally, this book raises crucial questions about how science is incorporated into policy and what it actually means for regulations to be scientific, thereby building off previous work showing that science is not an objective truth, which can be dispassionately piped into an equation in order to output optimal policies.[43] In the course of debates over whether a given regulatory standard is legitimate under WTO rules, nations have frequently been asked to prove that their standards are not a veiled form of protectionism. The central question in the adjudication process often comes down to whether the standard is based on science. The problem is that when science is a function of what data firms are or are not willing to provide, it becomes nearly impossible to say what is and is not scientific. By highlighting how regulatory institutions that seemingly prioritize science can help the primary producers of scientific information bias regulatory outcomes, this book sheds new light on the fundamental impossibility of arriving at a universally agreed upon scientific solution.

42 E.g., Kapstein (1989); Nielson and Tierney (2003); Keohane, Macedo and Moravcsik (2009); Mattli and Woods (2009).

43 See, e.g., Coglianese and Marchant (2003); Jasanoff (1987*a*,*b*, 1998); Wagner (1995).

1.5 OUTLINE OF BOOK CHAPTERS

In order to demonstrate the ways in which private actors leverage scientific information to acquire regulatory barriers to competition domestically and internationally, the book begins, in Chapter 2, by providing a broad overview of the sorts of information asymmetries that exist between producers of potentially dangerous products and those who are tasked with regulating them. Leveraging insights from a diverse set of industries – aerospace, direct-to-consumer products, pharmaceuticals, and industrial chemicals – and spanning a range of countries, this chapter establishes the surprising degree to which regulators not only are at a disadvantage relative to firms when it comes to acquiring information about product risk but also, as a result, depend on firms to be the primary source of information required to regulate. The chapter then considers the ways in which and conditions under which this might allow producers to influence regulatory change.

After establishing the pervasiveness of information asymmetries and dependencies at the domestic level, as well as the potential space for regulatory bias, the chapter next demonstrates why we should expect the very same information asymmetries and biases to be replicated and even exacerbated at the international level. The chapter concludes by outlining several broad takeaways and key questions that then serve as the foundation and motivation for the remainder of the book.

The next chapter (Chapter 3) introduces the book's theory. The theory explicates the conditions under which information asymmetries between regulators and producers will contribute to regulatory barriers. The chapter produces three central hypotheses, which are then tested empirically in the remainder of the book. First, innovative producers – those that develop and patent novel products – not only have incentives to seek lenient regulations on their most profitable products, but they also have incentives to acquire regulations that push their less profitable, competitively produced products off the market. These incentives will, at times, lead innovative firms to proactively reveal damaging information about their own products in order to acquire stricter regulations on them.

Second, institutional rules requiring product reevaluations during which lack of data is viewed as equivalent to harm (a precautionary standard, applied retroactively), while seemingly intended to ensure consumer safety in a world in which regulators struggle to acquire adequate information about product risk, will actually be supported by some of the very companies these rules are intended to regulate. This is because such institutions can assist innovative firms in eliminating older, competitively produced products by making the continued sale of these products dependent on whether or not their producers provide evidence the products are safe. In other words, retroactive precaution puts greater power into the hands of those who hold the information that regulators need: the innovative producers.

Finally, as suggested by the second hypothesis, once these precautionary rules are put in place, regulations will systematically become stricter on older, less profitable products for reasons that cannot solely be justified by appeals to the public interest. This, in turn, can explain existing regulatory barriers to trade that have been the subject of considerable disagreement between developed and developing countries. An important implication of this final hypothesis is that such regulatory bias need not be restricted to the domestic level. To the extent that domestic information asymmetries and dependencies are replicated at the international level (as Chapter 2 shows that they are), the incentives to implement retroactive precaution and the resulting ability of private actors to influence outcomes should look quite similar domestically and internationally.

Chapter 4 tests the first of the three hypotheses. Focusing on firm-level behavior in the US pharmaceutical and agrochemical industries, the chapter provides evidence that companies do indeed seek stricter standards on their own, out-of-patent products in order to boost sales of newer, patented substitutes, even providing negative information about their products in pursuit of this goal. In order to show this, the chapter leverages petitions submitted by pharmaceutical and agrochemical companies to the US FDA and EPA, respectively, requesting that the agencies place stricter standards or all out bans on products that these companies themselves developed. In the case of the pharmaceutical petitions, the chapter provides evidence that all but one of the requests for a product ban directly targeted a drug that was about to lose or had lost patent protection and for which the company had a more recently patented substitute. This suggests that such requests are not publicly minded attempts to ensure dangerous products remain off the market but, instead, are strategic gambits to boost profits of exclusively produced alternatives. In addition, the chapter provides a statistical analysis of petitions submitted by agrochemical companies requesting changes to existing pesticide standards. These petitions show that whereas farm lobby groups that petition for adjustments to pesticide regulations are no more likely to seek stricter standards on out-of-patent pesticides, agrochemical companies systematically request stricter standards on these products, while requesting more lenient standards on products still enjoying patent protection.

Armed with evidence that producers' preferences and behaviors accord with the theoretical expectations, Chapter 5 takes a deep dive into the history of US pesticide regulation in order to evaluate the next two hypotheses. In order to test the hypothesis that innovative companies will at times support sector-wide, precautionary reevaluations, the chapter uses primary and secondary sources to trace the evolution of American regulatory institutions as they progressed toward the retroactively precautionary system that exists today. Testimonies from congressional hearings offer evidence that, whereas the large, innovative companies joined forces with environmentalists in favor of the precautionary shift, even offering to help underwrite the cost of the new system, smaller, generic producers and those who relied on their products provided a counterweight, complaining that systematic, precautionary reevaluations would serve to eliminate generic products and push those who produced them off the market. In addition to offering direct evidence that innovative producers supported retroactive precaution in the case under study, the first half of the chapter also provides suggestive evidence that innovative producers' support for the regulatory change stemmed, at least in part, from the anticipation that the new rules would help eliminate generic products in favor of patented alternatives.

The second half of the chapter tests whether innovative producers received what they bargained for. Using an original dataset that tracks changes to US pesticide regulations over a two decade period, the chapter provides evidence that regulations have indeed become stricter on older less profitable chemicals over time for reasons that cannot be attributed to health, safety, or obsolescence alone. This has resulted in precisely the barriers to trade that motivated Argentina in 2007 to accuse its wealthier trading partners of disadvantaging poorer agricultural exporters. In addition, the chapter shows that the mechanism behind these barriers is not the lobbying power of producers but rather their ability to leverage their information advantages under a more precautionary regulatory regime.

Having provided evidence for the theory's plausibility domestically, the final empirical chapter turns to the international level in order to determine whether delegation to an international standard-setter ameliorates or exacerbates the regulatory biases previously identified. Looking at the Codex Alimentarius Commission, the most important international standard-setter in the realm of food hygiene, contamination, and safety, Chapter 6 explores how this organization operates and the role that information asymmetries play in its standard-setting process. The chapter then asks whether the information asymmetries found under Codex have resulted in similar regulatory deficiencies to those seen at the domestic level.

In order to answer this, the chapter leverages the fact that Codex puts forward agrochemical standards that are equivalent to those found in the United States. This makes it possible to replicate the analysis conducted in the previous chapter, this time looking at changes to standards under Codex. Like the United States, Codex previously transitioned to a retroactively, precautionary system for evaluating agrochemical standards in order to combat the problems associated with the organization's inability to acquire updated information about the risks of pesticide products – information to which firms have far better access. According to the theory, just as occurred at the domestic level, this precautionary system ought to lead to regulatory bias at the international level in the form of stricter standards on more affordable, out-of-patent chemicals. Chapter 6 shows that even though Codex standard-setters are relatively removed from the domestic political process and even though developing country members of the Codex Commission are heavily dependent on out-of-patent pesticide products the Codex Commission has mirrored the EPA in its tendency to systematically impose stricter standards on out-of-patent agrochemicals, even after accounting for health, safety, and environmental considerations. As such, the international standard-setter has ended up placing more onerous rules on more affordable products for reasons that are less based on science than they are based on the absence of scientific information. In addition to showing that international standards have been vulnerable to similar biases as domestic regulations, this chapter also explores how developing countries and generic producers have sought to combat the regulatory biases that have arisen at the international level and how the innovative firms have, thus far, thwarted them.

Finally, Chapter 7 concludes by revisiting the book's central contributions in more detail, exploring the normative implications of the findings, and providing some practical proposals for how policymakers might address the regulatory dilemmas that the book identifies.

Taken as a whole, the book offers a new perspective on the political economy of regulation in a globalized world. By expanding our understanding of how regulatory barriers to trade develop and why regulations frequently fail to reflect the public interest, the book challenges our assumptions about how private actors capture the regulatory process, while also raising new questions about what it actually means for regulations to be scientific.

2

Private Information in the Regulation of Risk

There can be no product safety regulation without accurate information about the product in question. Much of the scholarship on regulatory bias and regulatory barriers to trade has focused on governments' incentives to cater to interest groups. However, the centrality of information to the regulation of risk suggests that if we want to understand how bias and barriers arise, we might alternatively begin by looking at where the information that undergirds regulatory policymaking comes from. One could be forgiven for assuming that most of this information originates with the national or international body in charge of setting standards. After all, national regulatory agencies routinely hire scientists and other qualified authorities theoretically well-positioned to determine appropriate regulations. Likewise, international standard-setting organizations frequently assemble panels of scientific or technical experts. In addition, both national and international regulatory bodies engage in various types of oversight and surveillance activities that can help them gather information about potential dangers. Despite this, to a surprising and at times disturbing degree, both domestic and international regulators are regularly at a substantial informational disadvantage relative to those they regulate. This leads them to depend heavily on producers for the information necessary to set, monitor, and adjust product regulations.

This chapter offers an overview of the types of information asymmetries that bedevil the regulation of product safety. In doing so, the chapter aims to establish several stylized facts. First, it shows that information asymmetries about product risk between regulators of potentially dangerous products and producers of those products are far more extensive than most people realize, pervading the regulatory process both domestically and internationally. Second, these information asymmetries provide producers with the opportunity to withhold or otherwise suppress information in ways that can influence the timing of regulatory rules. Finally, the degree to which producers are able to use their information advantages in ways that are problematic for the public interest is a function not only of regulatory capacity and of the types of institutions governments put in place but also of the characteristics of the products being regulated. These three insights are a necessary foundation for the remainder of the book. Not only do they motivate the importance of looking to information asymmetries when seeking to explain the emergence of regulatory barriers and bias, but they also help establish the theoretical scope conditions regarding when we might expect regulations to most strongly reflect firms' ability to leverage private information.

2.1 AN OVERVIEW OF INFORMATION ASYMMETRIES

This is by no means the first piece of research exploring the consequences of information asymmetries between regulators and those they regulate. However, to date much of the focus in the literature has been on process regulations – rules dictating the process through which a product is manufactured rather than applying to the end product itself. In this domain, the information disadvantages of the regulator are readily apparent. Producers are clearly better positioned to observe their own actions than is a government agent. Producers can directly assess the extent to which they engage in risky behaviors and the level of effort they deploy toward meeting a particular requirement. While in the case of a single potential violator, a regulator's inability to witness actions or intent on the part of the firm might be partially mitigated by the regulator's ability to direct all of their resources toward catching a breach of responsibility, as the number of potential violators grows, the challenge of monitoring them grows concomitantly. This inherent difficulty of tracking process compliance has been discussed extensively in the social science literature, particularly as it relates to the regulation of polluting firms,[1] and it can help explain why regulators opt for one type of regulatory rule over another, such as choosing a design standard versus a performance standard for achieving pollution reductions.[2] Such difficulties also help explain why legal liabil-

[1] See, e.g., Braden and Segerson (1993); Schmutzler (1996); Baron (1985).

[2] Besanko (1987).

ity may at times serve as an important complement to or substitute for regulation,[3] helping to dissuade behavior that a regulator may not be able to observe.

While it may be apparent and while it is certainly well-documented that firms have an information advantage when it comes to monitoring their own production processes, at times less obvious and certainly less well-studied[4] is the fact that producers are also typically at a significant advantage when it comes to determining whether the end result of that process (the product) is safe and what regulatory standards ought to apply to it. The source of firms' advantage here is not simply the result of poor bureaucratic personnel quality or a lack of expertise. Although it may be true that in certain sectors, those with the best qualifications are unlikely to be found in government thereby contributing to cooptation by the better qualified party,[5] a potentially greater problem is that producers simply know more about their products than do regulators. Economists have noted this asymmetry particularly as it relates to the regulation of product costs, with researchers observing how monopolists' private knowledge of their own costs of compliance can help them win preferred pricing regulation from government overseers.[6] In addition, political scientists have recently begun to explore how information asymmetries in complex industries between firms and bureaucrats may allow firms to bias regulations more generally.[7]

One area that has received less sustained attention in the realm of political science or economics is how asymmetric information about product risk, in particular, might help producers influence the relative safety standards to which different products are held.[8] Yet this type of information

[3] Viscusi (1989); Shavell (1984*a*,*b*).

[4] Coglianese, Zeckhauser and Parson (2004).

[5] For example, in the realm of banking regulation, Griffith-Jones and Persaud (2008) argue, "Regulators are intelligent and hard working. However, they are generally not as expert in the conduct of banking as the bankers" (p. 267).

[6] See, e.g., Baron and Myerson (1982); Laffont and Tirole (1986); Joskow and Schmalensee (1986).

[7] McCarty (2017).

[8] Much of the work that does focus on information asymmetry in regards to product risk can be found in the legal and science and technology studies literatures, which tend to take a more qualitative approach, often problematizing the issue from a product-specific or historical perspective (e.g., Collins (2010); Pelaez, da Silva and Araujo (2013)). There has also been some work investigating how legal institutions and administrative processes might be designed in order to encourage better disclosure of product risks, given that regulators lack some degree of information regarding the risks of the product (Coglianese, Zeckhauser and Parson (2004)).

asymmetry is a defining feature of the domestic regulatory environment, with producers almost universally enjoying superior knowledge about the qualities and risks of their products than government regulators. This is a direct consequence of the fact that in order to manufacture a successful good, producers must invest extensive time and effort into ensuring that product's effectiveness, while also experimenting with alternative designs, studying consumer usage patterns, and analyzing customer complaints. As a result, particularly to the extent that regulatory oversight relates to individual goods or formulations – as is the case when it comes to product-level approvals, bans, residue levels, or dosage requirements – producers' unique knowledge of their own goods' characteristics both encourages and, in many cases, necessitates regulators' dependence on producers' private information.

The extent of both the information asymmetry between regulators and producers and the resulting dependence of government regulators on those they regulate for relevant information about risk often goes unnoticed by the general public, only occasionally surfacing in the face of tragedy. For example, in the wake of back-to-back crashes of two Boeing MAX 8 aircraft in 2018 and 2019, resulting in the deaths of 346 individuals, journalists began to observe with alarm that US regulators had delegated the task of determining whether the Boeing MAX 8 was safe to Boeing,[9] a decision that directly stemmed from regulators having determined that company employees were better situated to evaluate the safety of Boeing planes than they were.

Yet, as the remainder of this chapter lays bare, dependence on producers for critical information is not just restricted to US aviation. In fact, it is not even restricted to the most technologically complex products. Although technological complexity can exacerbate information asymmetries, making it particularly difficult for regulators to conduct independent evaluations, even in the realm of seemingly straightforward goods, regulators are consistently at a disadvantage relative to producers when it comes to verifying and monitoring product safety. This leads regulators to depend on producers for these tasks. Indeed the dependence on producers to determine which products are or are not safe is often explicitly built into the national regulatory system, such that producers are not only tasked with providing any studies necessary to show a product deserves approval (and under what conditions), but they are also relied upon to

[9] Gates (2019).

be the primary source of information should evidence emerge that a prior approval ought to be amended or withdrawn. Although producers may be reliable sources of information about risk when the odds of getting caught suppressing or otherwise fabricating relevant information are high, there is ample evidence that companies become less reliable and less timely purveyors of information when these conditions do not hold – a problem that will be explored in greater depth herein.

At the same time, given that domestic regulators are frequently thought to cater, rather deliberately, to those they regulate,[10] one might still wonder whether these same sorts of dynamics describe international standard-setters. After all, international organizations are one step removed from the domestic political process; thus, to the extent that regulatory bodies *can* reduce information asymmetries and dependencies, it is plausible that international standard-setters would be more inclined to do so. Moreover, as outlined in Chapter 1, the recommendations put forward by international standard-setting bodies have often been viewed as a means of addressing some of the biases that emerge domestically, particularly biases that result from interest groups' attempts to acquire regulatory barriers to trade. To the extent that national regulators' dependence on producers for information might help producers acquire regulatory outcomes that create barriers to trade, it is, therefore, crucial to ask whether international standard-setters are able to reduce them.

This chapter shows that they are not. The reason is that the information dynamics identified in this chapter are less the result of regulators' affinity for the regulated than they are the result of structural features of the regulatory environment, and the same structural features that exist domestically also exist internationally. In fact, if anything, the information asymmetries and dependencies faced by domestic regulators are exacerbated at the international level, as a result of international standard-setters' reduced legal authority and smaller operating budgets.

In order to shed light on the scope of regulators' informational disadvantages and how this impacts regulatory outcomes and design, the rest of this chapter provides a descriptive account of the role that information asymmetries and dependencies play in regulatory policy-making, unpacking the ways in which both domestic and international standard-setters regularly depend on developers of potentially dangerous products to promptly and faithfully reveal privileged knowledge about

10 This is, after all, a dominant theme in the "regulatory capture" literature.

those goods. Starting at the domestic level, the chapter examines the types and extent of information imbalances across four broad sectors, ranging from the highly technical to the relatively straightforward. The chapter begins with aerospace, an industry falling at the most technologically demanding end. Due to its complexity, aerospace is a sector in which regulators' information disadvantages are particularly clear-cut and acute. Aerospace is, therefore, useful as a jumping off point to establish what extreme information asymmetries look like and how these lead regulators to depend on producers for necessary expertise.

Having illustrated the extreme form that information asymmetries can take and the consequences for regulatory dependence, the chapter then asks whether these patterns are reserved for the most technologically complex industries or whether they are replicated elsewhere. In order to answer this, the chapter turns to a decidedly more quotidian sector: direct-to-consumer products, such as furniture, lawn mowers, and children's toys. Using data on product recalls, combined with evidence collected from government reports as well as personal communications with regulators, it is demonstrated that, much as in aerospace, the regulation of consumer products is overwhelmingly defined by producers' information advantages and regulators' resultant dependence on them. These findings then make it possible to turn to two questions that are central to the remainder of the book: How might producers be able to use these advantages, and under what conditions will producers be most successful? In order to begin to answer these questions, in the remaining sectors analyzed – pharmaceuticals and industrial chemicals – special attention is paid to a particular type of information imbalance, one already hinted at by the direct-to-consumer product recall data: regulators' dependence on producers to report discoveries of risk. While the data on recalls suggests that producers are the party most responsible for revealing newly uncovered product dangers, the discussion of pharmaceuticals and industrial chemicals helps elucidate what this might mean for firms' ability to shape the timing of regulatory change.

Having offered an examination of the sources, types, and potential consequences of information asymmetries domestically, the chapter finally asks whether the conditions that give producers an information advantage at the national level are replicated internationally, offering both theoretical and empirical reasons to expect the two levels of governance to look similar. The chapter concludes by examining the broader factors that seem to allow firms more or less leeway to leverage the information asymmetries identified in the preceding pages. This, in turn, helps to establish the scope conditions for the theory that follows in Chapter 3.

2.2 ASYMMETRIES AT THE EXTREME: THE REGULATION OF AEROSPACE

The recent crashes of two brand new Boeing MAX 8 aircraft have led to increased scrutiny of aircraft regulators over the past few years, particularly regulators at the United States' Federal Aviation Administration (FAA). While both Boeing planes involved in the accidents were operated by non-US companies, because the MAX 8 was manufactured in the United States, the FAA played a central role in verifying its safety. This is due to the fact that in addition to ensuring that aircraft are safe for domestic operation, the FAA-much like its European counterpart, the European Aviation Safety Agency (EASA)-also certifies aircraft that are manufactured domestically but sold abroad, certifications that are then accepted by foreign regulators thanks to a series of bilateral agreements that commit nations to recognizing other countries' certifications as equivalent to their own. Given that the USA and Europe are home to Boeing and Airbus, respectively, the two largest airplane manufacturers in the world, the FAA and EASA are effectively responsible for determining the safety of the vast majority of commercial aircraft worldwide.[11]

In the immediate aftermath of the MAX 8 disasters, many in the media blamed the tragedies on regulatory capture.[12] According to these accounts, FAA regulators had developed too cozy of a relationship with Boeing, leading them to put the company's interests ahead of the interests of the general public. Indeed, such concerns about capture had been expressed long prior to the MAX 8 crashes. For example, a 2002 journal article observed "that the private interests of the airline industry had, at least by 1999, overtaken public policy concerns as the primary motivating imperative of the FAA."[13]

This narrative of regulatory complicity is an appealing one. It caters to the human impulse to blame a terrible outcome on the malfeasance or negligence of a set of individuals. Nevertheless, the narrative is misleading, in that it ignores the larger, structural problem that contributed

[11] As of 2019, Boeing and Airbus combined made up a whopping 91 percent of the commercial airline market (Trefis Team and Great Speculations (2020)).

[12] See, e.g., Germain (2019); Economist (2019); Kitroeff and Gelles (2019).

[13] Niles (2002), p.424.

to the MAX 8 disasters. The larger problem is that the FAA, much like EASA or any other aircraft regulator, simply does not have the ability to independently evaluate all planes under its purview, and this, therefore, necessitates dependence on the manufacturers to provide the relevant information to verify that each jet meets the appropriate level of safety. In order to understand why aircraft regulators are so dependent on aircraft producers, one first needs a basic understanding of what airplane regulation entails.

Before a new model of airplane is allowed to transport passengers, it must acquire what is known as a type certification. Type certifications are the regulating body's affirmation that the aircraft design conforms with all relevant requirements and regulations. Individual aircraft must then receive a separate airworthiness certificate in order to be operated. In other words, flaws in the overarching design of a line of aircraft (as existed in the case of the MAX 8) must be identified during the type certification. Flaws related to wear and tear or improper maintenance of an individual craft fall under airworthiness certification.

Although issuing type certificates is one of the most important core functions of the FAA, much of the process is delegated to the airline manufacturers. This is partially due to the sheer number of aircraft the FAA must oversee. As noted by the National Research Council as far back as 1986:

> FAA engineers cannot review each of the thousands of drawings, calculations, reports, and tests involved in type certification. But it [sic] must be certain that each design for a new aircraft meets all appropriate regulatory requirements. Thus, the system relies not only on the FAA staff, but also on the assistance rendered by aircraft company employees called designated engineering representatives (DERs), who review the design and design process to ensure, on behalf of FAA, compliance with all aspects of the appropriate regulations.[14]

Thus, the incredible size of the task of overseeing aircraft approval necessitates some level of delegation, and this entails not only conducting the relevant tests but verifying their outcomes. The necessity of delegation, however, cannot simply be attributed to issues of workload. According to two separate reports prepared for Congress by the United States' US Government Accountability Office, US regulators have, for some time, actually delegated the *vast majority* of the testing and certification process to the aircraft manufacturers through the designee program.[15] A 1993

14 National Research Council (1986), p.65.

15 Government Accountability Office (1993, 2004).

GAO report found that under this program, "[the] FAA now delegates up to 95 percent of the certification activities to manufacturers."[16] Moreover, in 2005, the process of delegation was further institutionalized into law under the so-called Organization Designation Authorization Program, which "expands the scope of approved tasks available to organizational designees; increases the number of organizations eligible for organizational designee authorizations; and establishes a more comprehensive, systems-based approach to managing designated organizations."[17]

Even if part of the explanation for delegation is a desire to decrease the workload of an agency whose budget has increased only modestly over the years relative to its responsibilities, the huge percentage of regulatory duties that are outsourced suggests that budgetary pressures are only part of the problem. The other part relates to information. According to one scholar, "The complexity of modern aircraft has long passed a level where regulating it is within the FAA's budget and manpower, and yet the FAA would be ill-placed to make informed judgments even with infinite resources; they simply lack the 'tacit knowledge' to make the requisite judgments about the technologies they certify."[18] This author goes on to note that "Tacit knowledge ... refers to the information, skill, and experience that [is] vital to a task but difficult to codify."[19]

Tacit knowledge, as this author conceives it, is not simply a function of technical training or competence, though competence and training certainly play a role. Tacit knowledge also relates to the ability to collect the information needed to accomplish proper oversight. This information comes in large part from the day-to-day process of developing a product in need of certification. Without spending the hundreds of hours alongside the manufacturers inspecting the intricacies of designs and evaluating the impact of minor changes, how could a regulator possibly hope to have a full understanding of which individual elements could pose a subsequent problem? While an experienced engineer ought to be able to identify some of the obvious flaws in a new aircraft model, relative to those who have been charged with actually designing, building, and redesigning the aircraft, even the most skilled engineer would be at a massive disadvantage. This is why internalization of the oversight process by the FAA is nearly impossible without mandating that regulators, themselves, become

[16] Government Accountability Office (1993), p.3.
[17] Federal Register (2005, October 13).
[18] Downer (2010), p.86.
[19] Ibid. p.87.

involved in the design process from start to finish, a requirement that would be both burdensome and inefficient.

Moreover, the problem goes even deeper than the FAA's inability to adequately certify individual aircraft designs. As it turns out, these regulators lack even the necessary information to determine what certification ought to require. The previously mentioned GAO report from 1993 noted, for example, "that [FAA] staff were not sufficiently familiar with the Boeing 747-400's flight management system to define requirements for testing it or verifying regulatory compliance."[20] Given this, the suggestion of regulatory capture in the form of complicity at the FAA seems almost quaint; if the regulator isn't even capable of defining what regulatory oversight should be, let alone executing that oversight, any additional affinity for the manufacturer's interests is almost beside the point.

It should be observed at this point that although much has been made of the unique failings of the FAA, both prior to and especially in the wake of the MAX 8 crashes,[21] the notion that the FAA is substantially more dependent on manufacturers' information than equivalent agencies elsewhere would be incorrect. While other countries may not always speak of delegation in quite the same terms as the FAA, for which the designee program is a central feature of its official operations,[22] this does not mean other aviation regulators do not operate similarly.

Indeed, the other most influential aircraft regulator in the world, EASA, also relies quite heavily on manufacturers, not only for type certifications – for which it generally has sole responsibility relative to the national aviation authorities of EU member states – but also for a large array of additional regulatory tasks, including designations of airworthiness. In a direct parallel to the United States' Organization Designation Authorization Program, EASA has what is known as the Design Organization Approval (DOA) program. Under this program, manufacturers can acquire something known as DOA status, which then allows the company "to design, to validate the design to show compliance with applicable requirements and to perform airworthiness

20 Government Accountability Office (1993), p. 5.

21 Following the MAX 8 incidents, for example, a number of other aviation authorities, such as Europe's EASA, pledged to execute their own oversight in the future and not rely solely on the FAA's determinations (Katz (2019)).

22 The United States legal code specifically allows the FAA to "delegate to a qualified private person, or to an employee under the supervision of that person, a matter related to (A) the examination, testing, and inspection necessary to issue a certificate under this chapter; and (B) issuing the certificate" (49 USC 44702 2018).

and certification activities on behalf of EASA under granted privileges."[23] This is not to say that holders of DOA have carte blanche to operate independently without the oversight of the regulatory agency. Particularly when it comes to major design changes, EASA still plays a central role in requesting, validating, and overseeing compliance. Nevertheless, the explicit "aim [of DOA] is to promote the self-control of the organization on its way to designing safe products, independent from the surveillance of the Agency [i.e., EASA],"[24] an intention that highlights the very deliberate steps that EASA has taken to delegate the task of information collection and, albeit to a slightly lesser extent, even evaluation, to the manufacturers. Not surprisingly, both Boeing and Airbus hold DOA,[25] suggesting that EASA likely could have fallen victim to the same failings with the Boeing MAX 8 had it been in charge of certification, rather than the FAA.

Further, when it comes to the certification of individual aircraft as airworthy – a responsibility EASA shares with national aviation authorities – EASA relies on manufacturers to an even greater degree, allowing manufacturers to acquire Production Organization Approval (POA), whereby the actor can "[o]btain, in the case of complete aircraft and upon presentation of a Statement of Conformity (EASA Form 52), an aircraft certificate of airworthiness and a noise certificate without further showing."[26] During communications with one of the top officials in charge of airworthiness and certification at Airbus, the individual conveyed that it is both broadly understood and entirely accepted that there is no airworthiness authority in the world that could possibly verify compliance across all applicants, making a certain degree of delegation not only necessary but also preferable.[27]

The general takeaway from this discussion is that aircraft regulators place substantial responsibility for overseeing aircraft safety on the manufacturers themselves. In particular, regulators delegate the responsibility for designing appropriate tests, running the tests, evaluating the tests, and submitting the results of those tests. While part of the reason for this is undoubtedly an effort to reduce workload on agencies that simply lack the resources to validate the safety of all aircraft designs, let alone every

[23] Kun and Cunxi (2011), p. 390.
[24] Nita and Scholz (2009), p. 1.
[25] See www.easa.europa.eu/download/doa-adoa/List-of-Approved-DOA.xlsx.
[26] COMMISSION REGULATION (EU) No 748/2012, Annex I.
[27] Based on communications with Didier Robin, VP of Airworthiness and Certification at Airbus.

individual aircraft, even more central to this outcome is the fact that the regulators lack a sufficient degree of technical knowledge about the aircraft they are overseeing. The only parties with access to this information are the manufacturers.

Notably, none of this discussion is meant to suggest that this process of regulatory delegation makes air travel dangerous. The MAX 8 disasters aside, airplane travel remains one of the safest forms of transit, and it has only become safer over time, even as regulators have increasingly delegated their oversight responsibilities to airplane manufacturers. Considering the high visibility of failures and the substantial reputational consequences for Boeing and Airbus should their planes fail, these two companies clearly have substantial incentives to ensure that whoever is involved in overseeing safety, they are doing a good enough job to avoid what occurred with the MAX 8. Nonetheless, it is telling that even in a sector in which safety failures have extremely high stakes in terms of lives lost and reputational damage to the agency in charge of oversight, regulators are not internalizing the process of regulatory monitoring, nor are they collecting relevant information themselves.

At the same time, one could argue that aerospace is a relatively unique sector, due to aircrafts' technical complexity as well as the strong incentives manufacturers themselves have to ensure safety. These characteristics might not only necessitate greater reliance on manufacturers but also make regulators more comfortable doing so. Therefore, the next section turns to the direct-to-consumer products sector, an area that tends to have far less technological complexity than the aerospace sector, as well as typically less visibility in the case of product failures. Yet once again, as we shall see, asymmetric information problems and dependence on producers for safety information remain the norm, suggesting that these dynamics are not limited to sectors of high complexity or in which failures make for instantaneous headlines. Rather, information asymmetries and dependencies pervade the national regulatory space.

2.3 A CONSISTENT THEME: CONSUMER PRODUCT REGULATION

In theory, consumer products can include anything sold directly to consumers and intended as a final good. In practice, nations frequently separate out the responsibility for the regulation of certain consumer goods, such as clothes, furniture, home appliances, and children's toys from that of others, including food, pharmaceuticals, medical devices, and automobiles. For the present purposes, therefore, the focus is on the former types of consumer products, which typically fall under the purview of consumer product regulators, while omitting the latter types of products, which are more commonly handled by other, specialized agencies.

Considering that determining the safety of a toaster or a couch is less technically demanding than evaluating the safety of an airplane, one might assume that government regulators are more capable of internalizing the regulatory oversight of these simpler types of goods, such that they implement independent testing and evaluations prior to a product's approval. One might also assume that regulators are continuously monitoring existing products in order to ensure that any new revelations about a product's risk are rapidly and appropriately addressed. In reality, despite the low complexity of many direct-to-consumer products, regulators across countries still substantially rely on the firms involved in manufacturing and selling these products for much of the information necessary to determine their safety.

When it comes to the introduction of new products onto the market, consumer product regulators at times play little to no role. A *Washington Post* article investigating a baby sleeper that proved deadly quoted the US Consumer Product Safety Commissioner as saying, "People assume we bless a product before it comes to market. That isn't the case."[28] As for monitoring those products already on the market, there seems to be a near universal tendency for regulators to rely heavily on the information of firms. This is most clearly illustrated by examining the process that typically leads to a product recall.

A recall is one of the central tools that regulators have at their disposal should they discover that a consumer product is unsafe. It entails publicly announcing that a product safety issue has been discovered and then encouraging consumers to bring in the product for a repair, exchange, or refund. According to the OECD GlobalRecalls portal, which aggregates data on recalls across OECD countries, in 2020, there were more than 3,000 consumer recalls issued by regulatory agencies in the monitored nations.[29]

28 Frankel (2019).

29 The country with the most recalls was Australia (431), followed by Germany and Korea (349 for both), and then the United States (257). However, these numbers are not directly comparable, since Australia and Germany, for example, both include automobiles in their consumer recalls, whereas the United States does not. Likewise, Australia also includes pharmaceuticals in its consumer recalls, whereas most other countries list drug recalls

So from where does the information leading to these recalls arise? The OECD portal itself provides limited details, usually only listing the hazard in question but not revealing how the regulatory agency became aware of it. In order to help answer this question, therefore, regulatory agencies that participate in reporting recalls to the OECD portal were contacted, using information available through the various regulatory agencies' websites. Regulators were asked about the percentage of recalls issued in each country that were initiated as a result of information provided by the manufacturer or distributor as opposed to as a result of either market surveillance by the agency or consumer complaints that were reported directly to the regulatory body. Among those agencies that responded with the requested information, the answers were surprisingly consistent. Croatia's consumer products' oversight body observed that "product recalls generally come from manufacturers or distributors." Similar observations were made regarding recalls in the United Kingdom, Australia, Sweden, Slovakia, and Poland. Data provided by the Polish Office of Competition and Consumer Protection revealed that in 2019, 257 out of 564 (approximately 46%) of recalls were the result of company-provided information, while in 2020, 319 out of 704 (or 45%) of recalls fell into this category. Likewise, data provided by Slovakia's regulatory agency revealed that in 2020, 233 out of 293 total recalls were based on notifications by companies, while only 57 of these were the result of market surveillance activities by the Slovak Trade Inspection, and 3 were the result of consumer complaints.[30]

In fact, the only countries contacted for which company reports did not appear to spur a substantial portion, if not the majority, of recalls were Hungary and Israel, with Israeli regulators speculating that the low percentage of firm-initiated recalls could be a feature of Israel's rigorous testing of imports at the border and a robust system of consumer complaints that are generally delivered directly to the agency. As for Hungary, the official contacted estimated that manufacturer-initiated recalls only made up a tiny proportion of total recalls, yet she also observed that her agency does not keep accurate statistics on the initiation of recalls and that they are not always informed about voluntary recalls by manufac-

elsewhere. If one excludes automobiles, American recalls take the number two spot, after Korea

30 A majority of recalls from 2019 were also initiated by firms (110 out of 199 total recalls), as have been recalls thus far in 2021 (71 out of 84 recalls in 2021 so far have been initiated as a result of firm reporting).

turers, making it difficult to determine the true state of play. Moreover, to the extent that manufacturer-initiated recalls really do make up a small percentage of total recall activities, a cynical interpretation might be to attribute this to the low capacity of Hungarian regulators and manufacturers' calculations that failures to report suspected dangers or defects are unlikely to be uncovered.

Overall, the information collected from regulators suggests that these agencies – which, if anything, have an incentive to understate the level of company involvement in the oversight process – substantially rely on firms for ensuring that dangerous products are removed promptly and faithfully from the market. At the same time, much of the information received from regulators was fairly anecdotal or only covered one or two years. Therefore, in addition to reaching out to regulatory agencies directly, an effort was also made to collect more systematic data on where information leading to recalls typically originates. Whereas most countries do not list on their recall websites how the information for the recall arose, the US Consumer Product Safety Commission (CPSC) frequently does provide information of this nature. In order to supplement the information attained through direct communications with national regulatory agencies, data was also scraped from the CPSC website on product recalls issued between 2013 and the end of 2019, which was the last full year available at the time of collection. This resulted in a total of 2,003 individual recall announcements. Recall announcements often contain information about the circumstances leading to the recall, for example noting that the company in question had received a certain number of reports about incidents (which it then relayed to the CPSC) or that the CPSC itself had received a certain number of reports from consumers. This made it possible to analyze the circumstances leading up to each recall, looking specifically at whether the information eventually leading to the recall was reported to or otherwise originated with the firm, was collected by or otherwise reported to the CPSC, or whether the source of information was unspecified. As seen in Figure 2.1, across every year in the sample, at least 50 percent of recalls were based wholly on company-reported safety incidents. Moreover, this percentage, if anything, understates the percentage of recalls resulting solely from company disclosures since the vast majority of remaining recalls did not have the source of information specified.[31]

[31] Some recall announcements note that incidents had been reported abroad but do not indicate whether that information reached the CPSC via the firm, the foreign regulator, of the CPSC's own monitoring of foreign recalls.

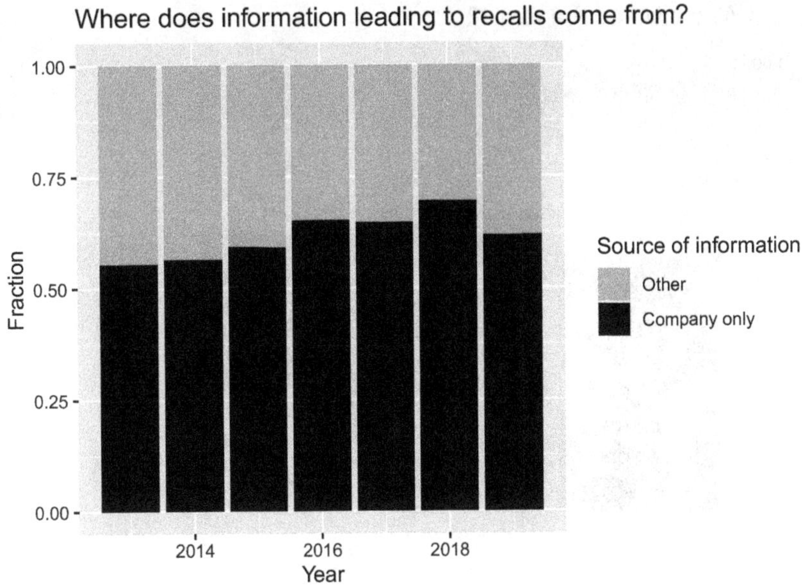

FIGURE 2.1 Source of recall information in the United States

A similar pattern emerges if we look at whether the recall itself was initiated by the firm or by the regulator. Beginning in 1995, the CPSC implemented the so-called "Fast Track" program. Under this program, companies agree both to submit the initial report of a defect when they discover it and also to institute a recall within 20 working days. In return, the CPSC agrees not to engage in its own preliminary determination regarding whether the product presents a substantial hazard.

The CPSC website records whether a product was recalled under the Fast Track program from partway through 2016. This made it possible to evaluate the percentage of recalls that occurred under this program on an annual basis between 2017 and 2019.[32] While the vast majority of the Fast Track recalls are the same as those for which the information for the recall solely came from the firm, making the Fast Track results similar to those presented in Figure 2.1, Fast Track recalls also include cases in which the source of information was otherwise ambiguous while excluding cases in which the information may have come from the firm, but the firm, for whatever reason, was not registered in the Fast Track program or was not willing to issue the recall within the required time period. As such,

[32] This time period contained 781 individual product recalls.

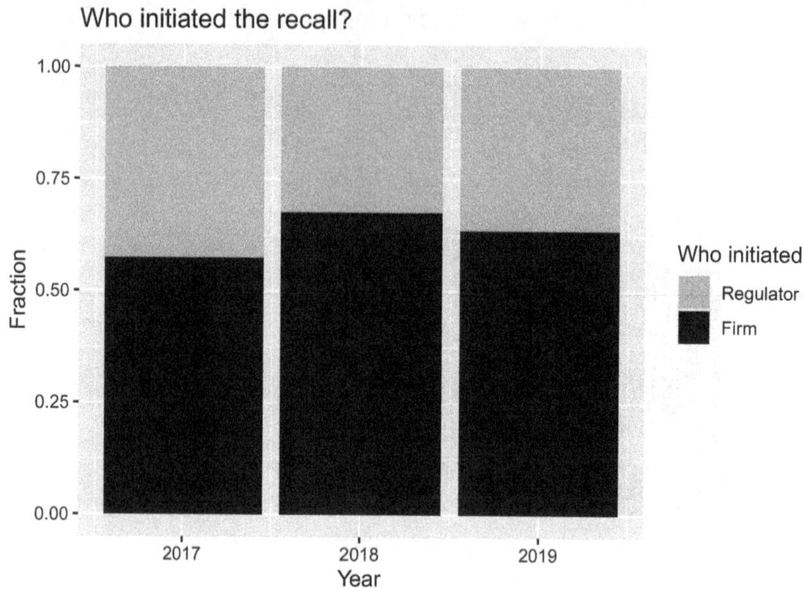

FIGURE 2.2 Who initiates recalls in the United States?

Fast Track recalls can offer an alternative way of confirming whether it is indeed true that producers provide the majority of information necessary for product recalls in the United States. In addition, the Fast Track program offers insight into how frequently recalls themselves are initiated by the firm as opposed to by the regulatory agency.

As can be seen in Figure 2.2, the majority of recalls not only rely on firms' private data but are also entirely firm-initiated. Taken together, analysis of the more systematic US recall data, therefore, suggests a substantial dependence on companies to promptly and faithfully reveal potential risks as they arise.

These findings raise the question of why regulators of consumer products around the world are so dependent on the information of producers to uncover emerging risks. As in the case of aerospace, part of the answer relates to resources. A 2014 report from the US Government Accountability Office, for example, noted that, "it would be unrealistic for the agency to implement a premarket approval process for all consumer goods given the vast number of products under CPSC's jurisdiction."[33] This same report found that despite a 10 percent increase in the value of imports that

[33] Government Accountability Office (2014), p. 20.

CPSC oversaw between 2010 and 2012, the number of staff has generally been decreasing, such that in 2014 the agency had 41 percent fewer staff members than in 1975.[34] Although not all regulatory agencies have seen a similar reduction in personnel, lack of capacity is a general problem across countries.[35] This lack of resources not only makes it difficult for agencies to conduct independent assessments of new products before they enter the market, but it also contributes to the impossibility of monitoring every product once it has entered the market.

Yet there is another problem as well, one that goes beyond resources. Simply stated, producers are better positioned than regulators to receive information about product risks first. If a toaster catches fire, destroying the toaster but causing no further damage, what is a consumer likely to do? With the possible exception of Israeli consumers, most consumers are unlikely to respond by reaching out to the regulator. They might not even know which regulatory agency oversees toasters. Rather, the average consumer will contact the company directly, demanding a refund and, assuming the spontaneous combustion hasn't put them off the brand, a replacement. The producer now, unlike the regulator, has information that its products can catch fire. The regulator will only learn of this if the producer reveals it or if a subsequent toaster fire either leads a consumer to report the situation directly to the regulator or leads to a broader tragedy and eventually an investigation.

Indeed, this is directly borne out in the information garnered from communications with national regulatory agencies, as well as in the data reported from regulators in Poland and Slovakia and collected from the United States, all of which shows that recalls are frequently the result of reports submitted by firms and not the result of the regulatory body's independent efforts. Notably, of the 1,326 recalls issued in the United States between 2013 and 2019 for which it was explicitly indicated that one or more safety incidents were reported prior to the recall, fewer than 2 percent listed the CPSC as the recipient (either sole or joint) of an incident report. Given this, it makes perfect sense that regulators, even in the case of relatively nontechnical products, would rely predominantly on producers to uncover and report product dangers. Meanwhile, producers' decisions about whether to relay the risks of which they are made aware will at least partially depend upon the likelihood that any given malfunction or design flaw could lead to greater financial losses down

34 Ibid. p. 15–16.
35 See, e.g., Australian Government Productivity Commission (2006), p. 117.

the road – due to damaged reputation, liability claims, or both – than a timely confession and rectification.

The discussion of consumer goods thus reveals some similarities between the regulation of these products and that of aircraft, despite the very different nature of the two types of goods. Most importantly, in both cases regulators are clearly at an informational disadvantage when it comes to evaluating or monitoring safety. In response to this, regulators in both areas have tended to delegate, either officially or unofficially, a substantial part of the regulatory process to the regulated. In the case of aircraft, manufacturers can officially acquire designee status, allowing them to play a direct role in assessment and verification, while in the case of consumer products, producers, at least in some countries, effectively operate on an honor system when it comes to verifying product safety initially, and it is also predominantly producers' responsibility to quickly and faithfully report newly uncovered product risks and malfunctions as they become apparent. This latter dependence on producers to monitor the safety of goods that have already entered the market is in many ways related to the sorts of dependencies that exist prior to market approval. In both cases, dependence stems from regulators' lesser familiarity with or capacity to oversee producers' products. At the same time, as subsequent chapters of this book will lay bare, dependence on the information of firms for post-market monitoring introduces some unique and perverse dynamics that dependence on producers for initial approval does not. Therefore, when examining the next two cases of pharmaceutical and industrial chemical regulations, particularly close attention is paid to the role of informational dependencies during the post approval period. This will make it possible to begin considering not only what informational dependence on producers looks like during the post-approval phase but, crucially, how producers might leverage this in order to manipulate which products receive what standards when.

2.4 TIMELY DELAYS? INFORMATION PROVISION IN PHARMACEUTICAL REGULATION

Pharmaceutical regulation around the world today is, in many ways, an outgrowth of a historical tragedy. In the late 1950s, thalidomide, an over-the-counter sedative, was widely distributed as a cure for morning sickness, gaining market access in 46 different countries. Unbeknownst to the countless pregnant women who took it, thalidomide had a devastating impact on fetal development, greatly contributing to miscarriages and severe birth defects, such that by the time the drug's consequences were broadly understood, it had already caused more than 10,000 infants worldwide to be born with major physical deformities.[36] The massive scale of the disaster contributed to a global reckoning, with governments around the world taking action to ensure they would be protected against such a catastrophe in the future. Under new legislation spearheaded by the United States – one of the few countries that had refused to approve thalidomide in the first place[37] – and quickly enacted across a broad swath of nations, pharmaceutical companies were required to prove that their drugs were not only safe but also effective before winning market approval. In addition, many governments under which regulatory oversight of pharmaceuticals had previously been minimal established national regulatory bodies tasked with guaranteeing that drugs targeted the conditions they were intended to target without causing undue risk. These new regulatory agencies were also given broad powers to monitor existing drugs to ensure that there would be swift rectification should information about a product's hazards emerge.

So how did these newly empowered agencies carry out their responsibilities? Who provided the data necessary to make a determination about a drug's safety and effectiveness, and who was primarily responsible for monitoring drugs on the market? The answer, of course, was the developers of the drugs.

Around the world, drug companies are responsible for conducting their own testing, clinical trials, and monitoring prior to and in the wake of receiving product approval. To be fair, there is a strong case to be made that, at the very least when it comes to new drug applications, reliance on the company's research is, in fact, optimal. The cost of testing a drug in the lead-up to first approval is astronomical, with two recent studies estimating the average at around $1.4 billion.[38] With the potential to realize substantial profits should their drug eventually be approved, pharmaceutical companies have strong financial incentives to shoulder the costs of evaluation. Moreover, regulators themselves benefit from requirements that producers report back on each stage of testing. As Carpenter has noted while writing about the US Food and Drug Administration (FDA), "The requirement that firms provide all information to the FDA

36 Vargesson (2015).
37 Carpenter (2014), ch. 3.
38 DiMasi, Grabowski and Hansen (2016); Wouters, McKee and Luyten (2020).

drastically reduces the agency's information costs and reduces the variance of product uncertainty in drug review."[39] As such, there is nothing inherently problematic about delegating initial testing to the producer. So long as the testing process is fully transparent and rigorously verified, producers have every incentive to provide all requested information, and given that the tests themselves are heavily documented, the ability of producers to suppress unfavorable information ought theoretically to be limited.

Where the dependence on pharmaceutical companies' information becomes potentially more problematic is during the post-approval process. This is because once drugs are released onto the market, the system for monitoring safety is far less standardized or closely analyzed than during the pre-market stage.

Officially, of course, drug companies have a legal obligation to report adverse reactions to their products. In the European Union, for example, drug companies must "record all suspected adverse reactions in the Union or in third countries which are brought to their attention."[40] Likewise, in the United States, the law states that "Any person whose name appears on the label of a marketed prescription drug product as its manufacturer, packer, or distributor must report to FDA each adverse drug experience received or otherwise obtained that is both serious and unexpected as soon as possible, but no later than 15 calendar days from initial receipt of the information by the person whose name appears on the label."[41] Nearly identical requirements are codified into law in developed countries around the world.[42]

Such requirements are, in some sense, an acknowledgement that drug companies are frequently privy to post-marketing information that the regulator is not. Indeed, although there are ways for physicians and (to a lesser extent) patients to report adverse events directly to regulatory agencies, in practice it seems that the companies themselves are more often the recipients of such information. One reason for this may be the logistical hurdles frequently involved in reporting adverse reactions. A meta-analysis of articles investigating the under-reporting of adverse events by physicians to official systems across a wide range of countries shows just

39 Carpenter (2002), p. 491.

40 Directive 2001/83/EC, Article 107.

41 21 CFR 310.305(c)(1).

42 Developing countries often rely on the pharmaceutical approval and monitoring activities of developed nations and thus may not always make this requirement explicit.

how pervasive this problem is, finding a median under-reporting rate of 94%.[43] Such a high under-reporting rate means that without company participation, regulators are unable to independently acquire information about potential safety issues as they arise. Such a high under-reporting rate also helps explain why, just as in the case of consumer products discussed previously, the majority of the reports about adverse events that do make it into the US reporting system (which itself represents approximately half of adverse event reports collected at the international level by the World Health Organization) come directly from the drug companies.[44]

What makes this potentially problematic is that because regulators may be unable to monitor drug companies' internal reporting systems, it opens the door to firms withholding reports or submitting them at convenient times. Bolstering these concerns, it has been observed, for example, that Canadian regulators have "a limited ability to ensure continued compliance with regulations once a drug enters the market."[45] Similarly, a study of post-market surveillance in Europe noted that "in general, time frames for reporting are relatively loosely handled [by regulatory agencies],"[46] a feature that may partially result from regulators' limited ability to engage in post-market surveillance themselves and one that suggests firms have some leeway in deciding when to reveal potentially concerning drug reactions.[47] Moreover, in the United States, pharmaceutical companies have been known to test the limits of the FDA's tolerance for delayed reporting, with failures to report adverse events in a timely fashion in some cases leading to warning letters and even criminal prosecutions.[48]

This is not to say that pharmaceutical companies indefinitely suppress information they are officially obligated to report. Particularly in the case of major adverse reactions that are likely to become publicly known and could seriously harm a company's reputation, even a purely profit maximizing firm ought to be incentivized to divulge fairly quickly. If one analyzes when in a drug's lifecycle it is most likely to be withdrawn from the market as a result of serious side effects, one finds that the most common timing of the first global withdrawal is within the first five years

43 Hazell and Shakir (2006) provide a survey of such studies.

44 Ahmad (2003).

45 Lemmens and Gibson (2012), p. 5.

46 Koster, Teeuw and Cockburn (2000), p. 476.

47 More recent legislation in the E.U. has attempted to improve the post-market surveillance process.

48 Ahmad (2003).

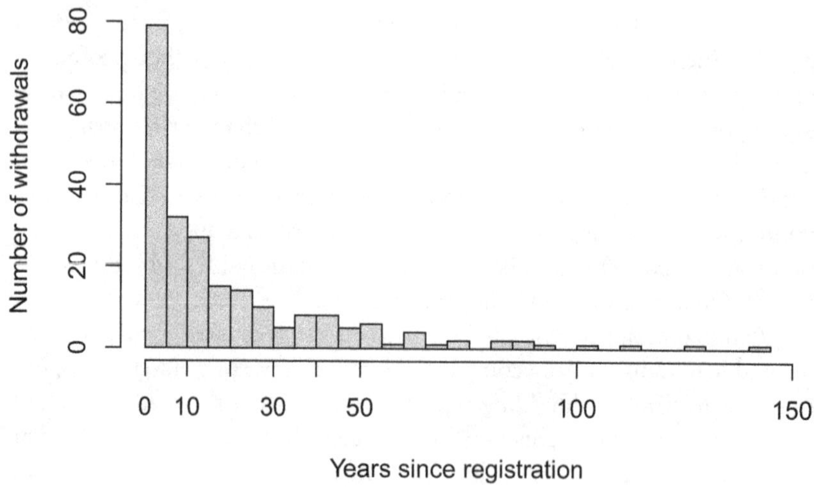

FIGURE 2.3 Withdrawals of pharmaceuticals

after a drug's approval (See Figure 2.3),[49] a time frame that falls squarely within a drug's most profitable period, when firms would undoubtedly like to avoid such an event. To the extent that firms are the primary distributor of adverse event reports, and given that such reports seem to play a central role in the withdrawal of drugs from the market,[50] the prompt withdrawal of most drugs that end up being withdrawn eventually suggests that firms do have incentives to reveal serious adverse events fairly promptly.

Nevertheless, the relative promptness of withdrawals stemming from the most concerning types of adverse reactions masks the degree to which drug companies attempt to and, at times, succeed in leveraging private information to affect the timing of regulatory change. In particular, concerns have been raised about companies' tendencies to strategically reveal the sort of information that falls short of the "serious" designation requiring immediate disclosure but that nonetheless is pertinent to regulatory decision-making. Along these lines, in a report to Congress by the FDA touching on pharmaceutical companies' utilization of citizen petitions in order to block the entry of generic competitors, the agency noted that, "Many of the petitions contained data that had been available to the

[49] Data is taken from Siramshetty et al. (2015) and is intended to capture all products that were recalled from the market due to toxicity concerns or side effects since the 1960s.
[50] Clarke, Deeks and Shakir (2006).

petitioner well before the date of the petition."[51] In other words, these companies intentionally timed the release of their information to try to maximize its regulatory benefit.

2.5 INDEFINITE DELAYS: INDUSTRIAL CHEMICALS AND THE BLACK BOX OF PRIVATE INFORMATION

The possibility that companies could delay releasing pertinent information so as to delay or manipulate the timing of regulatory change, while certainly present in the case of pharmaceuticals, seems to pose a significantly greater threat in the realm of industrial chemicals. In 2017, for example, *The Guardian* published an exposé detailing how Monsanto had known about the dangers of polychlorinated biphenyls (PCBs), which it produced in large volumes, for eight years prior to voluntarily deciding to halt the chemicals' production. Not long after Monsanto halted sales of PCBs, a number of countries implemented official bans on production of the chemicals in response to growing evidence showing their severe hazards.[52] In another instance, with many parallels to the Monsanto case, DuPont attempted to conceal the risks of perfluorooctanoic acid (PFOA) for more than a decade after discovering them.[53] According to subsequent investigations, Dupont had evidence as early as 1981 (32 years before it stopped using the chemical) that PFOA could enter the bloodstream of pregnant factory workers' fetuses, suggesting an obvious potential to harm fetal development, yet the company declined to reveal this information to regulators.[54] Making this omission particularly egregious was the fact that DuPont had been dumping PFOA into unprotected pits near its production site, thereby allowing the chemical to seep into the drinking water of nearby communities. The company continued this practice for more than a decade even after internal studies made clear the substance could cause birth defects in rats and humans. Perhaps not surprisingly, it has since become evident that PFOA contributed to adverse health outcomes near DuPont's factory as a result of the chemical seeping out of the unlined pits and into the ground water.[55]

While the PCBs and PFOA cases represent particularly flagrant examples in which industrial chemical manufacturers declined to share safety

51 Food and Drug Administration (2009).
52 Neslen (2017).
53 Rich (2016).
54 Government Accountability Office (2010), p. 8–9.
55 Rich (2016).

information to which they had privileged access, more broadly the examples highlight how, in the absence of companies' willingness to divulge internal data about chemical safety, it can take many years for regulators to become aware of what firms had known for some time. One of the features of industrial chemicals – as compared to pharmaceuticals and consumer products – that makes the information problem particularly acute following a chemical's initial introduction onto the market is the near total lack of opportunity for third parties to identify risks in a timely manner, even after they become obvious to the firm. As one author has observed:

> Toxicology information is too expensive for workers and consumers (or even unions and consumer organizations) to generate. Exposure and cost data may simply be impossible for these persons to obtain. Moreover, the benefit to any individual of developing the information is small. The information is a public good (that is, it is nonexcludable), which reduces to practically nil any return to these persons on investment in research.[56]

With no third parties in a reasonable position to identify chemical risks, regulators must either wait until the risks become broadly apparent (usually following years or even decades of harm), test all existing products themselves, or rely on the manufacturers to study the products they produce and faithfully reveal any and all information as it becomes available. The first option is clearly problematic, as it would lead to a substantial delay between regulatory updating and the knowability of risk. The second option, in which the regulator internalizes the risk assessment, suffers from many of the same problems already described in regards to the regulation of aircraft, consumer goods, and pharmaceuticals. For one thing, there are simply too many products for it to be practical for the regulator to continually assess their safety. A 2001 white paper produced by the Commission of the European Communities noted that there are approximately 100,000 chemicals registered for use in the European Union, yet "[t]here is a general lack of knowledge about the properties and uses of existing substances."[57] In the United States, a 2010 Congressional Hearing on toxic chemical regulation similary estimated that there are "more than 80,000 chemicals in the products we use every day,"[58] and of those 80,000 products, the EPA – which is the primary regulator of chemicals in the USA – had tested a mere 200. Beyond the sheer magnitude

56 Applegate (1991), p. 298–9.
57 European Union Commission (2001), p. 6.
58 111th Congress (2010, February 4), p. 1.

of chemicals in production, which alone would make it impossible for any regulatory agency to evaluate them all, there is also the fact that manufacturers frequently have a better sense of which chemicals ought to be prioritized for testing than regulators, meaning that any efforts by regulators to fully internalize the process of identifying and evaluating potentially dangerous chemicals would be a highly inefficient solution.

So this leaves the option of depending on manufacturers, sellers, and downstream users to provide the vast majority of necessary safety information, and indeed, this is what we see in practice, to varying degrees, across countries' regulatory regimes. In the United States, dependence on companies for information is codified into law, found in Part 15 of the US Code, which states, "It is the policy of the United States that ... adequate information should be developed with respect to the effect of chemical substances and mixtures on health and the environment and that the development of such information should be the responsibility of those who manufacture and those who process such chemical substances and mixtures."[59] The European Union has similarly made it the responsibility of manufacturers and downstream industrial chemical users to provide relevant safety information, a responsibility that has become more expansive following the implementation of Regulation (EC) No 1907/2006 - Registration, Evaluation, Authorisation and Restriction of Chemicals (REACH). Under this 2006 legislation, manufacturers, importers, and downstream users are expected to take on a greater information sharing burden, not only for new chemicals but also for those already in distribution. As one author pithily explains it, "REACH's objective is to move from 'no data, no problem' to 'no data, no market'."[60] In other words, REACH actually increases the extent to which regulatory updating responds to firm-level information provision, because it makes information a requirement of continued sales.

The theoretical downsides to a system in which regulations become stricter unless producers provide updated data are discussed in Chapter 3 and assessed empirically in Chapters 5 and 6. However, it is worth noting here that a central impetus for the European regulation was, on the one hand, the recognition that chemical producers and industrial users have better information about those chemicals than regulators and thus should be responsible for providing it and, on the other, that these actors have

59 15 USC 2601(b), 2020.
60 Applegate (2008), p. 1390.

taken few steps to provide necessary safety information to regulators about the products they sell. Indeed, in a white paper initially proposing the new legislation, the authors explicitly stated, "Responsibility to generate knowledge about chemicals should be placed on industry."[61] In support of this conclusion, the authors of the document observed that:

> Current liability regimes are insufficient to remedy the problems found by the review. Liability is usually based on the principle that those who cause damage should pay compensation for that damage. However, in order to be held liable, it is generally required that a causal connection be proven between the cause and the resulting damage. This is often virtually impossible for injured parties if cause and effect occur far apart in time and if adequate test data on the effects of substances are not available.[62]

In an earlier, unrelated academic paper that echoes the conclusions of the Commission, one author noted in regards to chemicals, "The tort system is predicated upon the existence of information linking cause with effect, but the manufacturer often is the only party in a financial position to perform the research necessary to prove a causal connection. Potential liability is therefore another influence that discourages manufacturers from producing this information."[63]

These observations about chemical companies' privileged information position and the resulting insufficiency of the liability system highlight one way in which the post-market information problems present for industrial chemicals tend to be more acute than those for consumer products, pharmaceuticals, or even aerospace. Specifically, the link between an industrial chemical and any harm it causes is often harder to establish than a link between, say, faulty battery design and a phone's spontaneous combustion or a diabetes medication and sudden heart failure. This may also help explain why manufacturers are seemingly quicker to recall or otherwise alert authorities about problematic consumer and pharmaceutical products than they are to take such steps with harmful chemicals, which in the absence of REACH-like legislation tend to be broadly underregulated, remaining on the market long after firms learn (or could have learned) their risks.[64] The fact that there is a lower probability that a chemical's harms will be discovered, at least in the near term, incentivizes producers not only to purposely avoid learning the specifics of the harms

[61] European Union Commission (2001), p. 8.

[62] Ibid., p. 6–7.

[63] Lyndon (1989), p. 1817.

[64] Lyndon (1989); Applegate (2008).

their products may cause but also to suppress what they do learn for an extended or even indefinite period, since the probability that the regulators themselves will uncover this information and be able to act on it is exceedingly low.

The case of industrial chemical regulation thus highlights the extent to which company suppression of private information can be an effective strategy for hindering regulatory change once a product has gained initial approval. Yet this does not mean that there is nothing regulators or governments can do to alter producers' incentives to reveal the information they have collected or are in a position to collect. Europe's implementation of REACH, for example, led to a substantial amount of new data on chemicals that had previously been understudied and poorly understood by regulatory bodies. Likewise, Wagner (2003) has observed that after the EPA changed its rules to grant amnesty to companies that had failed to report adverse effects, companies suddenly produced 11,000 previously undisclosed studies, which was four times the number that had been provided to regulators over the prior fifteen years.[65] This suggests that variation in information provision and, potentially, the degree to which or ways in which firms will use information to affect regulatory change are not only a function of different product characteristics but also of different institutional designs, meaning that even though information asymmetries and dependencies are universal, the consequences of them may vary.

2.6 NOT JUST A NATIONAL PROBLEM

This brief investigation of regulatory processes across four diverse industries reveals that information asymmetries between producers of dangerous products and those that regulate them are a pervasive feature of the domestic regulatory environment. In addition, it shows that these asymmetries not only encourage regulators to depend on producers for information about product risk; they effectively necessitate it. Finally, the discussion of regulation in the sectors of pharmaceuticals and industrial chemicals, in particular, hints that these informational dependencies are not without consequences. Rather, they may lead to inefficient or otherwise biased updating of regulatory rules.

65 Wagner (2003), p. 1648.

The reasons for the asymmetries and resulting dependencies identified in the previous sections are multiple. First, there is a problem of resources. Even the best-funded regulators simply do not have the resources to independently study every product on the market. This is true both for products entering the market and for those that remain on it. Second, there is an issue of both tacit and technical knowledge. Because producers have invested so much time, effort, and research into developing their products, they are better situated to understand potential risks. Finally, there is the fact that producers are the primary recipients of new information. Through a combination of consumer complaints, internal studies, and observations of adverse reactions, producers are constantly accruing knowledge about previously unknown dangers to which regulators are not directly privy.

Notably, these contributors to information asymmetries and dependencies are in no way specific to the national level. If anything, they are exacerbated for international standard-setters. This becomes readily apparent when one considers each of the factors in turn and asks whether or not these same conditions are likely to be replicated internationally.

First, there is the regulatory body's capacity. While international standard-setters may be better funded than regulatory bodies in certain developing countries, they generally do not enjoy greater resources than regulators in developed markets. This is partially a result of the fact that international organizations of all stripes have an inherent inability to coerce contributions from their members, leading to a free-riding problem. Indeed, as compared to the budgets of the wealthier national regulatory bodies, the budgets of international standard-setters are absolutely paltry. Take the relatively well-funded and highly influential World Organization for Animal Health (OIE), which is charged, among other things, with monitoring animal disease status globally and which "collect[s], analyse[s] and disseminate[s] veterinary scientific information" to member states.[66] The organization's total annual operating budget in 2020 was approximately €16 million (or around $18 million). By comparison, the US Department of Agriculture allocated $331 million to animal health inspection services in that same year,[67] suggesting the OIE could not hope to engage in any sort of comprehensive, independent monitoring of animal safety around the world, given it is operating on

66 World Organization for Animal Health (OIE) (2021).

67 US Department of Agriculture (2020), p. 57.

less than 5% of what the United States, alone, deploys for that purpose domestically.

Other international standard-setters receive even less in monetary allocations. For example, the Codex Alimentarius Commission, which is in charge of setting sanitary standards for all types of traded food, had a measly budget of $4.3 million in 2019,[68] while the Joint FAO/WHO Meeting on Pesticide Residues (JMPR), the organization tasked with providing scientific recommendations to Codex regarding agrochemicals, had an almost insignificant annual allocation as of 2002 of $80,000.[69] Given such miniscule budgets, it is little surprise that even finding competent individuals to staff these international agencies can prove challenging. A 2002 JMPR report noted, for example, "Over recent years, the FAO and WHO have had increasing difficulty in finding suitable experts that are willing to work on a voluntary basis in support of the work of the JMPR. This is particularly the case for the FAO Panel, where the pre-meeting workload in preparing the draft global monographs has become excessive and unsustainable."[70]

As for the second contributor to information asymmetries and dependencies, regulators' lesser tacit and technical knowledge, it seems hard to believe that overwhelmed technocrats, operating with paltry salaries or on a voluntary basis, would have any greater ability to acquire such knowledge than their better-paid and often better-qualified national counterparts.

Finally, when it comes to being the primary recipients of new revelations about product risk, international regulators again face equal or higher hurdles than domestic regulators. Like national regulators, international standard-setters suffer from the fact that they are simply unable to acquire the same degree of information that firms continuously generate in the course of research, development, and subsequent monitoring of performance. In addition, international standard-setters have no direct legal authority, unless directly granted it by national law. This reduces these actors' ability to demand scientific studies that domestic regulators might be legally authorized to obtain. Finally, with less name recognition in many cases than the competent national authority within a given jurisdiction, there is a low likelihood that international standard-setters would receive consumer or other third-party reports that their national counter-

68 Codex Alimentarius Commission (2019), CX/CAC 19/42/13.
69 Food and Agricultural Organization and World Health Organization (2002), p. 24.
70 Ibid., p. 24.

parts would not. All of this is likely why, when it comes to identifying product risks, many international standard-setting bodies do not even try to rely on their own surveillance. Instead, they depend on reporting from national agencies. Thus, the OECD portal for product recalls is purely an aggregator of recalls reported by domestic regulators. Likewise, when it comes to determining nations' risk statuses in terms of the prevalence of animal diseases, OIE relies heavily on self-reporting by each participating country. This means that to the extent that nations themselves rely on the information provided by producers of various products, this same information is simply being transmitted up to the international bodies through those bodies' national members. As for those cases in which international standard-setters do in fact bypass the information of national agencies and instead seek to make independent determinations about risk, for all of the reasons previously outlined they will have no choice but to remain heavily dependent on the information provided to them by private actors.

Taken together, this means that, if anything, international standard-setting bodies are likely to be at an even greater information disadvantage, as compared to their domestic counterparts. This suggests, in turn, that any national regulatory biases that result from the sorts of information asymmetries and dependencies described throughout this chapter ought to be mirrored internationally.

2.7 ANTICIPATING BIAS

This chapter has shown that across a broad range of sectors, nationally and internationally, those that manufacture and sell a given product have a far greater ability to gain insight into that product's risks than those tasked with setting the regulatory rules. As a result of this, regulatory systems are generally set up in such a way that regulators, both officially and unofficially, depend on producers to be the primary purveyors of information about their products.

What do these dynamics mean for producers' ability to influence regulatory outcomes? Certainly, when it comes to the most complex products, such as aircraft, producers wield substantial power over everything from the types of safety tests to which their craft are subject to determinations of whether their planes have passed the tests and ought to remain in operation. This clearly offers producers of complex products a substantial degree of discretion over regulatory rules. Yet what the case studies also reveal is that even when it comes to less complex goods, goods about which regulators ought to have a much greater understanding, producers continue to hold a significant information advantage. In particular, we saw that producers are in a privileged position when it comes to collecting information about newly discovered product risks. Thus, in the case of consumer products, manufacturers were frequently the primary source of information leading to a product recall. When it came to pharmaceuticals, drug companies were largely the ones in a position to discover and report adverse events. Finally, in the realm of industrial chemicals, chemical producers at times learned about the dangers of their formulations more than a decade before regulators became aware of the risks.

Producers' ability to learn about risks of their products before regulators, scientists, or the general public suggests that they have the opportunity to leverage this information in order to affect the timing of regulatory change. For example, producers might decide to suppress damaging information for as long as possible in the hopes of keeping a product on the market (as we saw with industrial chemicals), or they might selectively reveal certain risks at moments that are financially convenient (as pharmaceutical companies have seemingly done in the case of citizen petitions). At the same time, the cases revealed that there are limits to firms' ability to engage in these sorts of behaviors – limits that are partially a function of the characteristics of the products being regulated. In the case of pharmaceuticals, the timing of drug withdrawals implies that even if companies are willing to delay revealing certain types of information, the potential for discovery appears to pose a clear enough threat that serious adverse events tend to be reported, if not immediately, at least earlier than we might expect if firms thought they could get away with information suppression long term. By contrast, when it comes to industrial chemicals, a class of products for which it is much harder for regulators or third parties to link a harm to the product in question and for which there appears to be an excessively low probability that regulators or members of the public will uncover a harm for themselves in a timely manner, firms appear far more willing and able to delay regulatory change through the withholding of relevant information.

In addition to the role played by the characteristics of the products being regulated in informing firms' decisions around divulging or withholding private information, there is also undoubtedly a role played by regulatory capacity. Specifically, the greater the ability of regulators to internalize the oversight process, the greater their ability to uncover risks themselves and, one would assume, encourage timely reporting.

Finally, the industrial chemicals case briefly hinted at the importance of institutional rules to firms' information calculus. In particular, we saw that both Europe's implementation of REACH and the United States' decision to change reporting penalties led to a subsequent outpouring of privately held information. While the precise consequences of specific types of institutional structures for the sharing of information and, by extension, for regulatory updating will be explored in far greater depth in the chapters that follow, it is enough to observe here that producers' incentives to uncover new information or reveal what they already know is likely to be shaped by the legal and regulatory consequences of doing so. Thus, while producers may control the information, policymakers can play a central role in shaping what this means for regulatory change.

We can now consolidate the insights gathered in this chapter into four broad conclusions that will be central to the book's theoretical contributions. First, regulators' dependence on producers to be the primary source of reporting on the risks of their products means that producers' decisions about when or whether to reveal those risks has the potential to fundamentally influence the timing and shape of regulatory change. Second, products for which it is more difficult for regulators, citizens, or independent scientists to identify risks in a timely manner will offer more room for producers to manipulate regulatory change through the selective provision or suppression of information. Third, the institutional rules in place dictating how private information is treated and how regulations are updated in response to it are likely to play an important role in what firms choose or choose not to reveal. Fourth, the information asymmetries and dependencies found at the domestic level should be even more pronounced at the international standard-setting level as a result of international standard-setters' even lesser ability to collect information independently.

These four broad conclusions lead to several key questions that will be explored in the remaining chapters. First, how do producers seek to use their private information about product risks to shape regulatory change? Second, how do information asymmetries, particularly in sectors in which they are most acute, inform political preferences over regulatory institutions? Finally, given the similarities in information dynamics nationally and internationally, will regulatory biases look similar at both levels of governance, and, if so, what will this mean for the identity of the global winners and losers?

The next chapter seeks to answer each of these questions theoretically, while the subsequent chapters test the resulting expectations empirically.

3

A Theory of Regulatory Barriers

Governments around the world are constantly adjusting their regulatory rules. Many of these adjustments relate to highly detailed product-level standards. For example, they might entail revisions to how much of a chemical additive is allowed in food or new restrictions on a veterinary drug administered to livestock. Though often esoteric, these seemingly minor modifications can have significant implications for what products can and cannot be traded across borders. As a result, under WTO law, countries are required to ensure that the resulting standards do not arbitrarily impede imports, and they are expected to base their decision-making on science. But who provides the science on which these decisions are based? As the previous chapter revealed, producers of potentially dangerous products are frequently the primary source of information undergirding regulatory rules, and they also play a central role in informing any subsequent revisions. This chapter turns to the question of how producers leverage their information advantages to influence the timing and direction of regulatory change, thereby allowing those producers with the best access to scientific information to extract regulations that act as barriers to competition and trade. In addition, this chapter offers an argument for why, despite the introduction of a more diverse set of actors at the international level and the reduced potential for regulatory capture as it is traditionally understood, producers' regulatory influence via information replicates internationally what we see domestically.

In order to build out the argument, the next section begins by explicating firms' regulatory preferences. It develops a theory showing that innovative firms – which are defined as those that are involved in the patenting and production of novel products – may actually benefit from stricter standards on some of their own products. The section then explores how these firms might attempt to use their monopoly on information in order to acquire these stricter standards. It posits that firms may strategically reveal product risks at convenient times. In addition, it suggests that these same actors have incentives to seek out broader regulatory institutions that, while seemingly designed to ameliorate the sorts of information asymmetries discussed in the previous chapter, also end up conferring more power into the hands of those firms with the best access to scientific information. The result is a system in which more affordable products receive systematically stricter standards – standards that, in turn, create arbitrary barriers to domestic and international commerce. The final theoretical section asks how the international level does or does not look different from the domestic level. It argues that even if international standard-setting bodies are well-positioned to reduce trade frictions stemming from deliberate government efforts to keep foreign products out,[1] these same international bodies may still be highly susceptible to the sorts of regulatory biases identified here. The chapter concludes by laying out the observable implications of the theory that will then be tested empirically in the remainder of the book.

3.1 WHAT DO FIRMS WANT?

It is often assumed that firms prefer as little regulation as possible. After all, regulations introduce additional costs, circumscribing firm behavior and limiting what products are allowed on the market. As a result, it is not surprising to see examples of companies complaining about onerous or otherwise unfavorable regulatory rules. When Uruguay enacted mandatory labeling laws for cigarettes that limited branding strategies and required the enlargement of graphic health warnings, the tobacco behemoth, Philip Morris, filed suit in international court, not only countering the Uruguay law but also contributing to a broader regulatory chill on this type of legislation across the globe.[2] Similarly, oil and gas companies' attempts to block climate change regulation have been widely reported in the media, with estimates suggesting that these companies spend hundreds of millions of dollars on anti-environmental policy lobbying annually.

[1] Maggi and Rodriguez-Clare (2007); Bagwell and Staiger (2011).
[2] Moehlecke (2020).

At the same time, it is overly simplistic to assume that producers universally prefer lenient regulations. Companies have at times overtly lobbied for stricter health, safety, and environmental standards even when the requested standards would negatively impact their ability to sell products that they had been producing. For example, in 2015, Total SA and Royal Dutch Shell urged regulators to introduce an effective carbon pricing system that would make coal less attractive, despite their own participation in the coal business.[3] Likewise, starting in 2005, GlaxoSmithKline successfully lobbied to ban chlorofluorocarbon (CFC)-emitting inhalers even though GlaxoSmithKline was, itself, a major producer of these inhalers.[4]

Such instances in which companies have lobbied for regulations that make it harder for them to profit from some of their own products introduces a puzzle: What explains producers' occasional eagerness to back stricter safety standards on products that they themselves produce? In order to answer this, it is helpful to consider the case of CFCs in greater depth. Whereas inhalers containing these substances only received stricter regulatory oversight in the early 2000s, more significant sources of CFC emissions began to receive attention several decades earlier. CFCs are a type of chemical that used to be commonly found in refrigerators, air conditioning units, and aerosol cans. In the mid 1970s, evidence began to emerge that CFCs could potentially contribute to the depletion of ozone, a compound found in the atmosphere that helps filter harmful ultraviolet radiation from the sun. Following the 1985 publication of an article in *Nature* identifying an area of substantial ozone depletion over Antarctica, countries banded together to put in place regulations severely limiting the use of CFCs in industrial and consumer products. Not surprisingly, producers of products containing CFCs were quite resistant to both the scientific conclusions linking CFCs to ozone depletion and to the suggestion that a regulatory ban was the appropriate response. DuPont, a leader in the chemical industry and the world's largest producer of CFCs at the time, was one of the most vocal opponents of a CFC ban. DuPont not only spoke out against regulations curtailing CFC use but also engaged in various forms of opposition lobbying, such as submitting a report to

[3] Kent and Landauro (2015).

[4] Baumann (2011); see also comments submitted by the International Pharmaceutical Aerosol Consortium (of which GlaxoSmithKline is a member) to the US Food and Drug Administration, available at: regulations.gov, Docket number FDA-2007-N-0314.

the US Environmental Protection Agency in which it challenged both the need for regulatory measures and their feasibility.[5]

It may seem obvious that companies like DuPont would oppose regulations in this case, given that the CFC ban threatened to undermine a lucrative product space. Yet the CFC case is also one in which producer opposition eventually evaporated and even reversed in some quarters. Most surprisingly, DuPont completely abandoned its resistance to the ban in 1988, switching to a wholehearted public endorsement of stringent regulations. According to news reporting at the time, DuPont's change of heart was a compassionate response to new scientific evidence incontrovertibly linking CFCs to ozone depletion. A contemporaneous *New York Times* article noted that the manufacturing behemoth reversed its position and began to support new regulation "within hours" of a news conference by a scientific panel announcing its findings on the impact of chlorofluorocarbons on the ozone layer.[6]

While the narrative that DuPont's about-face was motivated purely by science is comforting, it is also misleading. Scholars have observed subsequently that DuPont's change of heart coincided not just with the output of new science but also with the company's recognition of an economic opportunity.[7] As it became increasingly clear that public opinion was moving toward a phase-out of CFCs, DuPont concluded that despite the fact that a CFC ban would prove expensive in the short term, in the longer term it could be quite lucrative. After all, DuPont was well-positioned to become a leader in alternative chemical production, and in the wake of a global ban, these alternatives would command a much higher premium than CFCs were then commanding. A regulatory measure that was initially resisted for its potential to harm profits in the short term now received enthusiastic support for its potential to raise them down the road.

The CFC case highlights the fact that regulations restricting one product may have the effect of increasing (or even creating) the market for another. This externality of regulation is not just restricted to CFCs, nor is it restricted to cases of outright bans. Rather, any regulation that makes it harder or more expensive to sell one product will tend to increase the market for partially substitutable products not impacted by the measure. Thus, a tax on e-cigarettes might inadvertently contribute to a rise in

[5] DuPont (1981).
[6] Glaberson (1988).
[7] E.g., Oye and Maxwell (1994).

traditional cigarette smoking,[8] and restrictions on trucking can bolster the fortunes of the railroads.[9]

Although DuPont first opposed and then eventually embraced the imposition of global regulations that removed the market for one of its products while opening it for another, the observation that a producer might stand to benefit from regulations precisely because they increase demand for a higher priced alternative suggests that there may be general conditions under which a firm will not only support regulations on its own products once it realizes such regulations are inevitable, but it will also enthusiastically seek out those regulations in advance of or entirely separate from popular demand. The next section specifies the conditions under which we might expect a producer to advocate for regulatory rules that reduce its ability to sell some of its own products. While these dynamics are formalized in Perlman (2020*b*), for the sake of readability, here only the qualitative intuition is presented.

3.2 THE PREFERENCE FOR STRINGENT STANDARDS

What are the general conditions under which a firm might support stricter standards or an outright ban on one of its own products? The answer relates to intellectual property rights. Intellectual property rights, in the form of patents, copyrights, and trademarks, have long been a feature of Western legal systems, with some of the earliest such laws surfacing in medieval Europe. Over the past several decades, these protections have been extended to and to some extent imposed on other nations, through the WTO's Agreement on Trade-Related Aspects of Intellectual Property Rights (TRIPS), as well as through additional bilateral and multilateral treaties. In theory, these protections are intended to encourage innovation. Under intellectual property laws, inventors are granted a monopoly on their creation, allowing them to sell their product at a higher price than they could if they faced direct competition. Yet this monopoly is not typically indefinite.[10] Governments have sought to balance their desire to incentivize innovation with the need to make products affordable for consumers. In the case of patents, once intellectual property protections

8 Saffer et al. (2020).

9 Along these lines, Stigler (1971) discusses how the railroads have sought and benefitted from weight restrictions on trucks.

10 Whereas patent and copyright protections are time-limited, trademark protections are not.

expire,[11] the innovator loses their monopoly and must contend with the entry of so-called generic competitors, typically forcing the innovator to reduce the now out-of-patent product's price in order to retain customers.

Or at least, this is how intellectual property law works in theory. In practice, innovative companies have sought numerous means of delaying or diluting the impact of the entry of generics. For example, firms might file additional, related patents several years after the patent for the original invention was introduced. These subsequent patents might cover chemical delivery mechanisms, product mixtures, or additional design features without which the product cannot be properly utilized. If executed effectively, these subsequent patents can block potential entrants for many years beyond the initial patent's expiration. At the same time, producers have engaged in a strategy known as "product hopping." Product hopping is when a company anticipates patent expiration by developing a very similar but newer (and crucially, patented) substitute product, which it then pitches to consumers as an upgraded alternative. Thus, when Schering-Plough lost patent protection on its internationally best-selling allergy medication, Claritin, it quickly introduced the new and "improved" Clarinex. Likewise, when AstraZeneca's patent on Prilosec was set to expire, it compensated by releasing an update in Nexium. In certain cases, the product-hopping company may stop selling the original, out-of-patent product upon the introduction of the newer version. Yet in many cases, it does not, instead selling both products together but at different price points.

Of course, none of these strategies involve regulation or really government participation of any kind, except to enforce the patent period. Why then would these companies seek out regulatory intervention? The answer is that, under certain conditions, innovative companies that have both an out-of-patent product and a similar, patented alternative to which they have "hopped" can actually maximize profits by acquiring stricter standards or, better yet, a regulatory ban on the original product *even if they would otherwise continue to sell it.*

The logic is as follows. When a patent expires and generic competitors enter the market, the original patent holder not only loses market share but also typically per-unit profits, as it is forced to lower its price in order to compete with the generic good. This does not necessarily mean the

[11] Under the WTO's Agreement on Trade-Related Aspects of Intellectual Property Rights (TRIPS), members agreed to impose a 20-year patent period for technological products.

firm will lower its price to cost. Innovative firms frequently benefit from branding or trust advantages that allow them to differentiate themselves from generic producers and thereby sell their products at a profit. Thus, GlaxoSmithKline can sell Advil at a higher price than generic companies can reliably list ibuprofin, even though Advil and the unbranded ibuprofin may be chemically identical. However, even if the innovative firm can derive positive profits from its out-of-patent product, given certain market conditions and the development of a newer, patented alternative, the firm may still be able to increase those profits if the out-of-patent formulation is banned through government intervention, thereby eliminating not only the generic versions of the product but also the innovator's branded one. In particular, imagine that some subset of consumers who would prefer to purchase the less expensive generic or branded, out-of-patent product in the absence of regulation would be willing to pay the higher price for the more recently patented substitute in the presence of a product ban on the older variation.[12] While it may also be the case that a ban would lead some prior purchasers of the out-of-patent, branded product to buy nothing, meaning the total number of consumers purchasing the innovator's products might remain flat or even diminish, so long as enough consumers of the now-banned product were willing to shift to purchasing the patented alternative, the innovator could end up increasing profits in the wake of a regulatory removal – or any other regulatory action that shifted some portion of consumer demand from the lower-priced good to the higher-priced alternative. This holds even though regulation in this case undermines sales of a product that the company would otherwise prefer to continue selling.

At the same time, just because innovative firms might *like* to acquire regulatory restrictions on some of their out-of-patent products does not mean they will be able to do so. If we want to understand the conditions under which innovators will be more or less successful at acquiring such regulations, we need to consider the various strategies at their disposal.

3.3 SEEKING A SYMPATHETIC EAR

In order for innovative firms to acquire regulations that disadvantage their older, out-of-patent products while in turn favoring their more recently patented alternatives, firms need to convince a regulatory agency

[12] In other words, if demand is somewhat inelastic

to impose stricter standards or an all out ban on the older products. This is where the information advantages enjoyed by producers can come into play. Specifically, by strategically revealing privately held information about the risks of their own products, information that, as the previous chapter showed, firms are uniquely situated to uncover, firms may be able to convince regulators to impose stricter standards on out-of-patent products at beneficial points in time. In fact, so long as regulators have some interest in protecting the public from harm – for which there are both intuitive and scholarly reasons to expect that they do[13] – then it would follow that if companies present valid safety concerns justifying the imposition of stricter standards on out-of-patent products, regulators will generally respond by providing those stricter standards. The implication is that firms may have incentives to reveal negative information about their own products when doing so could help bolster a more profitable substitute.

At the same time, a strategy of revealing dangers in a blatantly disingenuous way does face constraints. For one thing, as hinted at in the previous chapter, particularly when it comes to sectors in which it is more challenging for firms to suppress information for long periods of time, due to the possibility of discovery by regulators or other third parties, producers' ability to ensure that information only comes to light following patent expiration will be limited. There are also reputational risks to revealing negative information at convenient times. Companies' interactions with regulators are not isolated encounters but repeated games.[14] While companies may be able to benefit from strategically revealing information in certain cases and while we therefore might expect them to do this when acquiring a ban is particularly lucrative, to the extent that regulators do care about pursuing their mission of keeping dangerous products off the market, a firm's strategy would need to be applied in a way that avoided appearing as though they had knowingly allowed a dangerous product to remain on the market longer than advisable. As a result, there necessarily will be limits to when a strategy of strategically revealing damaging information about one's own products can be employed and how successful it will be.

There are, of course, alternative approaches firms could take. For example, rather than relying on their informational advantages to win stricter standards, companies could rely on the revolving door of

[13] See, e.g., Hird (1993); McFadden (1975); Thomas (1988).
[14] Carpenter (2004).

private–public employment,[15] political donations, or good old fashioned corruption. In the case of these latter strategies, firms wouldn't need to reveal any product risks, thereby protecting their safety reputations with regulators. Yet here again, although such strategies may work in specific types of cases, companies may still face an uphill battle due to the fact that bureaucrats inclined to comply with company requests are, themselves, likely to face pushback from both consumers and generic producers if they regularly ban products the moment they come off patent, without adequate justification. Consumers will oppose such bans because they raise consumer prices without making consumers safer in any obvious way. Generic companies will oppose such bans because they bar generic products from the market. In fact, even if, in line with theories of collective action, we were to assume that consumers might not be an effective political force, generic producers should still be reasonably well-positioned to mount a counter to their innovative competitors, given their intense and unified preferences.

Thus, although firms do have incentives to seek out stricter standards on some of their own products, and while the strategic leveraging of information may be one of the more effective methods for this in certain cases, the risks that companies face in a repeated game scenario, combined with the potential difficulty of convincing regulators to go along with their requests in instances in which the evidence does not support them, means that companies may also benefit from a more reliable method of acquiring the outcomes they seek.

3.4 THE PRIVATE BENEFITS OF PRECAUTION

How might innovative producers achieve a more systematic phase-out of those products that compete with their patented alternatives? One possible answer is under regulatory institutions that make the removal of existing products depend not on the presence of information showing those products to be dangerous but on the absence of information proving them to be safe. Specifically, institutional rules that require the reevaluation of existing products using a precautionary standard (no data, no market) could allow innovators to acquire stricter standards on less profitable, competitively produced products for which they have a more lucrative alternative without requiring firms to engage in product-by-product

[15] Gormley Jr (1979).

lobbying or strategic information revelations about product risk. Innovators would only need to *not* provide the information required during reevaluations, and they would receive stricter standards *automatically*. So long as no other third parties stepped in to provide this data, innovators could ensure that only their preferred, patented products retained market share.

What this suggests is that innovative producers may have reasons to support institutional rules that apply a precautionary standard retroactively to existing products, an institutional design that this book frequently refers to as "retroactive precaution." Such an institutional design is most likely to appeal to innovative producers when it is implemented in sectors in which innovators regularly would like to eliminate competitively-produced products and in sectors in which those actors most interested in keeping these products on the market are not in a position to provide the information required during reevaluations. Yet what this discussion does not explain is why or under what conditions governments would actually implement such regulatory institutions.

Ironically, some of the same information asymmetries that make it difficult for third parties to provide data during precautionary reevaluations, thereby making retroactive precaution attractive to innovative producers, also make these institutions attractive to public interest groups, bureaucrats, and politicians.

3.5 THE PUBLIC BENEFITS OF PRECAUTION

Chapter 2 revealed that information asymmetries between regulators and producers are pervasive, and these asymmetries compel regulators to depend on producers for much of the information about product risk necessary to set appropriate rules. This introduces a potential problem. Even if certain firms may have incentives to proactively reveal product risks in cases in which this could bolster sales of higher priced alternatives, firms' concomitant incentives to retain lenient regulations on most of their products means that they may frequently suppress or deliberately avoid learning information about product dangers. The result is that dangerous products may remain on the market for extended periods of time. This, in turn, can result in scandals, and scandals have the potential to hurt both bureaucrats in charge of regulation and elected officials.

Governments have various means at their disposal to try to address this problem. For example, more robust market surveillance can increase the odds that firms will be discovered should they choose not to disclose what they know, while legal liability laws, combined with severe penalties, ensure that firms will face consequences when they are caught dissembling.[16] Both intuition and prior research suggest that the higher the chance of discovery and the more severe the associated legal or reputational costs, the more incentive firms will have to reveal product risks early.[17]

This implies that, to some degree, the extent to which regulators' dependence on firms for information about product risk is likely to lead firms to suppress that information is endogenous to government policy; the more governments invest in monitoring the market and the more severely they punish information suppressors, the less problematic the information asymmetry problem becomes.

Nevertheless, as the previous chapter highlighted, there are also factors entirely outside of government control that drive the extent to which asymmetric information contributes to suboptimal regulatory outcomes. When products like baby sleepers, lawnmowers, and pharmaceuticals cause injury or death, it is often fairly straightforward to trace the bad outcome back to its cause. Regulators' direct monitoring of the market in such cases will, therefore, be partially supplemented by consumers or, in the case of pharmaceuticals, physicians, who can report serious risks directly to them, creating an alternative source of information outside of the firm and (perhaps more importantly) creating a credible threat of discovery, should the firm receive consumer reports and fail to share them. This can help explain why, as seen in the previous chapter, producers do seem to act as a fairly robust source of information for consumer product recalls and severe adverse drug reactions, even if they may not *always* reveal risks promptly and faithfully.

Yet there are other types of goods for which the link between a product and its risks is harder to identify by the general public, instead only emerging as the result of extensive scientific research or following many years of accumulating pieces of evidence. Such products are those that look similar in their risks to industrial chemicals, a case that was discussed in the previous chapter. They include goods like pesticides, food additives, veterinary drugs used in livestock production, and genetically

16 Though empirical research suggests that size of penalty is frequently less effective at reducing bad behavior than the odds of getting caught (see, e.g., Gray and Scholz, [1989]).

17 This basic intuition regarding firms' calculations has been described or referenced in various works, such as Gray and Scholz (1989); Shavell (1984*a*,*b*); Kip and Zeckhauser (1979).

modified organisms. For goods like these, legal liability will prove far less effective, since both tying the product to its ill effects and proving the company could have or should have known about those ill effects is often far from straightforward.[18] In the absence of any real ability on the part of consumers to supplement regulatory oversight, governments would need to internalize far more of the regulatory costs in order to introduce a viable threat of discovery. Given that the products for which these problems arise also tend to be ones for which determining the risks they pose requires expensive research, even for well-funded governments, the cost of investing in regular, independent studies of these products will prove prohibitive. As a result, companies will often (rightly) calculate that the risk of getting caught suppressing or avoiding negative information is fairly negligible and certainly passingly small in the short term.

In other words, the more severe the asymmetric information problem and the harder it is for regulators or other third-parties to connect a resulting harm to the product in question, the less incentive firms will generally have to proactively uncover product risks (at least when it comes to more profitable products) and the less effective inducements such as legal liability and market surveillance will be. In addition, the harder it is for regulators to study the risks in question, the more inefficient and likely ineffective it would be to try to solve the problem solely by increasing regulatory capacity. This is where the implementation of retroactive precaution becomes appealing to public interest groups – who want to ensure dangerous products are subjected to strict regulatory oversight – as well as to those regulators and politicians who are worried about the potential for a scandal. Retroactive precaution is attractive in these cases because it switches the institutional approach from a *fire alarm* to a *police patrol* strategy,[19] and it does this in a way that is explicitly intended to leverage the fact that, unlike regulators, producers have both the means and theoretically the motive to provide safety information about their products if failing to do so would mean the removal of those products from the market.

At the same time, requiring reevaluations of all existing products is an expensive solution, not only for the bureaucrats who need to oversee the process but also for the producers who must provide the data and potentially for the consumers to whom producers may pass on some of their costs. Therefore, it is hardly surprising that while retroactively

[18] See, e.g., Shapira and Zingales (2017).
[19] McCubbins and Schwartz (1984).

precautionary institutions have been adopted by some countries for the regulation of some products that introduce substantial information problems, such as industrial chemicals, pesticides, food additives, and genetically modified organisms, this precautionary solution is hardly universal. What then explains why this solution is adopted for some products in certain countries but not for others?

3.6 EXPLAINING THE ADOPTION OF PRECAUTION

Considering that the implementation of precautionary reevaluations constitutes a legal requirement that must be passed into law, if we want to understand what explains the passage of such laws, we must consider where and when we are most likely to see winning coalitions in support of precaution. As mentioned in the previous section, when it comes to public interest groups, we might generally expect support for such legislation in the sorts of problematic information environments that retroactive precaution is meant to address. In addition, given that individuals in wealthier nations tend to prioritize quality of life concerns over cost,[20] we might also expect there to be particularly strong public support for precautionary legislation in wealthier nations.

Of course, even in democracies, public pressure alone is often inadequate to drive policy, particularly when met with strong resistance from industry.[21] This is where the private benefits of precaution become relevant. It was stated previously that innovative firms may be able to benefit from precaution in cases in which they regularly want to eliminate competitively produced products and in cases in which those who want to retain the competitively produced products face difficulties in providing the information required during reevaluations. The former condition will generally hold any time patents are particularly lucrative, while the latter condition is most likely to hold in the same instances of high information asymmetries that make retroactive precaution attractive to public interest groups. Why? Because the harder and more expensive it is for third parties to acquire information about risk, the more difficult it will also be for them to produce the evidence necessary to prove safety during reevaluations. This is true not only for consumers, who may value some of the out-of-patent products for their lower prices, but also for generic producers whose business it is to sell out-of-patent products.

20 Inglehart (2000).
21 Gulotty (2020).

It may seem surprising that generic producers would face high hurdles when it comes to providing information about products that they play a role (or hope to play a role) in producing. Indeed, at times these hurdles are surmountable. Yet in the sorts of sectors that already present substantial information problems for regulators and consumers, generic producers will also face a number of impediments to providing the information required during precautionary reevaluations. These impediments exist for several reasons. First, because generic producers were not involved in the original development of the product in question, they do not have access to the detailed, proprietary safety studies required for initial approval; nor would they be privy to the observational safety data accrued by the original developer during the post-marketing patent period. Furthermore, since this data would also not be a requirement for winning generic approval, generic producers' information starting point will always be significantly lower than that of the original developer. Second, since non-innovative producers, by definition, invest fewer resources into research and development than innovators, they face a higher startup cost to doing research on a product in order to verify its safety, and since products that introduce substantial information problems are also ones for which studying them is expensive, this startup cost can become prohibitive. Finally, because out-of-patent products are often sold by multiple firms, these firms face a collective action problem when it comes to investing in the research necessary to keep the products on the market. Given the low or nonexistent profit margins on competitively produced products combined with the high cost of studying them, the incentive to overcome this collective action problem is often fairly low.

With generic producers, regulators, and consumers in poor positions to provide the necessary information for precautionary reevaluations, innovators stand to benefit from such rules, as they will contribute to a more systematic elimination of out-of-patent products that compete with patented alternatives. This suggests that we should see reduced opposition and even support for precautionary reevaluations from innovative firms in some of the same sectors in which these institutions appeal to the public. In addition, because the sorts of innovative firms most involved in developing and patenting novel products tend to be located in developed countries,[22] the combined backing of public interest

[22] One recent exception here is China, which in the past few years has become increasingly competitive in the patent filing space in areas like chemicals and pharmaceuticals (https://www3.wipo.int/ipstats/IpsStatsResultvalue).

groups and innovative producers means that we should also be most likely to see winning coalitions in support of retroactive precaution in those wealthier nations in which innovative firms have a strong financial and political presence.

On the flip side, noninnovative, generic producers ought to universally oppose retroactive precaution, precisely because one of the central consequences of it is to push generic products off the market. Given that generic producers tend to represent more significant percentages of the market relative to innovative producers in developing countries, we should generally expect to see industry in developing countries resisting or otherwise objecting to the implementation of precautionary institutions.

The argument thus far can be summarized as follows. When regulators are unable to solve the information asymmetry problem by encouraging firms to voluntarily reveal product risks, policymakers will have public interest motivations to put in place a system in which products are reevaluated on a precautionary basis, meaning that failure to prove safety is treated as equivalent to proving harm. At the same time, innovative companies, recognizing the potential for these institutions to privilege patented products at the expense of out-of-patent alternatives will have incentives to support these institutions. The implementation of retroactive precaution can thus result from a Baptist–bootlegger coalition of public interest groups, genuinely worried about consumer safety, and innovative firms, looking to use these institutions as a barrier to generic competition. On the opposing side of this coalition will be generic producers and price-conscious consumers, the former of which will oppose the institutions because they force their products off the market, and the latter of which will oppose them because they threaten to eliminate affordable goods. The composition of these coalitions suggests that we are more likely to see support for retroactive precaution in developed countries, whereas opposition should occur most strongly in developing nations.

The most crucial part of the argument, though, is what happens after precautionary institutions are implemented. Under the new institutions, the burden is no longer on the regulator to prove that products are dangerous in order to subject those products to stricter regulations. Rather, it is now the responsibility of the producer to provide data demonstrating that its products are safe. If all producers were equivalently well-positioned to provide such data, this might pose little problem, and it would almost certainly not be relevant from the perspective of international trade. A problem arises because innovative producers are uniquely situtated to provide data on the products they have developed. Once those products go out of patent, these producers have substantially reduced incentives to provide the data necessary to keep them on the market, and in cases in which these producers have already developed newer substitutes, they may actively want to impose stricter standards on the older alternative, since it is only through government intervention that these producers are able to reduce competition from generic firms. This means that a system of precautionary reevaluations allows innovative producers to use their privileged access to private information about product risk to systematically force out generic products and producers. Moreover, once precautionary institutions are in place, innovators can do this without resorting to any sort of potentially damaging information revelations, additional lobbying, or political capture. Simply withholding information is all the leverage these actors need.

3.7 HOW THIS CREATES BARRIERS TO COMPETITION AND TRADE

The resulting outcomes create regulatory barriers in two ways. First, the precautionary rules lead to stricter standards on out-of-patent relative to patented products for reasons that cannot be justified by science alone and that are arbitrary in their differential treatment of risk across product types. This has the result of discriminating against generic producers within those markets that implement the precautionary rules, and since generic products are frequently traded across borders, this also creates a barrier to trade for generic producers located outside of the precautionary market. Second, and perhaps more concerning, is what happens when the products being regulated are inputs into other goods. Now the stricter standards affect not just the generic producers but also those producers who rely upon the inputs in question. So long as the regulations dictate both whether the regulated products can be sold and whether they can be present in final products for which they act as inputs, then any final goods that contain the more stringently regulated out-of-patent products will face trade restrictions as well. This greatly expands the number and type of producers subject to the regulatory barrier. It in turn, will disproportionately impact poorer producers who use the restricted out-of-patent good as an input and for whom trading up to a patented alternative is prohibitively expensive – producers that, again, are disproportionately likely to be located in developing countries.

The biased regulatory outcomes that result from the dynamics outlined above thus create regulatory barriers to competition and trade that disproportionately impact exporters in developing countries. At the same time, these outcomes serve the interests of a small subset of innovative producers, most of which are concentrated in wealthier nations and whose novel products receive additional market share as alternatives are subjected to increased regulation.

Given the international trade implications of these outcomes, one might wonder whether those institutions explicitly charged with eliminating arbitrary regulations that act as barriers to international trade might be able to ameliorate some of the regulatory biases predicted to occur. Of particular relevance here are international standard-setting bodies, bodies whose recommendations under WTO law are automatically assumed to be nondiscriminatory. Can these standard-setters reduce the biases that develop out of retroactive precaution?

3.8 THE SHORTCOMINGS OF INTERNATIONAL STANDARDS

International cooperation has long been viewed as a means of helping nations escape the prisoner's dilemma inherent to international trade, through which, in an attempt to cater to domestic interest groups via the imposition of trade barriers, each nation makes itself, as well as the broader international community, worse off.[23] By requiring that any future policies be agreed upon by an international body representing the preferences of more than one country, trade agreements can help governments resist the pull of special interests to which they otherwise might be tempted to cater. In much the same way, international standard-setting bodies that bring together delegates from multiple nations are thought to reduce the sway of any given domestic lobby seeking to use regulations as a disguised barrier.[24] In addition, although international organizations are known, at times, to cater to their most powerful national members,[25] developing countries should, nonetheless, have greater voice in an international forum than in the policymaking process

[23] See, e.g., Grossman and Helpman (1994).

[24] See, e.g., Nielson and Tierney (2003), p. 250. Also see, e.g., Kapstein (1989); Keohane, Macedo and Moravcsik (2009).

[25] This tendency has been shown in the case of the United Nations Security Council (Vreeland and Dreher [2014]), the International Monetary Fund (Stone [2004; 2008]), and various standard-setting bodies (Krasner [1991]; Drezner [2004]).

of individual, developed nations. This suggests that developing countries should have more opportunities at the international level to prevent scientifically arbitrary regulations that harm their interests.

But what does all of this mean for international standard-setters' ability to ameliorate the sorts of regulatory barriers that result from innovative companies' incentives to undermine generic products? First, when it comes to the implementation of retroactive precaution, we might expect the influence of the innovative firms to be more muted than it would be in individual, wealthy countries. Because these firms are predominantly clustered in a subset of developed nations, they ought to face more countervailing pressures from generic producers at the international level than in those nations in which they are politically dominant. Second, to the extent that price-sensitive consumers or price-sensitive producers who use generic products as inputs are more likely to be located in developing countries, and to the extent that they recognize the potential for retroactive precaution to raise their costs, we should again expect more push-back against precaution internationally than in individual, developed nations. This suggests that retroactive precaution ought to be a harder sell under international standard-setting bodies than in those developed countries in which consumers prioritize safety over price and innovative producer groups can exert significant financial and, thus, political pressure.

At the same time, it is important to remember that a system of precautionary reevaluations is not necessarily against the public interest; nor will it, necessarily, be opposed by developing countries all the time. This is because reevaluations do have the very real benefit of ensuring that the existence of asymmetric information problems will not result in dangerous products remaining on the market indefinitely. Although these reevaluations are still certain to be opposed by generic companies, their ability to reduce the likelihood of a health and safety scandal down the line may still make these institutions, if not attractive to governments in developing nations, at least not entirely objectionable. Moreover, to the extent that international standard-setting bodies reflect the interests of their powerful (developed) members over those of their less powerful (developing) participants, the lack of strong, unified opposition from developing countries could be enough to allow those developed nations that have already implemented precautionary institutions and prefer to replicate these same rules internationally to win out.

All of this suggests that while retroactive precaution may not always be instituted as readily at the international standard-setting level, the political compositions of international standard-setting bodies in no way preclude the implementation of such institutions. Moreover, once the political bargain is struck and precaution is in place internationally, the same dynamics will play out as those seen domestically, despite the fact that these dynamics disproportionately harm developing nations and perpetuate arbitrary barriers to trade. This is because even though international standard-setting bodies bring together a broader array of actors, this does not significantly enrich the information environment. This becomes clear when we consider who is actually involved in the international standard-setting process and their ability to contribute information.

First, there are the generic producers. Generic producers, be they from developed or developing countries, will suffer from all the same information deficiencies that they do in a purely domestic regulatory environment. In both cases, these producers lack access to the internal studies and years of accrued data held by the innovators, and they continue to face collective action problems should they seek to band together to try to replicate this data themselves. Second, there are the national regulators. These are the very same national regulators that the previous chapter revealed universally rely on producers for safety data, and just because there are more of them does not, in and of itself, change how they operate vis-a-vis producers.

This leaves the international standard-setters themselves. In theory, such standard-setters might solicit funds from their participating members and take on more of an information-collection burden than their national counterparts. Alternatively or additionally they might encourage the individual national regulators to coordinate in a way that divides the information collection process and allows these regulators to reduce their information dependence. Unfortunately, as outlined in Chapter 2, if anything, international standard-setters tend to be more poorly funded than their national counterparts, rendering them entirely incapable of taking on a greater information collection burden than their national counterparts.

As for the second possibility, that these standard-setters might help national regulators coordinate on collecting and sharing safety data themselves, despite some bilateral and multilateral agreements between nations encouraging mutual recognition of each others' regulations, there has simply been little appetite to date for the type of cross-national coordination that would eliminate dependence on firms for information, either within or outside the auspices of international standard-setting bodies. Undoubtedly this is partially a function of the fact that no amount of effort by regulators will allow them to replicate the sort of knowledge that producers accrue through product development and production. Thus any attempts by regulators either individually or in coordination with one another to produce such knowledge themselves will still lead to less information production than might occur if regulators could instead create inducements for firms to share this information. Moreover, it should be recalled that precautionary institutions lead to biases that are particularly harmful to actors in developing nations. Yet regulators from these nations will generally have the least capacity to produce the science necessary to evaluate the safety of complex products. Thus, even if national regulators from these countries were particularly incentivized to coordinate to overcome their information deficiencies, they would face significant financial and technical impediments well beyond what regulators in developed nations already confront.

For all of the above reasons, we should not expect international standard-setters to be more capable than domestic regulators of protecting against the sorts of regulatory biases that occur as a result of retroactive precaution.

3.9 TESTABLE IMPLICATIONS

The theory outlined in the preceding pages offers a number of concrete, testable implications that will be the focus of the remaining chapters. First, if the hypothesis regarding innovative firms' preferences is correct, then rather than seeking similarly lenient standards across all of their products, innovative producers – those that are regularly updating the products they sell – will at times seek stricter standards on their own products when those products face generic competition and compete with newer, exclusively produced alternatives. Moreover, to the extent that private information plays an important role in allowing producers to win their preferred outcomes, we should see producers providing negative information about their own products strategically to argue that stricter standards are supported by science.

Second, we should see concerns about information asymmetries and, specifically, regulators' inability to acquire information to which firms have superior access driving public demand and government officials' support for retroactive precaution in sectors in which these information problems are acute. In addition, because such a system has the potential to benefit innovative firms at the expense of generic producers, we should see innovative firms supporting these regulatory institutions, in opposition to their generic competition. Likewise, we should see these institutions predominantly being championed by developed countries and being opposed by developing ones.

Third, once the precautionary institutions are implemented, the result should be a systematic regulatory bias against out-of-patent products for reasons that are orthogonal to concerns about health and safety alone. In addition, this bias, despite disadvantaging producers and consumers in developing countries, should be replicated any time that these precautionary rules are in place, regardless of whether this is at the domestic or international level of policymaking. This is because the bias that results from these precautionary institutions stems from the same problem that drives their implementation: domestic regulators' and international standard-setters' inability to acquire information about product risk themselves. This fundamental problem allows those with the best access to the relevant information to shape the regulatory process in unexpected and discriminatory ways.

The rest of the book seeks to assess each of these observable implications. The next chapter (Chapter 4) evaluates firms' preferences. It explores whether firms lobby and actively reveal information in ways that allow them to acquire stricter standards on out-of-patent or soon-to-be out-of-patent products for which they have a more lucrative alternative. Chapters 5 looks at the domestic coalitions that have supported retroactive precaution and their motives. It also examines the consequences for regulatory change at the domestic level. Chapter 6 explores coalition formation at the international level and more broadly, across countries, while also looking at whether international standard-setting bodies have been able to ameliorate precaution's bias.

4

Seeking Stricter Standards

The previous chapter laid out a theory suggesting that producers have incentives to acquire stricter standards on older, less profitable products in favor of newer, more profitable alternatives. In addition, it hypothesized that producers could use their monopoly on information about product risk in order to acquire these standards. But do producers' observable preferences and behaviors actually accord with these theoretical predictions?

The idea that firms would seek out regulations that impede the sale of their own products, let alone that they might, at times, be willing to reveal negative information about those products in order to acquire stricter standards on them, is in no way obvious. If anything, the conventional wisdom suggests quite the opposite: that firms will seek to suppress any information that might damage sales of their own goods. Indeed, there have been countless stories of businesses deliberately hiding evidence of product dangers or deficiencies in order to keep those products on the market. For example, during criminal proceedings against Takata Corporation in 2017, following the discovery that Takata airbags were liable to explode without warning in hot and humid environments, it was revealed that the company had known for years that its airbags were not operating as expected and could cause injury or death. In another incident that roiled the automobile sector a few years prior, investigators found that the German carmaker, Volkswagen, had gone so far as to install a "defeat device" in its cars in order to bypass emissions tests in the USA and Europe, thereby allowing the company to sell vehicles that did not meet environmental requirements. Similarly, tobacco companies are well-known to have aggressively suppressed knowledge of smoking risks for years, adamantly denying and discrediting all studies hinting at a link between smoking and lung cancer. A recent paper even uncovered new evidence of for just how long the tobacco industry deceived the public, showing that companies knew as early as 1959 that cigarettes contained carcinogens, meaning that these companies were aware of the carcinogenic potential of cigarettes *decades* before the link was broadly understood by regulators or the general population.[1]

Companies' incentives to suppress negative information about the products they sell are easy to grasp. The revelation that a widely used product is in fact dangerous could lead to substantial financial repercussions for the manufacturer, as a result of lost sales, penalties, and legal fees. While in some cases the consequences of suppressing negative information and getting caught may exceed those of revealing the unpleasant reality in the first place,[2] in other cases companies seem to anticipate that the chances of regulators independently discovering product dangers are relatively low in the near term, particularly when third parties are ill-equipped to uncover risks themselves and the link between product and consequences is difficult to prove.

The incentives that producers face to hide product dangers, as well as producers' frequent advantage over regulators when it comes to learning about risks in the first place (see Chapter 2), make it somewhat surprising when companies not only voluntarily reveal newly discovered dangers in cases in which discovery by regulators or third parties in the immediate future is fairly unlikely but also go one step further and request a regulatory response. A favorable reading of this behavior might be that it is driven by civic duty, while a slightly more cynical interpretation could suggest that it is simply an attempt to get ahead of the situation, in anticipation of future discovery. While both of these explanations undoubtedly have merit in certain cases, particularly when the link between a product and its risks are readily apparent, Chapter 3 highlights a third possibility, which is that stricter regulations on a competitively produced product may actually help a producer increase profits through sales of a vertically differentiated substitute on which the producer holds a monopoly. If this hypothesis is correct, then the observable implication is that we should see companies requesting stricter regulations and at times strategically

1 Karagueuzian et al. (2011).

2 Volkswagen, for example, was forced to pay a record $2.8 billion criminal fine and is reported to have shelled out around $30 billion in total to make up for its misconduct. More broadly, liability laws are intended to encourage companies to come forward with their knowledge sooner rather than later.

revealing product risks in cases in which they produce a more profitable alternative. In addition, we should observe producers requesting stricter regulations even in cases in which the risk does not truly warrant a regulatory response and revealing risks even in instances in which there is an extremely low probability that regulators would have uncovered the risk without the firm's intervention.

In order to examine whether producers act in such a manner, this chapter begins with a qualitative examination of companies in the pharmaceutical industry. Analyzing petitions submitted to the US Food and Drug Administration, the chapter shows that despite a low probability of success, drug companies have, on various occasions, attempted to convince regulators through data provision and questionable argumentation that soon-to-be out-of-patent products are dangerous, specifically when this could help them boost sales of more recently patented alternatives. After providing qualitative evidence that this strategy has been employed by pharmaceutical companies, the chapter next introduces a more rigorous, quantitative assessment of the pesticide industry to show that, at least in some industries, attempts to gain stricter standards on less profitable products through strategic information revelations and official requests are a fairly common feature of the regulatory environment.

4.1 THE PHARMACEUTICAL INDUSTRY

The pharmaceutical industry is a useful starting point for assessing producers' incentives to use regulation to shift the market away from their less profitable products, because it is an industry in which in- and out-of-patent products command starkly different prices. Given the well-documented, substantial drop in revenue that occurs once a pharmaceutical patent expires (the so-called patent cliff), there is little doubt that drug companies stand to make substantially more on their products during the period of patent protection. It is, therefore, unsurprising to observe that drug companies regularly engage in aggressive strategies, such as filing adjacent patents and "product hopping," in order to delay or impede generic competition as the patent cliff approaches.[3]

Drug companies' overt attempts to protect their patented drugs, as well as their regular strategy of "hopping" to newly patented alternatives as earlier patents expire, suggest that the pharmaceutical industry is an

[3] Gupta et al. (2010).

area in which, in accordance with the theory from the previous chapter, producers ought to have strong financial incentives to use health and safety regulations against their own, out-of-patent products. At the same time, there are two main reasons why we might not expect to see frequent, obvious attempts by firms to leverage their private information about risk in pursuit of this goal. The first is reputational and not specific to pharmaceuticals: the only way drug producers can convince regulators to permanently eliminate a competing product, absent regulatory corruption, is if the regulator concludes that the older product is unfit to be sold. Yet, as noted in the previous chapter, there may be a cost to strategically highlighting or revealing the dangers of a product that a company has long kept on the market. On the one hand, if a company successfully conveys that the older product is dangerous, it could make it seem as though they had knowingly allowed an unsafe product to be sold for an extended period of time. On the other, if the newly revealed dangers seem exaggerated, and the company's true motives are revealed, it could lead to a public or regulatory backlash against the company's anticompetitive behavior.

The second reason that pharmaceutical companies may be wary of strategically revealing negative information is the fact that pharmaceuticals is an industry in which the information asymmetries between regulators and firms are less acute than in some other industries. Whereas adverse effects from industrial chemicals, for example, may be difficult to identify in a timely fashion by third parties, adverse effects from medication are theoretically monitored by physicians, who can report them directly to regulators, often through online systems. While a recent study found that in the United States, reports from health professionals and consumers were dwarfed by reports from drug manufactures themselves,[4] and while under-reporting by the medical profession is significant,[5] the specter of physician reporting still ought to provide some check on strategic revelations by drug companies. Moreover, to the extent that regulators can compare the information provided by drug companies to the information available through other channels, they may be more skeptical of strategic attempts by drug companies to claim that a product long on the market with few signs of major adverse reactions is dangerous.

The potentially high reputational costs and low expected chance of success suggest that drug companies' strategic leveraging of information

4 Moore et al. (2016).

5 As discussed in the previous chapter, under-reporting rates seem to hover around 94% (Hazell and Shakir [2006]).

to eliminate out-of-patent products should only occur in rare instances, when the financial incentives are particularly strong, all other strategies have been exhausted, and there is some anticipation that regulators will be accommodating. At the same time, if we do see firms engaging in this behavior, in spite of the downsides and long odds, it lends credence to the hypothesis that producers have something to gain financially by using health and safety information to acquire regulations undermining their own products, thereby supporting the need for more systematic study.

4.1.1 Strategic Revelations in the US Pharmaceutical Industry

How, exactly, might pharmaceutical companies try to use the regulatory system to privilege newly patented products over older alternatives? Assuming the company had already developed a more recently patented substitute, the smartest strategy would be to convince regulators to ban the older formulation just prior to generic production. Such a strategy offers several benefits. First, we might expect there to be a higher barrier to convincing regulators to pull generic products off the shelves than to convincing them to prevent generic products from being placed on the shelves in the first place. Second, once generic products are broadly sold, their producers can begin to gather their own reports of adverse effects (or lack thereof). This means that any disingenuous claims about newly discovered risks from the innovative company seeking to undermine the formulation could be partially countered by evidence from generic producers. Finally, in the United States, where the analysis that follows takes place, regulatory rules surrounding the introduction of generic drugs offer a clear procedural opportunity for strategic claims of product risk just prior to competitor entry.

When a pharmaceutical patent is nearing expiration in the United States, generic entrants must submit what is known as an abbreviated new drug application (ANDA) before being allowed to introduce their generic product. In order for the ANDA to be approved, the applicant must be able to show that the generic drug is bioequivalent (i.e., identical in the way in which the active ingredient is released into the human body) to a drug that had previously received approval from the FDA. In addition, if the previously approved drug upon which the ANDA is based has been discontinued by the original manufacturer, the applicant must request the FDA to make a determination about whether the discontinued drug was removed from the market for reasons of "safety or effectiveness." Unless the FDA confirms that safety and efficacy did not factor into the original manufacturer's discontinuation decision, the ANDA cannot be approved.

Such a system provides innovative drug companies with an opportunity: if as a patent is expiring on one drug they come out with a newly patented variation, and if at the same time they not only discontinue the soon-to-be out-of-patent alternative but also argue that they did so for reasons of "safety or effectiveness," then they will successfully impede incoming generic competition. Of course, in the process they will also eliminate their own product, for which there may have been continued demand. Nevertheless, if the newer version is the same in terms of its usage and effect, while also commanding higher per-unit profits, the trade-off may well be in their interest, as elucidated in Chapter 3.

The question is whether companies engage in this behavior in practice. In order to answer this, a comprehensive search of the US Federal Register was conducted. The Federal Register is a publicly available government publication that lists changes and proposed changes to national regulations, while also providing information on bureaucratic agencies' decisions in the wake of any formal petitions requesting a regulatory adjustment. This means that any time a petition is filed requesting that the FDA evaluate why a drug was discontinued (a request the FDA then must fulfill), it would show up in the Federal Register. Using the Federal Register's online portal, a search was run in order to identify each documented decision that the FDA has made in relation to whether a drug was discontinued for reasons of "safety or effectiveness." This made it possible to capture cases in which the reason for a drug's discontinuation was subsequently brought into question, either by generic producers looking to copy the formulation, by concerned citizens, or by any other interested party.

The large number of instances in which a drug was discontinued and generic producers almost immediately requested a ruling on why suggests that drug discontinuation is not simply the result of low sales. Rather, it seems extremely likely that patent holders frequently discontinue drugs as a means of delaying generic entry in cases in which the patent holder has remaining exclusivity on another variation of the drug they have just discontinued. While this strategy deserves attention in its own right, in the great majority of cases, this discontinuation is not accompanied by assertions from the drug's developer that the decision was due to safety or efficacy concerns, meaning that the discontinuation is, at best, a temporary delaying tactic and does not reflect an attempt to acquire a permanent regulatory change. However, there have been a number of cases in which companies have gone beyond a simple discontinuation, additionally arguing, often quite emphatically, that the discontinued product was unsafe and ought to be permanently banned. An evaluation of these instances not only suggests that such claims are strategic, but it also hints at why such a strategy is far less common than the less permanent tactic of discontinuation without concomitant claims of safety or efficacy issues.

A search of the Federal Register uncovered approximately 200 cases since the year 2000 in which one or more actors requested the FDA to determine whether a discontinuation had occurred for reasons of safety or effectiveness. Of those cases, there are nine clear instances in which the company that had made the discontinuation decision insinuated or explicitly asserted either at the time of discontinuation or during FDA deliberations that its decision was based on safety or efficacy concerns. While the FDA only concluded that the product had been withdrawn for reasons of safety or effectiveness in three of these nine cases, in all three of the cases in which the FDA concurred that the drugs gave cause for concern, the discontinuation coincided with patent expiration. This suggests that safety concerns and financial interests aligned for the company in question, raising some questions about the timing of discontinuation and, by extension, the timing of drug companies' provision of information justifying the discontinuation. Indeed, for one of these three drugs, the wildly popular and increasingly controversial painkiller, Oxycontin, the FDA ruled against the introduction of generics on the *very same day* that the Oxycontin patent was set to expire, a decision that coincided with the introduction of a new, "harder to abuse" Oxycontin substitute that did enjoy patent protection and had recently been cleared for sale.[6] As for the two other products for which the FDA ruled that they had been discontinued for reasons of safety or effectiveness, the first involved the heart arrhythmia drug, Brevibloc (patented by Baxter Healthcare), while the second related to the conjunctivitis medication, Tequin (patented by Bristol-Myers Squibb). In a petition by Bedford Labs requesting a determination on why Brevibloc was discontinued, the petitioner observed that "the discontinuation in such close proximity to the [p]atent expiration provides question as to the cause."[7] Likewise, in the case of Tequin, Bristol-Myers actually admitted to the FDA that the impending arrival of generics factored into its discontinuation decision.[8]

[6] Food and Drug Administration (2013).
[7] Bedford Laboratories (2008).
[8] Federal Register (2008, September 9).

In the remaining six cases, those in which the FDA ruled the products had not been removed for reasons of safety or effectiveness, all but one present clear instances in which claims of risk by the pharmaceutical companies were overtly strategic attempts to reduce competition in favor of a patented alternative. And in many of these cases, expressed concerns about risk seem largely or entirely exaggerated.[9]

While the existence of instances in which companies have claimed that their own soon-to-be out-of-patent drugs ought to be banned from the market provides some support for the theory of firms' preferences, these cases also highlight two reasons why overt attempts at eliminating out-of-patent pharmaceuticals through the provision of negative information occurs only infrequently: the risk of reputational harm and the low probability of success.

One case that exemplifies the risk of reputational harm from a perceived exaggeration of risk is the case of Suboxone. Suboxone was initially patented by Reckitt to treat opioid dependence. According to the Federal Register, Reckitt notified the FDA in September, 2012 that it was discontinuing several of its Suboxone tablets, and "[s]hortly thereafter, Reckitt publicly announced that it was discontinuing the product for safety reasons."[10] However, upon investigating the matter, the FDA "found no information that SUBOXONE ... tablets ... were, or should have been, withdrawn from sale for reasons of safety."[11] The FDA was not the only one to reach this conclusion. As reported in *The Guardian*, Reckitt's decision was widely seen as an attempt to profit from the opioid crisis by blocking generic entry while shifting the market to a newer version of the drug, for which the company enjoyed an additional decade of intellectual property protection. In fact, so outraged was the general public about the deception that 35 US states subsequently filed a lawsuit against the company,[12] an outcome that not only had reputational repercussions but also very concrete financial consequences.

Of course, even when the drug in question is less of a lightning rod for negative publicity, companies hoping to eliminate their old product face the problem of needing to convince regulators that it is in fact unsafe. Chapter 2 suggested that drug companies do sometimes delay reporting

9 These remaining six cases are: Xibrom, Suboxone, Alphagan, Rowasa, Subutex, and Opana ER. Rowasa is the one case in which the strategic nature of the discontinuation is less clear-cut, since the producer was experiencing product quality issues.

10 Federal Register (2013, June 11).

11 Ibid.

12 McGreal (2016).

adverse events,[13] the eventual reporting of which might then support arguments for safety or efficacy concerns. However, in the absence of any serious adverse events, companies may face an uphill battle when it comes to convincing regulators of safety concerns, forced to resort to creative argumentation that seems to fail in the majority of cases. This makes it all the more remarkable when companies with little to no chance of success at convincing the FDA of their position nonetheless earnestly argue that a product they have long sold without major incident is dangerous and ought to be banned.

Perhaps the most flagrant example of a company disingenuously claiming that one of its products was unsafe is that of Alphagan 0.2%. Alphagan 0.2% is an eye drop for lowering intraocular pressure, originally patented by Allergan, Inc. and approved for sale in 1996. On August 20, 2002, Allergan notified the FDA that Alphagan 0.2% was being withdrawn from the market. One week later, two companies submitted petitions requesting that the FDA determine whether the discontinuation was for reasons of safety or effectiveness, presumably out of a desire to produce generic versions. In response, Allergan submitted its own petition, claiming that Alphagan 0.2% had a higher rate of allergic reactions than a newly approved alternative, Alphagan P 0.15%, thereby warranting the discontinuation on safety and effectiveness grounds.[14]

In the FDA's subsequent letter, denying Allergan's petition and laying out the FDA's determination that Alphagan 0.2% had not, in fact, been removed for reasons of safety or effectiveness, the FDA made it clear that it was well aware of the motivations underlying Allergan's claim. Writing directly to the company, the FDA observed, "As you know, Allergan's discontinuation of Alphagan 0.2% has implications for manufacturers who are interested in marketing generic versions of the product."[15] The FDA then went on to note that "nothing in the postmarketing history of Alphagan 0.2% indicates that it was withdrawn for reasons of safety or effectiveness ... In addition, none of the adverse events reported for Alphagan 0.2% would not also be expected to be associated with use of Alphagan P 0.15%."[16] The FDA concluded by stating, "Given the potential economic benefit to Allergan associated with the withdrawal

[13] Ahmad (2003), for example, finds that companies frequently delay adverse event reporting, though there has been no specific investigation into whether the times at which companies reveal adverse events is used to justify discontinuations.

[14] Federal Register (2003, June 6).

[15] Letter can be found in regulations.gov Docket No. 02P-0469/CP1, p. 3.

[16] Ibid. p. 5.

of Alphagan 0.2%, and the lack of evidence of an inferior safety or effectiveness profile of Alphagan 0.2% (as compared to Alphagan P 0.15%) … we conclude that Alphagan 0.2% was not withdrawn for safety or effectiveness reasons."[17]

Cases like Alphagan 0.2% highlight the difficulty pharmaceutical companies face in trying to use health and safety information to eliminate products they had previously marketed, in favor of patented alternatives. Under standard regulatory systems, in which products are assumed to be safe unless new evidence emerges suggesting otherwise, acquiring a ban on one's own product not only requires risking one's reputation, but it demands convincing a skeptical regulator that the safety concerns are valid. Despite these hurdles, the cases from the pharmaceutical sector reveal that companies do, at times, decide that the potential financial gains are worth the costs, and on occasion, this calculus may even pay off. More often, however, at least in the US case, pharmaceutical companies are rebuffed by the regulator, which clearly understands the financial incentives at play and appears willing and able to act in the public interest by denying these companies' disingenuous requests when the information producers present in support of them falls short.

Yet the pharmaceutical industry is not the only sector in which patents play an important role. Nor is it the only industry in which patent holders might seek to use regulations to nudge the market toward their newest inventions. The next section turns to the agrochemicals industry, a sector in which asymmetric information between regulators and producers is substantially more pronounced, reputational concerns are at least somewhat reduced, and the probability of success in acquiring beneficial stricter standards is greater. Again using data on petitions filed in the United States, this time by agrochemical companies, it is shown that, in certain industries at least, leveraging company-held information to lobby against one's own products is both systematic and quantifiable.

4.2 THE AGROCHEMICAL INDUSTRY

Similar to the pharmaceutical industry, the agrochemical industry is one in which patents play a centrally important role.[18] Because of this, pesticide

[17] Ibid. p. 11.

[18] One study found that the three industries in which patents are most effective at conferring monopoly power are agrochemicals, pharmaceuticals, and industrial organic chemicals (Levin et al. [1987]).

producers invest enormous sums of money into the research and development of novel pest control products, and they invest correspondingly large sums into defending and extending their intellectual property protections on those products. Much as pharmaceutical producers frequently develop updated versions of drugs to which they can "hop" just prior to or in the wake of patent expiration, pesticide producers similarly seek to develop and patent new variations of out-of-patent or soon-to-be out-of-patent chemicals.

Yet there are also some important differences between pesticides and pharmaceuticals that directly relate to firms' incentives to use private information against their older products. The first is the level of information asymmetry between companies and regulators. Although farmers and members of the public theoretically have the ability to report adverse effects from pesticide exposure, pesticides are more akin to industrial chemicals, in that there tends to be a far longer interval between when producers discover product dangers through observation of factory workers' exposure or internal testing and when regulators are themselves made aware of dangers through adverse reporting networks or scientific studies. Not only are the adverse effects of pesticides frequently longer term and harder to link to the pesticides themselves than is the case for pharmaceuticals, but even when reactions are acute, those most likely to suffer (farmworkers) tend to be less educated, with tenuous legal or financial status, making their odds of reporting such effects to a government official extremely low. In addition, while government-funded or independent scientists can and do at times study agrochemical risks themselves, such studies are expensive to conduct and frequently have only indirect implications for actual policy. For example, even if a study finds that a chemical is more toxic than previously reported, this does not necessarily mean that it is toxic at the levels at which farmers or consumers are exposed to it, making the appropriate policy response to such a study ambiguous. Indeed, chemical companies have been known to exploit the challenges of deriving policy decisions from external scientific studies in order to discredit risk assessments that do not suit their interests.[19]

None of this is to say that companies are the *sole* source of data on agrochemicals' properties or that they are the only parties capable either of lobbying or of using science to influence regulatory outcomes. Environmental and other public interest groups do, at times, campaign for

[19] Jasanoff (1987*b*).

pesticide bans, not only for individual products but also for clusters of them. In addition, studies from independent scientists uncovering the carcinogenic and environmental impacts of prominent formulations can lead to public calls for stricter oversight. Further, as discussed in the next section, farm groups are involved in petitioning for their preferred regulatory outcomes. Nevertheless, because of the types of health risks pesticides present, not to mention the fact that agrochemical companies are able to keep chemical data out of the public space during the exclusive use period, these actors continue to have significant information advantages, not only over regulators, farmers, independent scientists, and public interest groups but also relative to pharmaceutical developers, for whom the probability that they will be caught should they either exaggerate minimal risks or strategically delay revealing more substantial ones are significantly higher.

Another relevant difference between pharmaceuticals and agrochemicals is that reputational concerns are likely to be partially reduced in the latter sector, because unlike with pharmaceuticals, consumers are less directly impacted by the risks or costs of pesticides, particularly in developed countries in which only a small percentage of the population is engaged in farming. This makes the public more removed from the industry generally and should, therefore, provide an additional layer of cover for agrochemical companies to deploy information strategically without the public taking notice.

4.2.1 Strategic Revelations in the US Pesticide Industry

In order to evaluate whether agrochemical producers leverage private information to acquire health and safety regulations that force their less profitable products off the market in favor of more profitable alternatives, the analysis turns to industry lobbying around pesticide tolerance levels. Tolerance levels, which are also referred to as tolerances, maximum residue levels, or MRLs,[20] dictate the maximum amount of pesticide residue that is permitted to remain on an agricultural commodity at the point at which that commodity enters the market. These levels are set for the active ingredient(s) in each agrochemical product and are determined on a pesticide-by-commodity basis.

[20] In the United States, officials typically refer to tolerance levels or tolerances, but officials in most other countries, as well as those at international organizations, generally refer to maximum residue levels or MRLs.

Tolerance levels apply to both domestically produced and imported agricultural products, and they have substantial implications for farmers' willingness to use certain pesticides at all, as well as for the amount of a given pesticide that farmers apply. This is because if regulators discover that a crop has pesticide residue levels in excess of the legal limit, the offending product will not be allowed to be sold or, in the case of imports, will be refused market entry at the point of detection. Such refusals are not merely theoretical; one study investigating the cause of import rejections in the United States determined that pesticide residue violations were the most common form of adulteration-related refusals for vegetables and vegetable products between 1998 and 2007.[21] Given this, it is not surprising that, as highlighted at the outset of this book, countries frequently express concerns about the potential for strict tolerance levels to impede their exports during the course of international trade discussions.

Because of the potential repercussions from exceeding a tolerance, the lowering of a tolerance level can lead farmers to become extremely nervous about using the pesticide in question and may lead them to avoid certain uses of the product altogether.[22] This suggests that if companies wanted to encourage farmers to favor a more expensive, patented pesticide over a less expensive, out-of-patent alternative, one potential strategy would be to request stricter tolerance levels on the out-of-patent product. Doing so could make farmers' fear of exceeding the lower tolerance outweigh their reluctance to pay the higher cost of the alternative chemical, thereby shifting their preferences to the more expensive good. While changing tolerance levels may not be as impactful as acquiring an all out ban, one advantage of this strategy is its relative subtlety, a fact that may further reduce reputation concerns, as well as the possibility of opposition from those who would prefer regulations remain where they were.

In the United States, any time that an interested party seeks a change to an existing tolerance level, that party can submit a petition to the Environmental Protection Agency (EPA) requesting a revision to the Code of Federal Regulations (CFR), the document in which all US regulations are compiled annually. All petitions are then summarized and published in the Federal Register in order to allow the public time to comment on them prior to the conclusion of a final rule. Although petitions are only one method at an industry's disposal to influence policy, and while

[21] Buzby and Roberts (2011).

[22] Based on private communications with a senior member of a growers association, May 18, 2016.

more informal avenues of influence, such as private meetings, may offer additional or even greater leverage over policy,[23] these public submissions provide a valuable glimpse into the regulatory strategies and preferences of firms while also offering some insight into the rate at which agrochemical companies receive the regulations they seek.

In order to evaluate whether agrochemical companies systematically request stricter standards on older, out-of-patent agrochemicals, all petitions submitted to the EPA between 1999 and 2015 requesting changes to existing tolerance levels were collected.[24] Petitions not only serve to signal firms' underlying preferences,[25] but they also act as a form of scientific information transmission. In order to petition for a revised tolerance, petitioners first must pay a substantial fee, which can run into the hundreds of thousands of dollars. In addition to paying a fee, petitioners must also submit data to support their petition, data which is itself expensive to produce, is highly product specific, and that few parties outside of the agricultural industry have reason or the ability to replicate.

Because of these substantial monetary and scientific hurdles, the vast majority of petitions (and all those included in the dataset) come from one of two types of petitioners: registrant(s) of the pesticides in question (i.e., chemical companies)[26] or the Interregional Research Project No. 4 (IR-4), which is a non-profit group that lobbies on behalf of American specialty crop farmers. Specialty or "minor use" crops are those for which the overall US acreage is less than 300,000 acres or for which the government "determines that ... the use does not provide sufficient economic incentive" for pesticide companies to financially support research on pest control.[27] IR 4 is also the sole party that is exempt from having to pay a petition fee, an accommodation that is meant to facilitate the ability of specialty farmers to have their interests represented. A small number of petitions did not come from one of these two groups and were dropped from the sample. Specifically, a dozen petitions came from an international organization with the specific task of studying the pesticide lindane, and a handful of petitions came from generic chemical companies that solely replicate existing products.

23 Libgober (2020*a*).

24 The starting date was determined based on data availability and quality, while the end date reflects the last full year of petitions at the time the data was collected.

25 Libgober (2020*b*).

26 It should be noted that all petitions from chemical companies concern products that they, themselves produce.

27 7 USC §§136(ll).

2. *PP 9F7622.* (EPA-HQ-OPP-2010-0287). Valent U.S.A. Company, 1600 Riviera Ave., Suite 200, Walnut Creek, CA 94596-8025, proposes to amend the tolerance in 40 CFR 180.617 by decreasing the established tolerance for residues of the fungicide metconazole, 5-[(4-chlorophenyl)methyl]-2,2-dimethyl-1-(1H-1,2,4-triazol-1-ylmethyl)cyclopentanol, measured as the sum of *cis*- and *trans*-isomers, in or on nut, tree (crop group 14) from 0.04 ppm to 0.02 ppm. Independently validated analytical methods have been submitted for analyzing parent metconazole residues with appropriate sensitivity for all canola crop and processed commodities for which a tolerance is being requested. Contact: Tracy Keigwin, (703) 305-6605, e-mail address: *keigwin.tracy@epa.gov*.

FIGURE 4.1 Example petition

In total, the sample contained over 200 individual petitions. These petitions, in turn, contained nearly 900 specific tolerance amendment requests[28] and covered over 100 unique pesticide active ingredients. An example of one of these petitions is included in Figure 4.1. As shown in the example, for each petition the Federal Register lists the identity of the petitioner (in this instance, Valent USA Company) and what amended tolerance the petitioner is requesting. In some cases the Federal register also lists the existing tolerance. In cases in which the existing tolerance was omitted, however, it was possible to cross-reference the CFR in order to determine what the tolerance had been at the time that the petition was submitted. It was also possible to determine whether the petition was granted by searching the Federal Register and, where necessary, cross-checking the Code of Federal Regulations.

Once all tolerance amendment requests submitted during the relevant time period were collected, the sample of petitions was divided into two categories. The first category included all petitions submitted by innovative chemical companies (i.e., companies that research and develop novel formulations), a total of 622 individual tolerance requests. The other category included all petitions that were submitted by IR-4, a total of 253 individual tolerance requests. Separating out innovative company petitions from the farm group petitions is not only necessary in order to ensure that the analysis does not mix together actors with and without incentives to lobby against less profitable products, but it also provides an important comparison group. Unlike chemical companies, specialty farmers should have no incentive to systematically petition against generic pesticides and in favor of patented pesticides. Rather, if anything, farm

[28] The majority of petitions include requests for multiple tolerance amendments.

lobby groups should have an incentive to ensure that more affordable generic products retain reasonable standards. In addition, they may also have an incentive to ensure that regulators properly regulate dangerous products that could sicken either the consumers of their products or the field workers most likely to sustain high levels of exposure. Thus, to the extent that firms' petitions are driven in part by revelations from third parties, such as environmental groups or independent scientists, about product risks or to the extent that older products have simply been underregulated historically, leading to a need for stricter tolerances for safety purposes, we should see IR-4 also responding by requesting more stringent rules. In other words, if both farmers and producers similarly lobby for stricter standards on out-of-patent products, it might suggest that these actions are being driven by a factor outside of the theory, such as concerns about safety or quality. If, instead, farmers and firms behave differently in regards to older products, the firms' behavior is less likely to be driven by concerns related to risk.

In addition to determining the identity of the petitioner, it was also necessary to determine whether the pesticide in the petition was a high- or low-profit product. In an ideal world, we would want to know both whether the firm submitting the petition produced a patented substitute for the product in question and whether the firm had some form of monopoly protection on the pesticide about which it was petitioning. Unfortunately, determining the existence of a substitute can be quite difficult without extensive knowledge of farmer preferences and the chemical properties of each product. In addition, directly assessing monopoly protection is somewhat complicated by the fact that companies have a variety of means of effectively extending market exclusivity on an active ingredient, even beyond the original patent expiration date. Methods of patent extension include acquiring subsequent patents on mixtures or on manufacturing or delivery methods, as well as filing for usage on low-acreage crops, which, in the United States, wins developers several years of additional market exclusivity. This means that a simple dichotomous measure for whether the active ingredient is still under patent protection risks coding as out of patent products that still enjoy other forms of monopoly protection.

Likewise, even if one could consistently capture when market exclusivity rights fully expire – a difficult task in-and-of-itself, due to the fact that companies are extremely secretive about when this occurs, precisely because this makes it more difficult for potential generic entrants to determine at what point they can enter the market – the amount of effort that a firm invests into extending monopoly rights may itself be endogenous to the product's qualities. Moreover, even if the endogeneity problems were ignored, there is the fact that whereas some companies may develop substitutes in anticipation of patent expiration, the timing of the substitute is not guaranteed to coincide with the patent expiration date and could, instead, come many years later. Without a substitute, companies will have little incentive to undermine their existing products. Taken together, this suggests that solely focusing on patent period risks ignoring that the probability of a substitute increases over time and that the patent expiration on the initial active ingredient may not be the sole determinant of market exclusivity.

For all of these reasons, in order to capture producers' financial incentives to lobby for or against their own products, the analysis uses as the independent variable of interest the number of years that a pesticide had been registered in the United States at the time that the petition was submitted. Year of registration represents the moment at which a chemical was first legally allowed to be used or sold as a pesticide in the United States. Years since initial registration is, therefore, a plausibly exogenous proxy for whether or not a company enjoys exclusive use rights at the time of petition, and it accounts for the fact that certain methods of monopoly extension, such as filing for usage on low-acreage crops, only kick in once a pesticide actually hits the market.

4.2.2 Firms' Petition Behavior

Table 4.1 presents summary statistics on the petition behaviors of the two relevant groups of actors in the sample: farmers and firms. The data shows, not unexpectedly, that both firms and farmers petition for more lenient (higher) tolerances far more often than they petition for stricter (lower) tolerances, with approximately 85% of both groups' petitions for less strict tolerances. Yet, perhaps surprisingly, requests for stricter standards are not at all unusual, making up around 15% of both samples. Also notable is the likelihood of petition success. Specifically, both actors received a regulatory adjustment in the direction requested nearly 75% of the time. Firms were also particularly successful at achieving their requested outcome when they sought a stricter standard, getting the exact standard they requested more than half of the time, a slightly higher success rate than when companies requested a more lenient standard. This suggests that the strategy of requesting a stricter standard on one's own product has a reasonably high probability of success, perhaps

TABLE 4.1. *Summary statistics for petitions*

Description	Firms(%) N = 622	Farmers(%) 253
Higher tolerance request	85	86
Lower tolerance request	15	14
Outcome in requested direction	76	74
Outcome = Request (Overall)	49	50
Outcome = Request (When requesting higher tolerance)	49	53
Outcome = Request (When requesting lower tolerance)	53	31

explaining its relative frequency. At the same time, none of this illuminates the motivations behind firms' and farmers' requests for stricter standards. In order to understand firms' intent, we need to look at the characteristics of the products for which they request stricter standards and then assess whether these characteristics are or are not consistent across firm and farmer petitions.

As discussed in the previous section, if firms are strategically lobbying for stricter standards on products for which they have a more profitable substitute, then we should expect the products on which they request stricter standards to be further past their initial registration date than those products for which they request more lenient standards. This should also stand in contrast to the behavior of farmers, because farmers have no financial incentives to target pesticides that have been on the market longer for stricter regulations. In fact, if farmers were to lobby against older products in a manner similar to firms, then this would suggest that the mechanism driving firms' behavior may not be the one proposed.

In order to evaluate how time since registration correlates with the petition behavior of firms and farmers, it is helpful to begin with a simple forest plot. Figure 4.2 shows how years since registration relates to the percentage of requests for stricter tolerances from firms, relative to farmers. The plot groups petitions based on the number of years the pesticide to which the petition relates had been registered in the United States at the time of the petition, with firm petitions in black and farmer petitions in gray. The plot uses the cut point of 20 years past initial registration for each pesticide. Pesticides are typically registered between 1 to 5 years after they are patented, with initial patents lasting 20 years. Twenty years

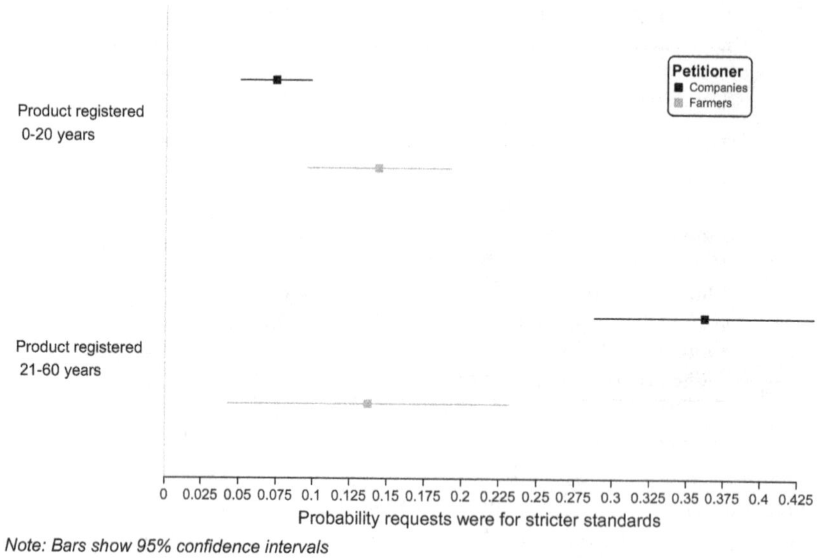

FIGURE 4.2 Petitions for stricter standards given product age

thus includes all pesticides that are still under their initial patent while also conservatively providing a small buffer period to include products that have experienced some patent extension. The plot shows, with 95% confidence intervals, the percentage of petitions in each group that were for stricter (as opposed to more lenient) tolerances.[29]

As we can see, companies are far more likely to petition for stricter tolerances on older pesticides than on newer ones. Whereas there is only a 7% probability that a company request was for a stricter standard if it related to a pesticide registered within 20 years of the petition, that probability jumps to 36% (a five-fold increase) for company petitions related to pesticides registered at least 21 years prior to the petition. By contrast, when it comes to the farm lobby group, there appears to be no overt relationship between pesticide age and the probability that a petition was for a higher or lower tolerance.

[29] Confidence intervals are calculated simply using the standard formula for proportions: $\hat{p} \pm 1.96 \times \sqrt{\frac{\hat{p}(1-\hat{p})}{n}}$.

Admittedly, we might want to look not just at the bivariate relationship between petitions and pesticide age but also at the characteristics of the pesticides themselves, taking into account the product's toxicity, carcinogenicity, and environmental impact. The challenge is that risk data of this nature is proprietary for newer pesticides, meaning that controlling for risk characteristics would lead to a temporally biased sample. This is part of the reason why it is so crucial to compare the petition behavior of firms to that of the farm group, IR-4. Because all of the pesticides used by IR-4 are also produced by companies, if the older pesticides present higher risks under prior standards or are lower quality than newer products, and if this, itself, incentivizes firms to lobby for stricter standards, then these factors also ought to play a role in the lobbying of farmers, as discussed in the previous section. The sharp divergence that we see between farmers and firms when it comes to their propensity to lobby for stricter standards, based on product age, is suggestive that pesticide risk characteristics are not the primary drivers of this behavior in firms. The forest plot, therefore, provides some initial support for the theory that innovative agrochemical companies strategically seek to use health and safety regulations as a means to move the market to more profitable products, leveraging their superior access to product information in pursuit of that goal.

At the same time, the forest plot has a major shortcoming, in that it relies on a single, somewhat arbitrary cut point. Given the degree of variability in how long firms enjoy effective exclusivity on their products, and given the expectation that the probability that a firm develops an alternative product increases over time, it is informative to evaluate both the continuous effect of age as well as the extent to which the model is robust to other cut points. Table 4.2, therefore, displays the results of a logit regression in which the binary dependent variable is designated as a 1 if the company or farm group requested a stricter standard and as a 0 if they requested a less strict standard. Model 1 uses a continuous measure for product age. This is the number of years that have passed since the pesticide was first registered in the USA at the time of the petition. Model 2 uses a dichotomous independent variable for whether the pesticide was (1) or was not (0) more than 20 years past registration at the time of the petition, while Models 3 and 4 use cut points of 19 and 18 years, respectively.

We can see that across all models, pesticide age has a strong and statistically significant effect on how a company petitioned while having no significant effect on farmer petitions. In accordance with the theory, companies are far more likely to request a stricter standard on older pesticides than on newer ones, while for farmers the effect is insignificant,

TABLE 4.2. *Company and farmer petitions for stricter standards*

	Petition Request: 0 = Less Strict, 1 = Stricter							
	Company Petitions				**Farmer Petitions**			
	(Model 1)	(Model 2)	(Model 3)	(Model 4)	(Model 1)	(Model 2)	(Model 3)	(Model 4)
Pest. Age	0.046***	1.959***	1.912***	1.810**	−0.006	−0.052	−0.052	−0.081
	(0.014)	(0.723)	(0.733)	(0.729)	(0.032)	(0.668)	(0.668)	(0.665)
Constant	−2.549***	−2.526***	−2.516***	−2.495***	−1.714**	−1.786***	−1.786***	−1.780***
	(0.488)	(0.327)	(0.332)	(0.333)	(0.753)	(0.496)	(0.496)	(0.496)
Observations	622	622	622	622	253	253	253	253

Note: * $p < 0.1$; ** $p < 0.05$; ** $p < 0.01$
Standard errors are clustered at the pesticide level

and in all cases the sign is actually reversed. To put the company results in perspective, whereas for a pesticide registered 5 years prior to a given petition, there is approximately an 8% chance that the petition was for a stricter standard under Model 1, the probability that a petition was for a stricter standard more than doubles for a pesticide registered 20 years prior, and it increases to over 50% for a pesticide registered 50 years prior.

Taken together, these results show that firms do indeed lobby for stricter tolerances on older pesticides, for which they are less likely to be the monopoly seller, while lobbying for less strict standards on their newer products, for which they presumably want to encourage increased usage. By contrast, farm groups, the other primary actor in this space, are no more likely to lobby for stricter standards on older pesticides than they are to lobby for stricter standards on newer ones.

The diverging behavior of firms and farmers bolsters the conclusion that the findings are a function of companies' profit motivations, yet there remain some alternative explanations. For example, given that regulators review pesticide safety on a recurring basis, it could be that older pesticides are those most likely to be reviewed by the regulator, and if petitioners frequently respond to pending reviews by preemptively requesting a lower tolerance,[30] then any result showing that companies petition for lower tolerances on pesticides that no longer have intellectual property protection might instead be driven by the fact that these older pesticides are more likely to undergo review. Alternatively, firms may have better knowledge about their products' risks than farmers, meaning they are petitioning for stricter standards in response to risks of which the farmers may not be aware.

While both of these alternatives are plausible, it seems unlikely that either would be the primary driver of the findings. First, if it is the case that older pesticides are more likely to undergo review, then farmers should have a similar incentive to preempt more onerous standards through the suggestion of minor adjustments, since farmers have a strong interest in retaining flexibility when it comes to the amount of pesticide they use. The fact that farmers do not do this makes such an explanation less credible. As for the possibility that firms simply know more about product risks than farmers, leading to the divergent petition behavior, this certainly could be the case, and the regression would not, itself, be able to rule out

30 Malhotra, Monin and Tomz (2019) demonstrate that firms might adopt private regulations to reduce calls for more stringent public standards. Analogously, they might propose stricter standards to forestall even harsher standards down the line.

such an explanation. At the same time, if a firm realized a product was extremely toxic and likely to lead to health problems, it seems unlikely they would respond by merely requesting the lowering of tolerances, a change that not only would flag the product's risks to regulators but would also not fully address those risks. Moreover, if farmers had not yet figured out the risks, and if regulators had not themselves initiated a regulatory change, it seems unlikely that companies would reveal such a risk without another financial motive, considering how challenging it is for third-parties to uncover pesticide risks for themselves. Finally, there is the fact that whereas petitions for lower tolerances on a subset of commodities represent a relatively veiled means of shifting the market toward certain products and away from others, pesticide companies are not always so subtle.

Agrochemical companies' less surreptitious methods have included dubious requests for bans of out-of-patent products, as well as requests for tolerance reductions across the board, rather than only on a subset of commodities. Whereas the petition results presented in this section may leave some room for ambiguity regarding firms' intent, the cases that follow are significantly more clear-cut.

4.2.3 Setting Subtlety Aside

The first case begins in 1996, the year that the chemical and pharmaceutical giant, Novartis, received approval for the registration of a new pesticide named mefenoxam, also known as R-metalaxyl. Mefenoxam was a revised formulation and close cousin of the wildly popular pesticide, metalaxyl, which had received approval nearly two decades prior and for which Novartis's patent was set to expire in that year. With mefenoxam approved for sale, Novartis canceled its registrations for metalaxyl, claiming its newer product was a safer variation and asking that the EPA deny all future approvals of generic metalaxyl products. Shortly thereafter, Novartis also submitted a petition to the EPA regarding existing metalaxyl tolerances.[31] Novartis argued that, "because of its systemic and intrinsic activity, effective disease control can be obtained with mefenoxam at one-half the rate required for metalaxyl."[32] Based on this claim, Novartis requested that all metalaxyl tolerance levels be

[31] This occurred two years prior to the start of the dataset and thus was not included in the analysis.

[32] Federal Register (1997, July 25), p. 40084.

cut in half, a move which would ensure an accelerated transition to mefenoxam at a time when farmers would not yet have exhausted their metalaxyl stocks. At this point, however, Nation's Ag, a company looking to sell its own generic version of metalaxyl, filed a lawsuit against both Novartis and the EPA. In the suit, the company observed that Novartis had relied on the metalaxyl safety data when registering mefenoxam in the first place, suggesting that "either [the] EPA violated the law by registering mefenoxam based on metalaxyl safety data if the products are different, or they violated the law by refusing to register metalaxyl if the products are similar."[33] The company's president also claimed that, if anything, metalaxyl was the safer pesticide of the two.[34] As a result, Nation's Ag concluded that Novartis' decision to cancel metalaxyl was simply meant to "prevent registration of a competing [generic] metalaxyl technical product."[35] In the end, Nation's Ag prevailed and was able to register and sell generic metalaxyl the following year. The EPA also eventually denied Novartis's request to halve the metalaxyl tolerances. Moreover, as of 2015, the EPA considered metalaxyl and mefenoxam toxicologically equivalent, with both pesticides identically classified as having low acute toxicity and as having no evidence of carcinogenicity in humans.[36]

A second, very similar saga played out a few years later, with another two pesticide products. In 1979, Ciba-Geigy – which was subsequently bought by the agribusiness giant, Syngenta – patented the compound racemic metolachlor, known simply as metolachlor. In 1999, six years after the metolachlor patent had expired, Syngenta came out with an updated variation, *S*-metolachlor. At the same time, Syngenta pulled its version of metolachlor from the market. Of course, this did not stop generic producers from continuing to manufacture and sell their own formulations of metolachlor, thereby reducing demand for Syngenta's newly patented alternative. In order to put a stop to this, Syngenta, like Nation's Ag before it, filed suit. But in this case the lawsuit was to ban a product, not to reinstate it. Specifically, Syngenta sued the EPA in order to force them to ban racemic metolachlor, the product that it, itself, had happily produced up until it manufactured a more expensive alternative. In the course of its lawsuit, Syngenta alleged, "The granting of this conditional

33 Tawasha (1998).
34 Paulsrud (1998).
35 Tawasha (1998).
36 New York Department of Environmental Conservation (2015), p. 17.

registration [of metolachlor] would be a clear statement to the public and to the agrochemical industry that EPA no longer values the environmental benefits associated with reduced risk products."[37] The disingenuousness of this claim was not lost on the judge in the case, who ruled against Syngenta in April 2002.

Even during my own conversations about agrochemical business practices with managers and other senior employees at major pesticide companies, I received confirmation that companies have an interest in using regulations to shift the market away from older chemicals. In particular, when asked whether chemical companies have an incentive to seek stricter tolerances on older products in order to favor patented alternatives, a senior manager at BASF responded directly, "Yes. It's all about the profits. Companies are constantly trying to phase out old products in favor of newer ones."[38]

Likewise, conversations with regulators suggest that they are also aware of companies' incentives to use health and safety regulations against older products. For example, during communications with a senior official at the EPA's Office of Pesticide Programs, he relayed the following:

> There have been cases where chemical companies have taken one of their existing products that is about to come off patent and come in with an "enriched" formulation to extend the patent. In that process, they often propose lower tolerances and request that the existing tolerances [on the old formulation] be revoked. On one of these applications, we got a lot of comments, so our general direction after that was not to lower or revoke the older tolerances.[39]

This quote, alongside the two cases discussed above, add further weight to the proposed mechanism behind companies' petitions. At the same time, the regulator's comments highlight the difficulty firms face in using more overt strategies in pursuit of their objectives. They imply that even when information asymmetries between regulators and firms are quite high, firms will likely be most successful at acquiring stricter standards if they obfuscate, perhaps by only requesting changes to a small subset of a pesticide's tolerances at a time.

37 Watkins (2002).
38 In-person discussion, June 1, 2016.
39 Email communication, September 16, 2016.

4.3 CONCLUSION

This chapter has provided evidence that innovative companies have in fact attempted to use health and safety regulations in order to undermine their own products in cases in which those products interfered with sales of higher profit alternatives, and these companies have been willing to wield information in pursuit of this. While the evidence has primarily come from the pharmaceutical and pesticide industries, the general incentives that we see here are not restricted to these two sectors. Similarly, although the focus here has been on the leveraging of safety regulations, environmental regulations can and have been used in comparable ways. For example, as mentioned in Chapter 3, GlaxoSmithKline and DuPont have both argued in favor of stricter standards on CFCs despite the fact that such standards would have eliminated some of the companies' popular products: an inhaler in the case of GlaxoSmithKline, and air-conditioning units in the case of DuPont. Likewise, in 2016, as nations debated placing restrictions on hydrofluorocarbons (HFCs), a chemical group that has largely replaced CFCs, one of the biggest proponents of the restrictions was Honeywell International Inc., which also happened to be one of the largest producers of HFC-containing air-conditioning units but had recently developed an HFC alternative.[40] In addition, in 2015, Total SA and Royal Dutch Shell, two oil and gas companies not known for their environmental consciousness, began making calls for an effective carbon pricing system that would raise the cost of using coal. The companies' environmental turn happened to coincide with a business decision to transition out of the coal mining business and into the business of liquified gas.[41]

Although the general strategy of using public interest regulation to push one's own products (and the products of one's competitors) off the market spans numerous industries, as several of the pharmaceutical and pesticide examples have illustrated, even when companies are willing to use information in pursuit of this strategy, it is not guaranteed to work, particularly when the disingenuousness of the request is readily apparent. In order to convince regulators to acquiesce to the request for a stricter standard, companies either need a regulator who is captured, clear evidence that the product is in fact harmful, or a subtle enough strategy that neither the regulator nor any potential losers catch on (or, if they do, they

40 Schlossberg (2016).
41 Jamasmie (2015).

do not consider it worthwhile to raise a fuss). In the absence of at least one of these conditions, attempts to eliminate competing products tend to be unsuccessful. Furthermore, even in the presence of such conditions, a company's strategy of trying to eliminate its own product may have reputational costs. The difficulties companies face in using public interest regulation to privilege patented products over out-of-patent alternatives suggests why companies may desire a regulatory system in which their chances of eliminating generic products are greatly enhanced, even if the institutional rules concomitantly raise company costs and make it more difficult to keep products on the market long term.

The next chapter traces the history of one such type of regulatory institution in order to show that large, innovative companies did, in fact, actively support its implementation. While such support, at the time, struck some legislators as surprising, in the context of the theory, it is perfectly consistent. The regulatory rules in question were projected to raise the costs of keeping generic products on the market, while also giving innovators the opportunity to selectively provide and withhold product data in order to influence which products would be subject to stricter standards and which products could continue to be sold, all with minimal risks to their reputation. Indeed, as the second half of Chapter 5 reveals, innovators received precisely what they bargained for: in the wake of the implementation of the new regulatory system, regulations have consistently become stricter on older, out-of-patent products, while regulations on newer products have become more lenient or remained the same – outcomes that, as will be shown, cannot be explained by the public interest alone.

5

How Precaution Begets Bias

The previous chapter provided evidence that innovative producers seek out stricter health and safety standards on their own less profitable products in order to privilege more profitable alternatives, at times leveraging private information about product risks in order to achieve this. Yet the chapter also revealed the challenges producers face in getting what they want. Not only can disingenuous attempts at revealing product dangers backfire by harming a company's reputation, but more overt requests for stricter standards are frequently unsuccessful, even in sectors in which producers are particularly well-positioned to leverage their information advantages. Given the difficulties producers face in using health and safety regulations to privilege certain products at the expense of others, under what conditions might these actors enjoy greater success? The theory in Chapter 3 provided one possible answer, highlighting how firms' information advantages could both encourage the adoption of and, in turn, help innovative producers exploit a form of precautionary institution.

Specifically, the chapter hypothesized that in the presence of substantial information asymmetries that make it unlikely that anyone other than the firm would be able to discover product risks in the medium term, public interest groups and regulators, particularly in developed countries, may rally behind laws that require producers of products already on the market to provide renewed evidence of those products' safety. Such laws apply a precautionary approach (no data, no market) retroactively, after products have already been approved, which is why this book often refers to these regulatory rules as "retroactive precaution." In addition, Chapter 3 suggested that the same conditions of high information asymmetry that make retroactive precaution attractive to public interest groups and regulators should also make these legal institutions attractive to innovative firms, who stand to benefit from a system that facilitates the tightening of standards on less profitable products, relative to more profitable ones. Finally, it was argued that non-innovative, generic producers will always oppose the implementation of these precautionary rules.

In order to test this next piece of the theory, the first half of this chapter uses historical evidence from US regulations of agrochemicals. By tracing the evolution of precautionary institutions in the US agrochemicals case, it becomes possible to evaluate the coalitions that supported and opposed these institutions in practice. In addition, one can assess the role of information asymmetries in shaping these coalitions. Unsurprisingly, the evidence shows that public interest groups, alongside regulators, were key advocates for a transition to precaution, with interested parties frequently referencing the role the new institutions would play in improving the ability of regulators to evaluate the risks of products for which information was generally not forthcoming. More surprising is that the large, innovative firms that stood to bear much of the cost of a precautionary system joined forces with the public interest groups to advocate in favor of precaution's implementation. A close reading of history suggests that this support was not simply an attempt to look amenable in the face of impending regulation, nor was it merely a backhanded attempt to reduce the regulatory burden through feigned acquiescence. Rather, innovative producers were instrumental in facilitating a system that raised their own costs while making it harder to keep many of their older products on the market. Moreover, innovative firms supported this system in direct opposition to generic producers, a divide that is difficult to explain if firms' intentions were simply to forestall more onerous government intervention or protect themselves from accusations of opposing the public interest. These findings offer qualitative support for one of the central observable implications of the theory presented in Chapter 3.

After walking through the history of retroactive precautions' implementation in the US agrochemical case, the chapter turns to the question of how this institution has impacted patterns of regulatory change. Using original data tracing the evolution of thousands of agrochemical standards over two decades, the chapter shows that, in accordance with the theoretical expectations, regulations have systematically become stricter on older, less profitable products for reasons that cannot be explained by appeals to public interest alone. Rather, these outcomes can be traced to the way in which precautionary institutions incorporate firms' private information, combined with innovative producers' differentiated profit incentives across their various product lines. The chapter concludes with a discussion of the normative implications of the chapter's findings, while also looking briefly at whether similar dynamics have emerged in other countries and sectors.

5.1 WHY AGROCHEMICALS?

Before turning to the evidence, it is first important to explain why the decision was made to focus on US agrochemical regulation. There are a number of reasons why this case presents an ideal opportunity to test the book's theoretical expectations. First, the regulation of agrochemicals is a clear example in which regulators depend on firms for relevant safety data and in which the potential health risks of the products are both complicated to research and difficult to identify without expensive and frequently long-term studies, thereby offering an unambiguous case of substantial information asymmetry, as conceptualized by the theory. Second, this is an area in which the institutional design has changed over time, moving from what was effectively a reactive system to a precautionary one. As a result, the case provides the opportunity to examine the actors and factors driving that change as well as how the shift did or did not impact regulatory outcomes. Third, because US agrochemical regulation is the first major example of an institutional shift toward retroactive precaution, adequate time has passed to allow for a full study of the regulatory implications. Fourth, the data for agrochemical regulation, particularly in the United States, is unusually detailed, quantifiable, and rich, offering the opportunity to draw rigorous, empirical conclusions about the impact of a precautionary regime on regulatory change.

Finally, the regulation of pesticides has important international economic implications, directly affecting more than $1.7 trillion in annual, global agricultural exports, which comprises approximately 10% of total merchandise exports.[1] For this reason, agrochemical regulations have been a major focus of international standard-setters. As discussed in previous chapters, scholars often assume that international standards follow fundamentally different patterns than their domestic counterparts. The central contention of this book, however, is that much of the variation and change we see in product-level regulatory standards can

[1] World Trade Organization (2015).

be explained by the systemic factors of asymmetric information and institutional design, factors that are likely to look similar domestically and internationally. By choosing a case for which there are both national and international standards, it becomes possible to evaluate whether or not the two levels of governance look similar in the ways suggested by this book's theory. Thus, the chapter that follows this one conducts a parallel empirical evaluation to that conducted in the current chapter, looking at how changes to international agrochemical standards have or have not mirrored changes found at the US domestic level.

5.2 US AGROCHEMICAL REGULATION: HISTORICAL BACKGROUND

Early regulation of agrochemicals in the United States aimed to achieve two distinct goals: to protect farmers from ineffective or dangerous products and to protect consumers from ingesting harmful levels of pesticide residues in their food. Prior to the establishment of the Environmental Protection Agency in 1970, these two tasks were divided between the Food and Drug Administration (FDA) and the Department of Agriculture (USDA). The FDA was responsible for protecting consumers by setting tolerances for the amount of pesticide residue permitted to remain on agricultural commodities at the point of market entry, while the USDA was responsible for ensuring the safety and effectiveness of chemicals for farmers, which in practice entailed registering and, if necessary, cancelling the registration of products. In 1970, partially in response to concerns that the existing setup catered too heavily to industry, both of these tasks were reassigned to the newly created Environmental Protection Agency.

While the shift in responsibility to a new regulatory agency undoubtedly had important implications for subsequent outcomes, an equally, if not more important change that occurred in the wake of this shift related to the procedures dictating how existing regulations would be reevaluated. Prior to 1972, producers of agricultural chemicals were only required to demonstrate safety of their products upon initial registration. If subsequent evidence emerged that a pesticide posed a hazard to humans or the environment, "the burden of proof was paradoxically shifted to the federal government. Each use, in essence, was considered innocent until proven guilty, and manufacturers could produce and sell the product until all appeals were exhausted, which could take years."[2]

[2] Bosso (1987), p. 156.

Under such a system, much as we might expect for an industry in which linking human harm to a specific chemical requires either expensive studies or years of accumulated evidence, the result was regulatory paralysis, with change only occurring in the wake of crisis. In fact, during the 15 years following the initial requirement that regulators establish pesticide tolerances for food and feed items, a mere 6.5% of the more than 500 pesticide tolerance levels in force became more strict in response to new scientific evidence.[3] Moreover, all but one of those changes related to the pesticide DDT, which was famously the subject of Rachel Carson's *Silent Spring* – a book that was to the pesticide industry what Upton Sinclair's *The Jungle* was to the meat packing industry. Moreover, DDT was only banned after approximately a decade of significant environmental group and public pressure in the wake of the scandal brought on by Carson's text.

By the early 1970s, there was a rising awareness that the system in place was unable to respond to scientific developments and was woefully unprepared to identify risk. During a 1971 Congressional hearing contemplating revisions to existing laws, Dr. Albert Kolbye, Deputy Director of the Bureau of Foods in the FDA, testified:

> It has become apparent ... that some of the decisions made on pesticides in the past deserve our attention ... in recent years, we have begun to ask some questions about certain biological effects of pesticides when humans are exposed ... In brief, we need to arm ourselves with better scientific understanding of the biological effects of pesticides.[4]

The proposed solution was something known as "reregistration," which came about in 1972 under the Federal Environmental Pest Control Act (FEPCA). Through this process, producers of existing products were required to submit updated data on their pesticides, proving that they were safe by modern standards. In theory, this meant that pesticide companies took on the burden of providing adequate information to prove that old chemicals were safe, flipping the USA from a reactive regime to a retroactively precautionary one. In practice, however, the lack of funds allocated to the effort meant that little had changed. Testimony by Senator Richard Lugar during a 1987 Congressional hearing revealed that, "Despite two mandates by Congress in 1972

3 This percentage was calculated by entering all tolerance levels listed in the US Code of Federal Regulations (CFR) in 1955 and comparing them to tolerances listed in the 1970 CFR.

4 US Cong. House Comm. on Agriculture (1971), p. 93–94.

and again in 1978 to review and reregister some 600 active ingredients, the EPA has reregistered less than one percent of these products."[5] As one scholar subsequently phrased it, reregistration "lay dead in the water."[6]

Finally, in 1988, following years of impasse and numerous Congressional hearings, the US government passed an amendment to regulatory law that successfully expedited reregistration, making the theoretical precautionary regime a reality. The amendment's primary innovation was that it required producers of existing pesticide products to pay the costs of reregistration, both through a fixed fee and, more onerously, through the provision of data that was expected to meet contemporary evidentiary standards. These requirements rejuvenated the reregistration process, assuring that the EPA could reevaluate chemicals in a far more efficient manner, eventually resulting in the removal of numerous registrations and revisions to a substantial portion of pesticide tolerance levels.

The public health motivation for the 1988 amendment was straightforward. With reregistrations stalled, the EPA remained hamstrung when it came to updating regulations quickly and appropriately in response to agrochemical dangers. As Ron D. White, speaking on behalf of the Commissioner of the Texas Department of Agriculture, phrased it during a 1986 Hearing, "We cannot depend on complaints to tell us when there is a chronic health problem with a product ... To depend on complaints is simply to use people as indicator organisms, like the canaries of the miners. The States and EPA need the information that reregistration will yield so they can do their basic regulatory work."[7] In other words, the public interest motivations for the legislation were fairly straightforward. Yet to understand why the law passed, more than a decade after the federal government initially tried to institute a system of precautionary reevaluations, it is necessary to look more closely at the coalition that supported the amendment and what its members hoped to gain from its passage.

5.3 THE PRECAUTIONARY COALITION

Some of the most active supporters of the 1988 amendment, not surprisingly, were consumer and environmental groups. These groups saw successful reregistration as a necessary step toward ensuring that pesticide

[5] US Cong. Senate Comm. on Agriculture, Nutrition, and Forestry (1987), p. 5.

[6] Bosso (1987), p. 200.

[7] US Cong. House Subcomm. on Department Operations, Research, and Foreign Agriculture (1986), p. 63.

standards provided adequate public protections. During a 1986 Senate hearing leading up to the legislative change, Albert Meyerhoff, a senior attorney for the Natural Resources Defense Council, drove this point home, expressing alarm at the lack of information available on pesticides in the absence of a more effective reregistration regime:

> The National Academy of Sciences ... found that only 10 percent of pesticide active ingredients that are marketed in the United States have adequate data to allow a full health and hazard assessment. And a 1982 House Agriculture subcommittee report previously found that 85 percent of the pesticide active ingredients sold in this country lack sufficient data to determine their carcinogenicity; two-thirds lack adequate data to determine if they cause birth defects; over 90 percent lack adequate data to determine if they cause genetic mutations. In short, we have been regulating out of ignorance.[8]

In light of Meyerhoff's concerns, it should not be surprising that consumer and environmental groups wanted a more responsive regulatory system; what *is* surprising is that a subset of agrochemical companies helped them get it.

Despite clear evidence that reregistration had stalled for lack of resources, and despite substantial pressure from a variety of public interest groups for regulatory reform, no new legislation had been passed to address the situation as of mid 1985. Had industry stayed the course and refused to cooperate with amendment efforts, it seems likely that the impasse could have continued indefinitely. Instead, representatives from the largest chemical companies sat down with environmentalists over the summer of 1985 and drafted a proposal. Notably absent from those meetings were the smaller companies,[9] a representative of which noted during one of the 1986 Congressional hearings, "I think it would be fair to say that we were not included [in the negotiations] ... we were not invited."[10]

What the large companies and the environmentalists came up with was a way of speeding up the reregistration process by levying a fee of $150,000 on companies for each requested reregistration. Carl J. Kensil, chairman of the board of directors for the National Agricultural Chemicals Association (NACA), a trade organization for the biggest pesticide producers, and an employee of CIBA-GEIGY Corp, one of the

8 US Cong. Senate Comm. on Agriculture, Nutrition, and Forestry (1986), p. 38.
9 Bosso (1987).
10 US Cong. House Subcomm. on Department Operations, Research, and Foreign Agriculture (1986), p. 52.

most successful developers of novel agrochemical products at the time, had this to say about the proposal:

We have heard and been sensitive to repeated criticism about the integrity of data supporting a few old commodity chemicals whose entry into the marketplace predated modern detection technology by several decades. And we have debated among ourselves how we might respond to publicly expressed concerns about ... EPA's missed reregistration deadlines ... We have come to recognize that we are more than simply manufacturers and formulators of products that enable our farmer customers to control ever-present insects, weeds, and diseases. We have come to accept that in one way or another, every American is exposed to the products of our industry. That recognition puts an even greater burden on us. What we are here to say to you, Mr. Chairman and members of the subcommittee, is that we accept our responsibilities to our customers and to the public at large. Their concerns [and ours] are really identical.[11]

If Kensil's avowed concern for the public seems somewhat disingenuous, that of his fellow NACA representatives should seem equally suspect. During the same hearing, Jack Early, the president of NACA, asserted the following:

The situation we are really trying to address ... is a situation that I think is unacceptable to our industry, to the public, and to the American farmer, and that is, EPA is projecting that the reregistration process will take up to 20 years. Now, that is too long, we believe, to leave products in the marketplace.[12]

Why would companies that had seemingly benefitted from the ability to sell old products indefinitely suddenly volunteer to pay a substantial fee to help the EPA get those very products off of the market? What makes the sudden generosity particularly suspicious is the attempt to avoid fees for initial registration of new products, despite the willingness to pay for the reevaluation of older products. As Early notes:

Now I differentiate between registration and reregistration. I think reregistration money is an appropriate thing to do to get the old products registered in an appropriate and up to new science and technology [manner]. We do not believe that this should translate to a registration fee, which we believe is still in the public's interest, the consumer's interest, and the farmer's interest.[13]

The eagerness of the large, innovative companies to volunteer a $150,000 reregistration fee that would help remove old products from the market struck at least some participants at the hearings as odd. Leon

[11] Ibid., p. 9.
[12] Ibid., p. 13.
[13] Ibid., p. 11.

E. Panetta, a California representative observed, "You are beginning to talk like us in Congress. I have a feeling, if I know most business managers, 150 grand is still 150 grand."[14]

Yet perhaps the best indication that the willingness of the large companies to help speed up reregistration came from a place of self-interest, rather than one of public spirit, is the fact that the smaller, and particularly the generic producers were extremely opposed, as were some of those who relied on their products. For example, Ralph Engel, the president of the Chemical Specialties Manufacturers Association, which represented smaller companies, many of which did not develop novel products, stated, "Any system of reregistration fees would in effect result in taxing a few to finance a regulatory system that benefits many. When Government services benefit society generally, the expense of these services should be borne by the taxpayer at large and not by individuals."[15] Moreover, a representative from the National Cotton Council observed, "Our biggest immediate concern is the threatened loss of many of our older pesticide products. Patents on many of them have expired, and many of the registrants are small businesses which are understandably reluctant to spend large amounts of money to save those products without having any market protection."[16]

This last quote, combined with the concerns of the smaller companies, points to two possible explanations for the larger companies' willingness to pay a fee to speed up the reregistration process. First, it seems likely that the larger companies knew that a fee that might be negligible for them could be enough to push smaller companies off the market. In that sense, the companies' eagerness to succumb to more onerous regulations partially follows the classic Stiglerian logic, in the sense that such regulations were seen as a way to reduce competition from the smaller upstarts. At the same time, Early's differentiation between registration and reregistration, combined with the concern of the cotton producers, suggests a second motivation as well: by accelerating and also increasing the cost of reregistration, the large, innovative companies could push generic producers of older products off the market, thereby making room for their own patented alternatives. Indeed, the innovators would have known that a $150,000 fee paled in comparison to the true cost of running the necessary tests for reregistration, costs that a 1990 study estimated to be,

[14] Ibid, p. 17.
[15] Ibid., p. 43.
[16] Ibid., p. 60.

at a minimum, $670,000 per product,[17] or $1.3 million in 2018 dollars. This also explains why a registration fee, by contrast, had little appeal: It would only serve to make the introduction of patented alternatives more expensive.

The fact that the large companies created a Baptist–bootlegger coalition with the public interest groups in order to change the regulatory system to one that placed more of a burden of proof on producers suggests that such a system was anticipated to benefit both players, albeit in different ways. From the perspective of the public advocacy groups, the revised system would help make it easier for regulators to acquire scientific evidence of harm. Albert H. Meyerhoff, the previously cited senior attorney for the Natural Resources Defense Council, effectively testified to this point when he noted that, "I think anyone that is familiar with pesticide issues realizes that probably the fundamental deficiency in regulating pesticides in the United States is the absence of adequate health and safety data."[18]

This suggests that the precautionary system that was put in place did reflect a genuine desire by public advocacy groups and, likely, also by politicians to address the inherent regulatory stasis that occurs under conditions of low information discoverability. Moreover, precaution was also viewed as a solution to a situation in which producers had an inherent advantage over regulators in discovering the characteristics of their own products. As Mike Synar, a representative for Oklahoma, noted, "[T]hese companies are the first to know when they have a problem because it is their studies that they are submitting to EPA that are telling them that they have some potential problems. So they know about the problems they are facing long before EPA does."[19]

At the same time, we also saw that certain companies supported the institutional changes. While some of this support likely reflected a desire on the part of the largest players to increase relative costs for their smaller competitors, part of the support also seems to have stemmed from the fact that retroactive precaution was anticipated to help innovative companies shorten the product life cycle of their own products, thereby forcing farmers to purchase more expensive alternatives that had come onto the market more recently. Notably, during the course of hearings, some generic

17 Fagerstone, Bullard and Ramey (1990).

18 US Cong. House Subcomm. on Department Operations, Research, and Foreign Agriculture (1986), p. 26.

19 US Cong. Senate Comm. on Agriculture, Nutrition, and Forestry (1987), p. 32.

producers directly sought ways to protect against this. For example, James K. Champion, the president of the Pesticide Producers Association, many of whose members "rely upon production of generic pesticides," requested that any legal amendments include a provision mandating cooperation among all companies seeking to reregister equivalent, generic products,[20] a request which was seemingly an attempt to overcome the free-rider problem inherent in a reregistration system in which many producers could benefit from an ingredient's approval, but few wanted to bear the costs.[21]

So what was the EPA's position on all of this? Throughout the legislative process, members of the EPA expressed substantial support for rules that would effectively act to help them achieve the task of reregistration. The basis of this support is not difficult to grasp. According to James Q. Wilson, one of the most heavily-cited scholars of bureaucratic politics, what agency executives care most about is autonomy and resources. To quote Wilson, "Autonomy is valued at least as much as resources, because autonomy determines the degree to which it is costly to acquire and use resources ... If autonomy can reasonably be assured, then the agency of course will seek more resources or an enlarged jurisdiction."[22]

Producer funding of reregistration offered the EPA precisely the two things bureaucracies value most. Prior to the 1988 legislation, the EPA had increasingly been under siege for its inability to tackle the enormous backlog of reregistrations. As a new agency less than a decade old, the EPA undoubtedly would have been intent upon staking out its jurisdiction and ensuring that it maintained relevance. At the same time, its utter failure to complete the task of reregistration, combined with a scandal in the mid-1970s revealing that the United States' primary pesticide testing firm, Industrial Biotest, had been engaging in fraudulent testing procedures,[23] threatened the EPA's central mission. Considering that the EPA was itself born out of the scandal following *Silent Spring*, a scandal that transferred responsibility away from the FDA and USDA to the newly created EPA, the agency would have been acutely aware of what might happen to its own autonomy (not to mention its jurisdiction) if a new scandal emerged or the public became overly dissatisfied with the agency's lack

20 Ibid., pp. 101–107.

21 Although the USA did implement a requirement of this nature, it does not appear to have fully solve the cooperation problem.

22 Wilson (2019), p. 195.

23 Bosso (1987), p. 199.

of oversight. Fees for reregistration thus offered the EPA the possibility of redemption from the Industrial Biotest scandal and protection from future failures by making it possible for the organization to complete its assigned task of reevaluating pesticides.

The legislation also offered protection of the EPA's valuable resources. John A. Moore, the assistant administrator in the EPA's pesticides and toxic substances division, attested to much of this during one of the 1986 hearings when he said:

> We invest large amounts of our own resources to identify gaps and inadequate studies. This process is very labor intensive ... We have been reevaluating whether or not this process must be done by the Agency. For a new chemical not yet on the market, the applicant seems to have no difficulty identifying, organizing, and submitting a complete data set to support that registration ... why should EPA be performing the preliminary work of organizing the data base on old chemicals which registrants can and do perform for new chemicals? ... There is ... considerable sentiment for having registrants pay the costs of the pesticide program.[24]

In other words, the new reregistration rules benefitted a number of key actors: the EPA wanted reregistration fees because such fees would not only increase the agency's resources but also potentially protect its autonomy, the two things bureaucracies care most about. Improved reregistration was sought by public interest groups because it could help solve problems of regulatory stasis and inadequate availability of information for those charged with protecting the population. Finally, the system was supported by large, innovative firms because it had the potential to disproportionately disadvantage smaller companies while also ensuring that older products did not linger on the market indefinitely. With the public, the bureaucracy, and the biggest players in industry all squarely behind the 1988 amendment, politicians had every reason to throw their weight behind the legislation.

So did these groups get what they bargained for? While the 1988 amendment has undoubtedly led to a more efficient reregistration system, which is what both the public interest groups and the EPA most wanted, less clear on the face of it is how these accelerated reevaluations have impacted the composition of products on the market. It is possible, for example, that the innovative companies underestimated the ability of generic producers to coordinate in support of older pesticides. As a result, it could be the case that the innovative firms lobbied for a system that

[24] US Cong. Senate Comm. on Agriculture, Nutrition, and Forestry (1986), p. 4–7.

raised their costs and eliminated the most dangerous products without necessarily shifting the market in a financially favorable way.

In the end, the question of whether precaution has played out in the way the innovators might have hoped is an empirical one. In order to answer it, the remainder of this chapter evaluates how pesticide standards have changed since the implementation of precautionary rules. The sections that follow provide evidence that, as predicted by this book's theory, US regulations have indeed become stricter on older, less profitable pesticides, relative to their newer, more profitable counterparts, for reasons that are difficult to attribute to health, safety, or environmental concerns alone. Moreover, this outcome does not appear to be the result of bureaucratic corruption or regulatory capture, as it is traditionally understood. Rather, it is a function of a system in which the absence of information is treated as equivalent to evidence of harm and in which information comes predominantly from producers. This interpretation of the findings is further reinforced by the chapter that follows, which shows that under precautionary institutions, the imposition of stricter standards on less profitable, out-of-patent products is not restricted to the domestic level, where private actors might be expected to wield the greatest amount of political influence. Instead, these patterns are equally pronounced at the international standard-setting level.

Before turning to the data, the next section offers a brief description of where pesticide regulations stand in the United States today. The discussion of current rules helps justify the empirical strategy while also clarifying the observable implications of the book's theory in the case under study.

5.4 US REGULATION TODAY

Since the 1988 amendment that required companies to take on more of the financial burden of reregistration, there has been one major change to the regulatory process, which remains in effect today. In 1996, Congress passed the Food Quality Protection Act (FQPA), further enhancing the precautionary nature of existing institutions.

The FQPA has two notable components. First, it requires regulators to pay special attention to how pesticide exposure might impact pregnant women and infants. This means that all pesticide tolerance levels have had to be reevaluated for negative effects on these two groups. Second, and most important, the FQPA requires that all pesticides be reregistered on a fifteen-year, repetitive basis. This means that every fifteen years, pesticide companies are faced with a choice: they can pay the costs of reregistration or they can agree to drop their product from the market. Refusing to pay any reregistration costs would mean that tolerance levels on all crops would be "revoked," and the USA would move to having zero tolerance for that pesticide on all products. A company might alternatively opt to reregister the product but only pay the data collection costs of reevaluating tolerances on certain crops. In this case, tolerances might remain on some crops but be revoked on others. Finally, the company might reregister its product but at the same time provide evidence supporting higher (less strict) tolerances on some crops and lower (stricter) tolerances on others.

According to a variety of industry executives with whom I have spoken, the costs of each reevaluation are substantial, and they increase commensurately if the producer's products are under review in multiple national markets, each of which might require a slightly different data package. What is more, after spending the money on data collection, there is no guarantee that the outcome will be in the company's favor, since the regulator has the final say on how to interpret the data submitted.

The theory presented in Chapter 3 provides clear expectations for what will happen given a reevaluation process in which the evidentiary burden rests on the firm and the failure to provide evidence of safety results in the assumption of harm: low-profit, competitively produced products will be pushed off the market through regulation, as producers refuse to spend the necessary funds to defend them, while the most profitable products will be defended by producers and, in turn, receive more favorable regulatory outcomes. In the context of pesticide regulations, this suggests that, after controlling for other characteristics of the pesticide that influence regulatory change, tolerance levels ought to become stricter on older products relative to newer ones. The reason, as discussed in the previous chapter when looking at firms' petition behavior, is that the existence of intellectual property protections in the form of patents and exclusive use data (both of which provide firms with a temporary monopoly) make newer products far more lucrative than those that are no longer shielded by government-provided monopolies. Once an agrochemical product is no longer protected through patents or other exclusive use rights, profits typically decline precipitously, due to the fact that the manufacturing firm invariably must reduce its price while at the same time experiencing a decline in sales as the brand-name product loses market share to new entrants. In addition, the more time that has passed since a product was first developed, the more likely it is that a producer will have developed an alternative to its out-of-patent or soon-to-be out-of-patent product. These alternatives frequently consist of minor variations on the original formulation, variations that the initial inventor will have a substantial advantage in developing, due to a two decade head-start in researching the original chemical's performance and risk profile. This means that the same actor with the most knowledge of a chemical that has recently lost market protection and thus the one best positioned to steer that product through the reregistration process is also the actor that may be most incentivized to see reregistration fail.

The next section evaluates whether regulatory outcomes have behaved consistently with the theory using data on changes to domestic tolerance levels during a two-decade period following the Food Quality Protection Act.

5.5 EVALUATING HOW US REGULATIONS HAVE CHANGED UNDER PRECAUTION

In order to evaluate whether standards have become stricter on less profitable pesticide products relative to more profitable ones, under a precautionary system, the analyses use data on changes to US tolerance levels for over 100 widely-used pesticides, where pesticide here refers to the active ingredient, which is the entity to which tolerances apply. The pesticides were selected to be the same as those that were also regulated at the international level, by the Codex Alimentarius Commission, which is the premier international standard-setting body for food safety. Codex standards have international legal authority through the World Trade Organization, making them a crucial reference for WTO disputes. Focusing on pesticides that are also regulated under Codex helps ensure that the pesticides studied at the domestic level are major products, less likely to be abandoned due to low utility or limited commercial appeal. Additionally, it means that these tolerance levels are those with the greatest relevance for imported products, endowing the findings with broader importance beyond US borders. Finally, focusing on chemicals also regulated by Codex makes it possible to compare how US regulatory changes have or have not differed from changes at the international level, a question that is explored in the chapter that follows.

As mentioned previously, within the United States, tolerance levels are determined by the EPA, and they are set at the crop or crop group level for each pesticide. This means that there are frequently a large number of tolerance levels for a single active ingredient. In all cases, a higher tolerance reflects a less stringent standard (more pesticide residue is allowed to be present), and a lower tolerance reflects a more stringent standard. Using the Code of Federal Regulations (CFR), American tolerance levels were recorded for 1996. These tolerances were then traced over time in order to see how they had or had not changed as of 2015.

The time period was selected for three primary reasons. First, 1996 marked the year that the Food Quality Protection Act came into effect. As a result, starting the dataset in 1996 ensures that all pesticides in the US sample were subject to the same regulatory criteria. Second, because the FQPA mandated that pesticides be reevaluated on a fifteen-year basis (and because, in practice, these evaluations occurred slightly slower than every fifteen-years), it was possible to ensure that every pesticide in the sample had been reevaluated precisely once. This helps guarantee that the results are not biased by having some pesticides reviewed more often than others. Finally, the time period selection makes it possible to compare the Codex and US data. Because Codex data was lacking for nearly all of the interim years between 1996 and 2015 (the most recent year available at the time of data collection), it would have been impossible to compare the US and Codex outcomes either on an annual basis or for almost any other period.

Figures 5.1 and 5.2 provide an example of what the data collection strategy actually looked like. Figure 5.1 shows the 1996 US tolerance level for the pesticide carbaryl, on strawberry, in parts per million (ppm), while Figure 5.2 shows the same tolerance level for 2015. In the example, the tolerance moved from 10 ppm to 4 ppm, meaning that the standard became stricter. These two tolerances, along with the pesticide name and commodity, would be entered into the database, capturing the move toward a stricter standard. This strategy was then repeated for all commodities for which a carbaryl tolerance existed in 1996 as well as for all other pesticides in the sample. This resulted in a total of

Squash, summer	10
Squash, winter	10
Strawberries	10
Sugar beets, tops	100
Sunflower seeds	1

FIGURE 5.1 1996 Carbaryl tolerance

Soybean, seed	0.5
Spinach	22
Strawberry	4.0
Sunflower, seed	0.5
Sweet potato, roots	0.2

FIGURE 5.2 2015 Carbaryl tolerance

3,683 tolerances, corresponding to 103 pesticides and several hundred commodities or commodity groups, all tracked across time. While a handful of pesticides had only 1 or 2 tolerances as of 1996, the vast majority had over 10, with a median of 27 tolerances per pesticide and a maximum of 145.

In practice, tracing how a tolerance evolved was sometimes a simple matter of recording two numbers. In the example provided, we see that the tolerance for strawberry simply moved from 10 ppm to 4 ppm, and while the terminology for the commodity shifted from the plural to the singular, it is clear that the tolerance refers to the same agricultural product. However, two features of the CFR complicated the process. The first is that crop and crop group names have changed over time, and these changes are not always as simple as moving from the plural to the singular. For example, "Alfalfa, fresh" became "Alfalfa, forage," not to be confused with "Alfalfa, hay" or "Alfalfa, fodder," both of which refer to entirely different commodities in terms of how their tolerances are measured. Similarly, the tolerance for orange might be replaced by a group tolerance for "Fruit, citrus, group 10" or vice versa. To ensure that the tolerance in 2015 actually applied to the same crop as in 1996, therefore, it was frequently necessary to cross-reference the Federal Register, which notes all name changes. Since some of the name changes were overarching and some only applied to a single commodity/pesticide combination, nearly every pesticide entry required at least one reference to the Federal Register and usually several.

The second complication inherent to tracing standard changes has to do with revocations. When the EPA revokes a tolerance level, it means that the regulation moves to a zero tolerance for the presence of the active ingredient on the commodity in question. However, this does not mean that the CFR records a tolerance of zero in its pages. Instead, the tolerance simply disappears from the list of regulations, and it is understood that if a tolerance does not exist, the default permitted residue is zero. This is problematic, because tolerances can also disappear for other reasons. For example, whereas in 1996 the EPA set tolerance levels for pesticides on pineapple forage, over the next two decades this crop stopped being considered a major feed item, and all entries for the crop were removed. On paper, this looks like a revocation, but in practice, it means that the USDA, which is the agency responsible for evaluating compliance with tolerance levels, no longer tests for pesticide residues on pineapple forage, making the interpretation very different. In order to ensure that a standard was not coded as revoked in cases in which the USDA had effectively stopped testing those crops, for every single revocation, it was necessary to cross-reference the Federal Register (which records all revocations and usually their cause) so as to be sure that the absence of a tolerance in 2015 was actually due to a revocation and not to some other explanation. Recording the explanation for the revocation also made it possible to identify pesticides for which revocations occurred for health, safety, or environmental reasons, which was then incorporated into some of the empirical analyses.

In addition to collecting data on changes to tolerances, data was also collected on the characteristics of the pesticides themselves. This included recording when the pesticide was initially registered for use in the United States, as well as the product's toxicity, carcinogenicity, and environmental impact.

Summary statistics are displayed in Table 5.1. They show overall patterns in tolerance changes, broken down by commodity, year of registration, and pesticide toxicity level, which, as will be discussed in more detail in what follows, was recorded on a five-point scale from least toxic to most toxic. The data show that the most likely outcome for any tolerance that existed in 1996 was that it would remain the same. Nevertheless, there is substantial variation. 85% of pesticides in the sample had at least one tolerance change, with approximately half experiencing one or more tolerance increases and over 60% experiencing one or more revocations. We can also see from the summary statistics that among tolerances themselves, a little under half experienced no change, while the remainder increased, decreased, or were revoked.

The question is whether the profitability of the pesticide had any impact on the probability that a given change occurred. In order to evaluate this, the empirical analysis employs an ordered logit model, for which the dependent variable was comprised of four categories: tolerances that became less strict over the twenty year period (coded as 1), tolerances that remained the same (coded as 2), tolerances that became stricter (coded as 3), and tolerances that were revoked (coded as 4). These four outcomes lend themselves well to the statistical model chosen, as there is a clear ordering of the dependent variable, yet the distance between these outcomes is ambiguous. The reason that revoked received its own category is because this is an even stricter outcome than simply lowering a tolerance. Whereas a farmer could still use a pesticide for which a tolerance has been lowered, so long as the usage was adjusted to accommodate the change, once a tolerance has been revoked, it becomes very risky to use the pesticide on the crop in question,

TABLE 5.1. *Summary of US tolerance changes 1996–2015*

Outcome	All(%)	By Commodity[a]			By Pesticide Registration			By Pesticide Toxicity	
		Produce (%)	Grain (%)	Animal[b] (%)	Pre-1961 (%)	1961–1980 (%)	1981–1996 (%)	High[c]	Low[d]
Revoked	28	33	28	18	41	26	13	62	11
Stricter	10	10	6	11	17	6	9	4	10
Same	49	52	45	48	33	57	55	32	66
Less Strict	13	5	22	23	9	11	22	2	13
N	3,683	1,601	195	1,068	1,211	1,745	727	690	977

[a] Not included are feed, nuts, and miscellaneous crops.
[b] Refers to animal products.
[c] Includes two most toxic categories.
[d] Includes two least toxic categories.

because any detectable residue would make the crop ineligible for sale. Moreover, from a theoretical standpoint, the causes for a revocation and a tolerance reduction often look quite different. A tolerance may be reduced because the data suggests a lower tolerance is appropriate, yet if the data does not exist because the registrant(s) refuses to provide it, a revocation is the automatic outcome. As such, if financial incentives drive decisions about whether or not to provide data, and if data omission is viewed as an effective means of eliminating certain out-of-patent products without risking one's reputation, revocations should be even more heavily influenced by unit profitability and the existence of alternatives than tolerance level reductions. For these reasons, separating out tolerances that were revoked from those that were simply lowered is both reasonable and necessary.

The primary explanatory variable in the model is *Pesticide Age*, which captures the number of years that the pesticide had been registered in the United States as of 2015. As discussed in the previous chapter, years since initial registration is intended to capture both the pesticide's profitability as well as the likely existence of a patented alternative, with the assumption that older pesticides are less profitable and more likely to have a patented substitute. To briefly recap: Year of registration represents the first time that a pesticide can be used or sold in the United States, with registration typically occurring within a few years of initial patent filing. The moment a pesticide is registered, a legal clock starts, marking a period during which the developer has exclusive use rights. These exclusive use rights thus combine with patent protection to ensure the company can accrue monopoly profits. Companies have various ways of slowing the clock, sometimes extending the period for years through additional patent filings or the registration of new uses, but they cannot stop the clock indefinitely. Therefore, the longer a pesticide is on the market, the more likely it is that the exclusive use period has expired, thereby reducing the pesticide's profitability. In addition, the longer a product is on the market, the more likely it is that a patented substitute has been developed, further depressing the producer's financial interest in the product and potentially giving the producer an active incentive to eliminate it.

While the relationship between monopoly protections and profitability is well understood, actual data on sales and profits before and after protections expire is difficult to acquire. Nevertheless, there is little doubt that the reduction in profits following generic entry is particularly stark in the pesticide industry. For one thing, industry surveys have found that when it comes to the ability of patents to forestall competition and protect monopoly profits, the pesticide industry ranks at the very top, alongside pharmaceuticals,[25] an industry for which an abundance of studies attest to the substantially higher profits that can be earned before relative to after patent expiration.[26] In addition, innovative pesticide producers routinely devote a section of their annual report to trying to allay investor concerns about impending patent expirations, suggesting that such expirations pose real risks to company profits.[27] Finally, because failure to control pests results in full market exit for farmers, demand for high-quality pesticides is relatively inelastic when generic alternatives are lacking.[28] This, combined with the fact that commercial farmers are savvy consumers of inputs, helps guarantee a substantial plunge in profits and prices following generic entry.[29]

While time since initial registration is, therefore, a strong proxy for a product's profitability, an obvious problem with using this measure is that it could be correlated with other pesticide characteristics, such as toxicity, carcinogenicity, environmental impact, or effectiveness. These other characteristics, in turn, might be responsible for any observable effects. Prior research on the drivers of US pesticide regulation suggests that, as we might expect, pesticide risk characteristics do indeed matter for regulatory change,[30] making it crucial to incorporate each pesticide's risk profile into the analysis. As a result, significant efforts have been made to account for relevant pesticide characteristics in the model specifications, both through the use of controls as well as through a variety of robustness checks.

The first control included in the analysis is *Toxicity*. Toxicity is the acute risk a pesticide poses to human health and is, therefore, one of the primary factors determining safety. Beginning in 1975, the World Health Organization (WHO) began classifying chemicals on a five-point scale from "extremely hazardous" (5) to "unlikely to present acute hazard in normal use" (1). This classification is updated every few years. To make its determination, the WHO utilizes independent scientists from numerous countries. For every pesticide in the sample, its 1 to 5 WHO ranking,

25 Levin et al. (1987).

26 E.g. Cook (1998); Grabowski, Long and Mortimer (2014).

27 See e.g. Monsanto (2016).

28 Based on interviews with US farm representatives, who noted that unlike farmers in developing countries, US farmers can afford patented products.

29 For example, Monsanto's blockbuster pesticide, Roundup, went from selling at $44/gallon under patent protection to $28 three years later, when the primary patent expired (Barboza [2001]).

30 Cropper et al. (1992).

as of 2009, was recorded, since 2009 was the most recent ranking, both as of 2015 and at the time of data collection.[31] The 1996–1997 classification was also recorded,[32] as well as a dummy variable coded 1 if the classification became more hazardous over time (*Toxicity Increased*).

Controls were additionally included for the pesticide's carcinogenic potential (*Carcinogenicity*). Carcinogenicity, unlike toxicity, captures danger from long-term exposure. The USA, EU and WHO all publish classifications of carcinogenic potential. However, the WHO's list contains only a small portion of the pesticides in the sample, leading to issues of selection bias. The EU scaling, meanwhile, is less granular than the US or WHO versions. As a result, the USA's classification[33] is utilized here.[34] The US ranking is on a five-point scale, ranging from "carcinogenic to humans" (5) to "not likely to be carcinogenic to humans" (1). No pesticide in the sample ranked above a 4, where 4 equals, "likely to be carcinogenic to humans." Unlike the WHO's toxicity classification, carcinogenicity is not updated regularly by any of the documenting parties, thereby only providing a single data point for each pesticide.

A third set of controls captures environmental impact. The primary environmental concern relates to a pesticide's aquatic risk, should it seep into the ground water. The most recent and comprehensive recording of aquatic risk comes from the EU's Classification, Labelling and Packaging standards.[35] Using these classifications, each pesticide's acute aquatic risk, as well as its chronic aquatic risk were recorded. The first of these is a dichotomous measure for whether a short-term risk exists. The second ranges from "no chronic aquatic risk recorded" (0) to "very toxic to aquatic life with long lasting effects" (4) and measures long-term risk.

All controls related to pesticides' risk incorporate the most recent information available at the time of data collection, thereby ensuring that, to the greatest extent possible, we are capturing the products' "true" risk. This helps guarantee that any information that could have plausibly been available to regulators at the time of a decision is captured. It also means that to the extent that regulators accrue information about risk over time, potentially making them more likely to impose stricter standards on older products, the model directly controls for this.

31 World Health Organization (2009).
32 World Health Organization (1997).
33 Environmental Protection Agency (2018).
34 The Appendix shows that results are robust to instead using the EU's classification.
35 European Chemicals Agency (2018).

In addition to controlling for the characteristics of the pesticide, the analysis also controls for the type of commodity to which the tolerance applies. First, there is a dichotomous variable that captures whether the tolerance applies to a fruit or vegetable. The reason for this is that the FQPA mandated that regulators pay special attention to pesticides' impact on infants. As a result, residues on fruits and vegetables have been held to a higher standard, due to their prevalence in infants' diets, suggesting that fruit and vegetable tolerances may follow different patterns than tolerances for other commodities.[36] A second dichotomous variable records whether the tolerance relates to one of the three largest acreage crops in the USA (*Primary Acreage*). Since pesticides used across more acres are more profitable, companies may invest more in retaining these tolerances. It is also possible that they might seek to eliminate out-of-patent pesticides for which they have a patented alternative on large acreage crops, in particular, so an interaction term was included for large acreage crops and pesticide age.

The primary results are presented in Table 5.2. All standard errors are robust to heteroskedasticity and clustered at the pesticide level.[37] Most importantly, we find that even after controlling for a variety of factors that could influence regulatory change, *Pesticide Age* has an independent and statistically significant effect. This means that pesticides that were registered earlier and that, therefore, would generally have been less profitable at the time that their tolerances were reevaluated, were far more likely to see their tolerances revoked or reduced. In addition, all control variables have the expected signs (though many are not significant), suggesting that safety concerns have also played a role in the observed regulatory changes.

Regarding the magnitude of the effect that years since registration has on the projected tolerance change, if we hold each of the dichotomous variables at their modes and set *Toxicity*, *Carcinogenicity*, and *Aquatic Chronic* to their means, the model predicts that a pesticide registered relatively recently, in 1995, had only a 6% chance that its tolerance would become stricter and a 9% chance that it would be revoked. By contrast,

36 Environmental Protection Agency (2017).

37 Despite growing concerns about pesticide mixtures, tolerances are largely evaluated on a pesticide-by-pesticide basis (Standeven [2012]). This means the EPA does not jointly consider tolerances across pesticides, and once a pesticide is introduced, tolerance changes cannot be used to justify changes on other products, thereby reducing non-independence within the sample. One exception is that the EPA considers cumulative risk from products with similar toxicological mechanisms. The Appendix shows that results are robust to using higher order clustering that can account for this.

TABLE 5.2. *US tolerance changes 1996–2015*

	Tolerance Change 1996–2015: 1 = Less Strict, 2 = Same, 3 = More Strict, 4 = Revoked		
	(1)	(2)	(3)
Pesticide Age	0.049***	0.048***	0.043***
	(0.012)	(0.014)	(0.015)
Toxicity		0.647***	0.666***
		(0.194)	(0.193)
Toxicity Increased		0.243	0.254
		(0.369)	(0.373)
Carcinogenicity		0.082	0.091
		(0.141)	(0.144)
Aquatic Chronic		0.082	0.090
		(0.143)	(0.140)
Aquatic Acute		0.495	0.490
		(0.510)	(0.505)
Fruit/Veggie			0.367*
			(0.194)
Primary Acreage			−1.373*
			(0.772)
Pesticide Age*Primary Acreage			0.026*
			(0.016)
Observations	3,683	3,459	3,459

Note: $^{*}p < 0.1$; $^{**}p < 0.05$; $^{***}p < 0.01$
Standard errors clustered at pesticide level

a pesticide registered twenty years prior had an 11% chance that its tolerance would become stricter, while the odds of a revocation more than doubled to 19%.

We can visualize the results more clearly using a simplified, dichotomous model, where the outcome is coded 1 if the standard became stricter or was revoked and 0 if it became less strict or remained the same. The predicted probability plot (Figure 5.3) shows the impact of pesticide age on this dichotomous outcome, again holding *Toxicity*, *Carcinogenicity*, and *Aquatic Chronic* at their sample means, and setting *Fruit/Veggie*, *Primary Acreage*, and *Aquatic Acute* to their modes. The bands around the predictions reflect 95% confidence intervals, using the robust standard errors, clustered at the pesticide level, while the black hashes at the bottom depict the distribution of observations. The figure shows, quite

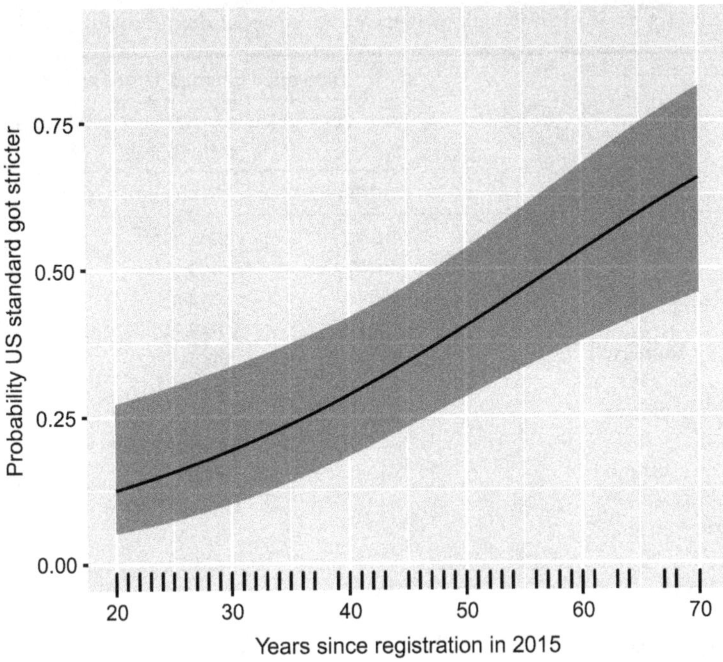

FIGURE 5.3 Probability US tolerance became stricter/was revoked

clearly, the strong relationship between time since initial registration and the probability that a tolerance became stricter or was revoked, even after controlling for other characteristics of the pesticide and commodity that we might expect to influence this relationship.

Nevertheless, we still might be concerned that the results presented thus far are driven by factors unrelated to pesticide profitability. For example, one reason the government might impose stricter standards on products registered earlier is that older pesticides are simply more dangerous and/or their dangers are more likely to be uncovered the longer they are on the market. Although using the most recent measures of toxicity, carcinogenicity, and aquatic impact should help address both of these concerns, we still might want to try to control for the possibility more thoroughly. In order to do this, the analysis leverages the fact that the Federal Register records the reason behind nearly all revocations. This makes it possible to document all pesticides for which health, safety, or environmental concerns factored into a single tolerance revocation. All tolerances for these pesticides were then dropped from the sample. This led to the removal of tolerances for 12 pesticides, leaving 91 pesticides remaining in the sample.

TABLE 5.3. *US tolerance changes dropping most dangerous pesticides*

	Tolerance Change 1996–2015: 1 = Less Strict, 2 = Same, 3 = More Strict, 4 = Revoked		
	(1)	(2)	(3)
Pesticide Age	0.047***	0.048***	0.042***
	(0.013)	(0.015)	(0.016)
Toxicity		0.541**	0.557**
		(0.235)	(0.233)
Toxicity Increased		0.150	0.158
		(0.360)	(0.363)
Carcinogenicity		0.164	0.170
		(0.152)	(0.155)
Aquatic Chronic		0.102	0.107
		(0.141)	(0.138)
Aquatic Acute		0.255	0.257
		(0.507)	(0.503)
Fruit/Veggie			0.353*
			(0.211)
Primary Acreage			−1.183
			(0.807)
Pesticide Age*Primary Acreage			0.024
			(0.016)
Observations	3,237	3,019	3,019

*Note:**p < 0.1; **p < 0.05; ***p<0.01
Standard errors clustered at pesticide level

The same logistic regression that had been run on the full sample was then re-run on this new sample. The results are displayed in Table 5.3. Notably, this had little impact on the size or significance of the coefficient of interest.[38]

[38] A related concern could be that the results are being driven by the oldest pesticides in the sample. In particular, we might worry that pesticides registered prior to the founding of the EPA might have been subject to less stringent oversight initially, thus necessitating a more substantial correction down the line. This possibility is evaluated in the Appendix by dividing pesticides into three age buckets, with those older than 1970 separated out. Results show that even when comparing pesticides registered within 10 years of the start of the dataset (thus products with the most patent protection coverage) and those registered prior to that but subsequent to 1970, products in the middle age group were still significantly more likely to receive stricter standards over time than those registered most recently.

TABLE 5.4. *US tolerance changes dropping revoked*

	Tolerance Change 1996–2015: 1 = Less Strict, 2 = Same, 3 = More Strict		
	(1)	(2)	(3)
Pesticide Age	0.027**	0.019	0.009
	(0.011)	(0.014)	(0.015)
Toxicity		0.054	0.082
		(0.164)	(0.160)
Toxicity Increased		0.122	0.152
		(0.371)	(0.359)
Carcinogenicity		0.258**	0.272**
		(0.122)	(0.121)
Aquatic Chronic		−0.104	−0.097
		(0.133)	(0.128)
Aquatic Acute		0.559	0.563
		(0.394)	(0.382)
Fruit/Veggie			0.646***
			(0.214)
Primary Acreage			−2.009**
			(0.922)
Pesticide Age*Primary Acreage			0.044**
			(0.021)
Observations	2,636	2,465	2,465

Note: *p < 0.1; **p < 0.05; ***p < 0.01
Standard errors clustered at pesticide level

Another possibility about which we might be concerned is that as pesticides become older, they lose some of their utility, meaning that the imposition of stricter standards should not be viewed as catering to the preferences of firms so much as the natural regulatory evolution. Indeed, pests do develop resistance to pesticides, and eventually products do become less effective. However, there are several reasons to be skeptical that this explanation could be driving the results here.

First, if pesticides become less effective over time, farmers would need to use more of them, not less. This would suggest that if we drop the revoked category, tolerances should actually be increasing over time, not decreasing. Yet as shown in Table 5.4, when the revoked category is dropped and we only focus on tolerances that became stricter, less strict, or remained the same, the sign on *Pesticide Age* retains the same direction, despite losing significance in two of the models.

A larger problem with the effectiveness explanation is that if pesticide tolerance levels became stricter simply because the pesticides became less useful, this would fail to explain the differential lobbying behavior of farmers and pesticide developers discussed in Chapter 4. Indeed, it is hard to explain why companies would need to lobby against less useful pesticides in the first place: If the products are no longer useful, they should fall out of the market naturally, without any need for lobbying. To the extent that petitions play any role in outcomes, therefore, the effectiveness explanation makes little sense.

Finally, as will be shown in the next chapter, the same regulatory patterns have occurred at the international level,[39] yet farmers in developing countries have been extremely vocal in opposing the revocation of tolerances for older pesticides, saying, for example, that the revocation of tolerance levels "of compounds which are still used by countries is very harmful to the international food trade since it can raise trade barriers without scientific justification."[40] The strong opposition of farmers internationally to a wide range of pesticide revocations suggests that many of the pesticides with revoked tolerances retain their utility at the international level. It seems unlikely that all these pesticides would have retained their usefulness internationally but lost it domestically. Further, even if this were the case, one would still have to explain why, as will be shown in the next chapter, outcomes at the international and domestic levels have mirrored each other in terms of the imposition of increasingly strict standards on older products.

5.6 DISCUSSION

The previous section provided evidence that under a system of retroactive precaution, standards have consistently become stricter on less profitable, out-of-patent products, relative to more profitable options. Yet how do we know that these outcomes are driven by information and institutions and are not simply deriving from some other form of influence? In other words, how can we be sure the patterns of regulatory change uncovered in this chapter stem from the interaction of producers' monopolies on product-level risk data and a system of retroactive precaution in which a lack of information is treated as equivalent to harm?

[39] In fact, at the international level we find that *Pesticide Age* retains its significance in all three model specifications after dropping the revoked category

[40] The Codex Committee on Pesticide Residues (2013), CRD 9.

On the one hand, we do know from Chapter 4 that innovative firms actively lobby for stricter standards on older products, even introducing data in order to support their requests for regulatory change. It is also the case that firms received the stricter standards they sought approximately 53% of the time between 1999 and 2015, the period for which petitions were collected. Although precautionary institutions were in place during these years, the mechanism through which stricter standards were acquired through petitions suggests that at least part of the results presented in this chapter can be attributed to avenues unrelated to the existence of precaution.

Nevertheless, it is difficult to avoid the conclusion that precaution itself and, specifically, the way in which precaution incorporates firm-provided data, has played a central role in the regulatory patterns identified. For one thing, prior to the implementation of the reregistration requirement, US tolerance levels changed at a substantially slower rate. As mentioned previously, between 1955 and 1970 only 6.5% of standards became stricter. Since the total number of tolerances in 1955 was just over 500, this means that on average, only around two individual standards actually became stricter per year, less than one half of one percent of existing tolerances, and all but one of these changes related to DDT, a pesticide that by any objective standard ought to have been subject to stricter regulations and for which there was enormous public, as opposed to just private, pressure to impose those stricter regulations. By contrast, in the wake of the 1988 amendment expediting the reregistration process, tolerance levels became stricter at a rate of approximately 2% of tolerances per year, well over a four-fold increase from before. This occurred despite the absence of a public push for stricter standards on specific products commensurate with what was seen in the wake of *Silent Spring*. The significantly greater amount of change that occurred following the implementation of a system in which a decision by firms not to provide information during reevaluations resulted automatically in stricter standards suggests that there has been much more opportunity for stricter standards to reflect profits, as well as safety, under precautionary institutions.

Moreover, there is ample evidence that firms' decisions about whether or not to provide information during reevaluations is heavily motivated by considerations of profit. This was a notable theme of the Congressional hearings leading up to the implementation of a more effective reregistration system. For example, during one of the 1988 hearings, a chemical producer testified,

> The use of [the pesticide] Mylogard was [for] a very minor crop area compared to major crops in the United States ... It was not a big market. And when we looked at the cost of doing all of the new studies that it would take to keep [Mylogard] on the market, the long-range cost did not justify continuation of the product. So we chose to drop it and not reregister it.[41]

In other words, even before reregistration was made more effective, in the rare cases in which products did come up for reassessment, the costs of the process could be enough to convince at least some registrants to abandon sales. While in this case, the decision was based on amount of use, in the case of the pesticides in the sample, all of which were regulated internationally and thus could be expected to enjoy broader popularity and substantial usage, profit considerations would be more likely to center on patent status.

Indeed, the relevance of patent status for making decisions about information provision during reregistration was highlighted during my own conversations with industry executives. For example, during a discussion with an executive from Bayer, one of the largest chemical producers in the world, the individual stated that once a pesticide goes out of patent, "it's really not profitable to continue to pay for the research" to retain lenient tolerance levels.[42] Moreover, given that the precautionary system initially put in place in 1972 and bolstered in 1988 and 1996 means that failure to pay for research leads automatically to stricter standards, firms' financial decisions about when to pay for reregistration research clearly plays a central role in determining outcomes.

Taken together, the results are consistent with the conclusion that given a system in which producers must defend the continued existence of lenient standards with updated data, regulations will become stricter on out-of-patent products for reasons that are partially orthogonal to the public interest. This is because the products in question are ones for which producers have a low incentive to continue paying for the research necessary to maintain stable standards. They also may be products for which certain firms produce a patented substitute, giving them an active reason to want stricter standards. While producers may seek and receive stricter regulations on some products under a system in which acquiring stricter regulations depends entirely on either being able to reveal negative information at strategic times or on finding a sympathetic regulator, a

41 US Cong. House Subcomm. on Department Operations, Research, and Foreign Agriculture of the Committee on Agriculture (1988), p. 94.

42 Private communications, June 1, 2016.

system that allows firms to acquire stricter standards by simply doing nothing undoubtedly makes the strategy of using regulations to push the market toward more profitable alternatives both more attractive and more successful.

So why does this matter? If all of this were simply about firms deciding to drop some of their products, our normative concerns might be limited. But this represents a much larger problem than that. First, the products in question are not simply being dropped by one firm, but rather their use is being impeded via regulation, even though there may remain other, generic firms eager to sell these products. The difficulty is that generic firms are disadvantaged relative to the innovators when it comes to keeping their products on the market. One challenge is that the generic firms suffer from a free-rider problem when it comes to providing the necessary data, with individual sellers often unwilling to invest in producing information that will then serve as a public good.[43] The generic firms are also at an inherent information disadvantage relative to the original developers in the sense that they not only do not have the years of data accumulation already available to the originating firms, but they frequently lack the large research and development arms found within the innovative companies. Because of these impediments, precautionary institutions act to hinder generic producers' ability to compete on the market.

The second reason that the dynamics uncovered here are problematic from a normative perspective is that they have international spillover effects, impacting not just foreign pesticide producers but, more broadly, foreign pesticide consumers (i.e., agricultural exporters). Fundamentally, tolerance levels are rules dictating the conditions under which different crops can be sold. As revealed in the opening of this book, tolerance levels are critical in shaping patterns of international trade. Indeed, this book began by asking what might be driving certain countries to impose stricter pesticide tolerances in ways that impede exports from developing nations. The question posed was whether this was the result of diverging national risk preferences, a deliberate attempt to privilege domestic producers, or something else. This chapter has revealed what that something else might be. On the one hand, legitimate concerns about risk and regulators' lack of information prompted the United States (and other

[43] This conclusion was bolstered during private communications with a senior member of a growers association, May 18, 2016.

developed countries) to move toward a more precautionary system, one that proactively reevaluates products to gauge their potential dangers. Yet these institutions only succeeded in being implemented because they garnered support from the most powerful industry players. This support was not a public-minded attempt to improve health and environmental outcomes. Instead, firms appear to have supported these institutions, at least in part, because they facilitated a regulatory environment in which more affordable products, some of which remained highly useful and highly demanded by downstream users, would be regulated off the market in favor of more expensive alternatives. In a global economy in which one nation's product standards dictate not only what can and cannot be sold domestically but also what can and cannot be traded internationally, the result has been a wave of regulatory barriers for traded agriculture that have proven to be some of the most contentious regulatory impediments during the WTO's existence.

Given all of this, one might be left asking why regulators haven't stepped in to stop it. As discussed in Chapter 4, both the EPA and the FDA have, in multiple cases, refused to grant firms stricter standards on their products when the regulators suspected ulterior motives. So why have some of these same regulators not required firms to provide the necessary data during reevaluations in cases in which the data was lacking? The answer is that even though the EPA seems to be aware of firms' incentives under retroactive precaution, there is little they can do to correct the problem. Under current US law, there is no provision by which the EPA can force companies to pay for regulations they do not desire. As it was expressed to me, doing so would be "akin to requiring someone to pay for renewing a hunting license they no longer want. Also, if we [the EPA] have inadequate data to make a safety finding under FFDCA [the Federal Food, Drug and Cosmetic Act] we would move to revoke the tolerance."[44]

At the same time, there are often no other groups with the resources, access to information, and desire to fill the gap. Although generic companies have, in some cases, overcome their free-rider and data disadvantage problems, hurdles to doing so remain. Likewise, while farm groups such as IR-4 can and do provide residue data to the EPA in some instances, such groups can only produce some of the data required to retain tolerance levels, and then only for certain crops; they themselves depend on pesticide

44 EPA official via email correspondence, November 15, 2016.

producers for much of the more expensive research, such as toxicological studies.[45] As for the EPA itself, it has made it clear that it does not view it as its responsibility to pay for the expensive studies that companies are far more capable of providing, and history has already shown that the agency is not particularly capable of taking on greater burdens under reregistration, in the absence of company cooperation. Furthermore, although the EPA may view the removal of generic pesticide tolerances as unfortunate, it has plenty of reasons to prefer the current system to the previous one, in which regulators were effectively hamstrung when it came to removing dangerous products. After all, the previous system helped create the problematic conditions that Rachel Carlson illuminated in *Silent Spring*, and the EPA would hardly need reminding how the *Silent Spring* episode ended: with the overseeing agencies being stripped of their regulatory responsibilities.

5.7 PRECAUTION BEYOND PESTICIDES

While the US regulation of pesticides is only one case, it illustrates how a coalition of innovative producers and public interest groups can create the necessary impetus for an institutional shift toward a system of retroactive precaution. This system, in turn, contributes to regulatory barriers via the phase-out of more affordable, out-of-patent products for reasons that cannot solely be attributed to health and safety concerns. Yet the case also raises some broader questions. First, why was the United States such an early mover toward precaution in the realm of pesticides, while at the same time it has been slow to implement an equivalent change in the realm of industrial chemicals, a sector with similar information opacity? Second, in those instances in which retroactive precaution has been implemented in sectors outside of agrochemicals, do the resulting coalitions accord with the theory?

As to the first question of why the United States has lagged behind in the realm of industrial chemicals, one possible answer is simply that there has not been an equally strong public coalition in favor of precaution in this sector. Although there have been various calls for improved oversight of the American industrial chemical industry, the dangers of industrial chemicals have not entered into the public awareness in quite the same way as the dangers of pesticides, a fact that may be partially attributable

45 Information based on discussions and emails with a senior staff member at Inter-Regional Research Project Number 4 (IR-4).

to the absence of a galvanizing force equivalent to *Silent Spring*. This may also help explain why "most legislators demonstrated little interest in amending the law" on toxic chemicals during the twentieth century.[46]

At the same time, there has been some movement in the direction of precaution in the past few years. The Frank R. Lautenberg Chemical Safety for the 21st Century Act, enacted in 2016, allows the EPA to determine that a chemical presents an unreasonable risk, even in the absence of information, while also requiring, in certain instances, that insufficient information to conclude that a chemical presents a low risk priority automatically means that the chemical must be designated as high priority, leading to further evaluations and potentially regulations.

Although the US Chemical Safety Act represents a more moderate move toward precaution than occurred under the pesticide legislation that preceded it, the two cases have some key parallels. First, as was true for the 1988 amendment to US pesticide legislation, the industrial chemicals legislation was motivated, at least in part, by policymakers' concerns about high information asymmetries in the chemical industry between regulators and chemical producers. House representative, Paul Tonko, observed as much during hearings in the lead-up to the new chemical safety law when he noted that "the [EPA] has insufficient resources and little authority to require manufacturers to produce information for an adequate evaluation of [] chemical risks."[47] In other words, the inability of regulators to acquire necessary information for themselves, and the apparent unwillingness of industry to share the private information they had, played a central role in the perceived need for institutional change. Second, and directly relevant to the question of whether this book's theory is predictive of precautionary coalitions outside of the US pesticides case, the Chemical Safety Act also received support from the biggest chemical developers, as conveyed through the endorsement of the American Chemistry Council,[48] a trade organization which boasts all of the largest, most innovative companies among its members.

Nevertheless, considering that the Chemical Safety Act represented only a moderate precautionary shift, it is difficult to know whether the American Chemistry Council's support for the legislation was a result of the law's strength or, instead, of its weakness, making it helpful to look to other cases. The case of industrial chemical regulation in Europe

46 Schierow (2008).
47 US Cong. House Subcomm. on Environment and the Economy (2015), p. 4.
48 American Chemistry Council (2015).

offers a little more clarity. In 2006 the European Union implemented sweeping changes to how it regulates industrial chemicals through legislation known as REACH, which stands for Registration, Evaluation and Authorization of Chemicals. Under this legislation, manufacturers and downstream users of all chemicals sold in the EU above a certain volume were required to register and provide risk information for their products. Failure to provide the required data results automatically in a ban of the chemical in question. This legislation, therefore, instituted a much stronger precautionary system than that found in the subsequent US Chemical Safety Act.

In the period leading up to the passage of REACH, the government solicited comments on the draft legislation. Analyzing the more than 2,000 comments submitted, including 1,135 from individual firms, Gulotty (2020) finds, consistent with this book's theoretical expectations, that the large, multinational firms generally supported the legislation, while smaller firms were broadly opposed. Gulotty makes a compelling case that the larger firms' support stemmed from their understanding that the legislation would impose fixed costs that, while affordable for them, would effectively push their smaller competitors off the market, and indeed he shows that in the aftermath of REACH, there was increased concentration in the number of firms filing patents.

Yet, much as was the case for pesticide regulation in the United States, there may have also been an additional reason why companies like Dow, DuPont, and BASF supported the European chemical regulation: These innovators expected that REACH would help shift the market toward their more profitable products. Such an expectation would have had merit. A 2009 study by RiskMetrics Group found that DuPont and Dow were both in a position to profit from REACH, thanks to increased demand for some of their compliant (and patented) chemicals.[49]

There was also at least some concern from those less well-positioned to benefit that the new law could favor patented products for the wrong reasons. In a comment submitted to the EU by a representative of OmniChem N.V., the writer of the comment worried that registrants might purposely use the mandatory review structure as a way "just to disfavour an existing substance, in favour of a new substance of which the competitor/importer has a patent or confidential production method."[50] In addition, several

49 Eid and Lotfipour (2009).
50 All comments submitted in response to the REACH draft legislation were helpfully provided by Gulotty upon request.

distributors and many smaller firms expressed strong concerns about the consequences of the legislation on products for which there was no patent protection. For example, one distributor noted, "You must remember that most preparations are not protected by patent. Manufacturers will therefore not supply within the EU and there is a very big risk that many of our key customers would be forced to relocate outside the EU in order to obtain these key preparations."[51] Meanwhile, several company representatives submitted comments suggesting that the data requirements would be detrimental for small and medium-sized firms that frequently could not afford to patent their products in the first place and would thus give up critical trade secrets if forced to share information with regulators.[52]

While this last concern about data-sharing requirements undermining sales of non-patented products highlights a somewhat different mechanism for how retroactive precaution might harm out-of-patent products than the one identified in Chapter 3, the REACH case, more generally, again seems to be one in which producers' differential incentives across patented and non-patented products played an important role in shaping the coalitions that emerged. Here again we find that the large, innovative firms came down in support of precaution, while their smaller competitors, many of which were less innovative and/or could not afford patent protection, were opposed.

5.8 GOING INTERNATIONAL

This chapter has shown how regulators' inability to acquire adequate data about certain products' risks can encourage a precautionary system that not only deepens the degree to which regulatory outcomes depend on firms' information but that creates regulatory barriers that favor more profitable, patented products at the expense of less profitable, out-of-patent alternatives. As a result of the potential for retroactive precaution to benefit innovators, relative to their generic competition, those companies in the business of producing patented products have been more likely to support these precautionary institutions, thereby helping to facilitate the institutions' implementation in some of the markets in which innovative companies are dominant. The question to which the book now finally turns is whether delegation to an international standard-setter can help eliminate the types of regulatory biases and barriers that have resulted from the implementation of retroactive precaution.

[51] Submission by Peter Short of VWR International Ltd.
[52] See, e.g., comment by Ian McRobbie, Associated Octel.

6

The Internationalization of Bias

Developed countries, such as the United States, Germany, Japan, and the Netherlands are among the most lucrative export markets for everything from agriculture to processed foods to industrial chemicals. These countries are also ones that have increasingly gravitated toward retroactive precaution in many of the sectors that directly impact these export markets.[1] The previous chapter demonstrated how such precautionary institutions can help innovative producers leverage their information advantages in order to win regulations that bolster their most lucrative, patented products by imposing stricter standards on out-of-patent substitutes. It showed, in the case of agrochemicals, how this leads to regulations that disproportionately hamper the use of more affordable pesticides for reasons that cannot be justified solely by appeals to safety. The impacts of these outcomes are widely felt, but developing countries often bear the brunt as a result of their greater proportion of generic producers relative to innovative ones, as well as their lesser ability to substitute away from the cheaper and more heavily regulated inputs necessary for exporting.

This chapter asks whether international delegation can offer a solution by, on the one hand, giving greater voice to those poorer nations most harmed by these dynamics and, on the other, by providing a forum that is potentially more removed from the political influence of special interests. In order to answer this, the chapter focuses on how standards have

[1] Most recently, Japan announced in 2018 that it was implementing a system of periodic reevaluations of pesticides, in which companies must provide data packages that contained the same level of detail as required for initial registration (Sato [2018]).

evolved under the Codex Alimentarius Commission (henceforth Codex), an international standard-setting institution charged with establishing recommendations for a wide range of food safety regulations. Since the founding of the WTO in 1995, Codex has become one of the most influential international standard-setters in existence, making the study of potential biases under Codex particularly important. Codex is also the international organization responsible for recommending agrochemical tolerance levels, making it possible to conduct a direct comparison between the outcomes uncovered in the previous chapter, at the US national level, and those that have arisen internationally.

6.1 CODEX ALIMENTARIUS COMMISSION: THE BASICS

Codex was originally established in 1963 by the Food and Agriculture Organization of the United Nations (FAO) and the World Health Organization (WHO), with the founding purpose of "protecting consumers' health and ensuring fair practices in the food trade."[2] The main responsibility of Codex is to provide detailed recommendations to nations on what their food standards should be. These recommendations are typically developed in specialized committees and then adopted by the full Codex Alimentarius Commission at its annual meeting, with recommendations ranging from general advice related to food safety inspection practices to highly specific numerical standards specifying, for example, allowable defects for frozen peas or acceptable maximum residue levels for veterinary drugs. As suggested by Codex's founding purpose, the goal of these recommendations is two fold. First, the recommendations are meant to ensure that traded food meets certain baseline safety requirements. Second, by acting as focal points to which nations might harmonize, the recommendations are supposed to encourage governments to resist the temptation to impose barriers to trade through the implementation of unnecessary or arbitrary regulations.

Throughout the first three decades of its existence, Codex standards carried little weight. During this period, several different standard-setting bodies, among which Codex was only one, offered competing recommendations in the food safety space, with nations free to adopt or ignore any of the proffered suggestions.[3] This all changed in 1995, with the

[2] Food and Agricultural Organization and World Health Organization (1962).
[3] Büthe (2009).

conclusion of the Uruguay Round and the establishment of the WTO. In the lead-up to the WTO's founding, nations had increasingly come to appreciate the potential for national regulatory measures to disrupt free trade flows, particularly in a world of diminishing tariffs. National Members of the WTO's predecessor, the General Agreement on Tariffs and Trade (GATT), therefore sought to encourage nations to take greater steps toward regulatory harmonization. This was done, in part, by naming certain international standard-setters as the official authorities in their substantive domains and then requiring that nations base their standards on the recommendations of these organizations. Under the WTO's 1995 Agreement on the Application of Sanitary and Phytosanitary Measures (SPS Agreement), the Codex Alimentarius Commission became one of just three international standard-setting bodies explicitly listed as an official authority,[4] thereby endowing Codex standards with "far reaching implications for resolving trade disputes."[5]

Since its naming in the SPS Agreement, Codex has indeed played a central role in international trade law, as reflected by the fact that nations have referenced this organization 6,473 times in the course of meeting their WTO obligation to notify members of changes to domestic regulations that could impact international commerce.[6] The number of references to Codex greatly surpasses references to any other international standard-setter, including the International Organization for Standardization (ISO), with 2,805 references, the World Organization for Animal Health (OIE), with 1,969 references, or the International Plant Protection Convention (IPPC), with 304 references. Also telling is how frequently Codex comes up in trade concerns under the SPS Agreement and under its companion for technical standards, the TBT Agreement. Trade concerns, such as those described at the outset of this book, are complaints that have not (yet) reached the level of a trade dispute and that are registered by one or more WTO members in regards to the regulations of their trading partners. As of this writing,[7] nations have appealed to Codex in 85 different trade concerns, making the number of references to Codex second only to

4 The other two are the World Organization for Animal Health OIE, and IPPC.

5 Codex Alimentarius Commission (2016).

6 This is as of November 10, 2020 and includes notifications made both under the SPS Agreement and the Technical Barriers to Trade (TBT) Agreement. Though reporting is variable across countries (See, e.g., Karlas and Parízek [2020]), notifications offer some indication of the extent to which Codex touches on areas of significant relevance for international trade.

7 November 10, 2020.

the OIE, which has arisen in 145 such concerns. Moreover, previous work has shown that Codex standards can directly influence how national regulations are set, not only in developing markets, which frequently adopt Codex standards in their entirety, but also in developed markets like the United States, which systematically gravitate toward Codex standards, at least on the margin.[8]

Codex's distinctive significance among other international standard-setting bodies offers a practical justification for why it deserves attention. Yet there is also a more theoretical reason that is particularly relevant to this book's aim. By listing Codex as the reference body for nations' food safety standards, the WTO explicitly concluded that national standards that accord with Codex are both "necessary to protect human, animal or plant life or health"[9] and do not "create an unnecessary obstacle to international trade."[10] In other words, Codex standards are automatically presumed to be nondiscriminatory. As laid out in previous chapters, there are indeed reasons to expect international standard-setting bodies to reduce the potential for arbitrary rules that serve the interests of a small subset of nations, and as an inter-governmental body with broad national membership and procedures that are open and transparent, one might hope that Codex, in particular, could live up to this potential. To the extent then that Codex actually replicates the regulatory barriers that exist at the national level, it would suggest that a central assumption undergirding the WTO system – that international standards represent necessary and nondiscriminatory rules – does not hold.

6.2 THE POLITICS OF CODEX

At first glance, Codex would seem to be well-positioned to reduce the sorts of regulatory biases often found at the domestic level. Final decisions on Codex standards are adopted by majority, with each nation or national member organization in attendance receiving a single vote.[11] Although consensus is encouraged, decisions do often get passed over the protests of one or more members, even when those members are powerful international actors like the European Union or the United States. In addition,

[8] Perlman (2020*a*).
[9] World Trade Organization (1995*b*), Article 3.1.
[10] World Trade Organization (1995*a*), Article 2.5.
[11] The European Union is currently the only member organization.

despite criticisms that Codex's rules frequently reflect the preferences of its wealthiest national participants,[12] researchers have shown that since the naming of Codex by the SPS Agreement as the relevant international standard-setter for food safety, developing countries' attendance at and involvement in Codex meetings has risen dramatically.[13] For example, whereas in 1991, the number of delegates from high-income countries at the annual Codex Meeting numbered 170, as compared to 143 delegates attending from low- or middle-income countries,[14] by 2019, delegates from low- and middle-income countries had risen to 239, significantly surpassing the 153 delegates from high-income nations.[15] In addition, both Codex documents and my own observations from attending a Codex meeting in 2016 suggest that developing countries do actively participate in Codex discussions, even if not at the same rates as developed nations,[16] and developing countries also regularly submit detailed comments expressing their agreement or disagreement with Codex proposals. All of this, combined with the fact that middle- and low-income countries actually make up the majority of Codex members, suggests that these countries should have some ability to block proposals that overtly harm their interests.

Codex also enjoys some characteristics that might help insulate it from the sort of political capture by special interests that can lead nations to impose regulatory barriers to trade. Unlike in the domestic arena, in which industry can use its superior resources to out-lobby opposing groups, at the international level, with decision-makers not elected officials but rather delegations of technocrats, industry's lobbying potential would seem to be more muted. This is not to say that industry wields no political influence under Codex. To the contrary, a number of scholars have observed that industry has been granted undue access to the Codex process.[17] Though voting on final adoption is limited to national or regional delegations, within those delegations one can easily

[12] Victor (2002).
[13] Veggeland and Borgen (2005).
[14] Most countries bring more than one delegate.
[15] Delegate counts based on Codex Alimentarius Commission meeting lists of participants. Only delegates listed for member countries were included. Country development categorizations were taken from the 2019 UN World Economic Situation and Prospects and the World Bank's 1991 World Development Report.
[16] Smythe (2009).
[17] See, e.g., Avery, Drake and Lang (1993); Rosman (1993); Smythe (2009); Sklair (2002); Victor (2002).

identify representatives from industry,[18] and industry groups frequently attend Codex meetings and working groups in an observational capacity. While the number of industry representatives on delegations is dwarfed by the number of government officials, the mere presence of industry has, at times, been viewed as evidence of corporate meddling.

At the same time, even among those who have suggested that Codex is bowing to corporate interests, concerns have been that this will lead to the prioritization of trade over safety.[19] Thus, those who perceive a strong potential for industry influence assume that this will result in Codex effectively eliminating unnecessary trade barriers, albeit to the partial detriment of consumer safety. While this might not be an outcome any of us would want, it also is not an outcome that would lead Codex standards to mirror the types of biases identified in the previous chapter, nor is it one that would disproportionately harm developing countries. After all, from a pure trade perspective, if anything, poorer countries often benefit from looser regulatory measures, as these countries are those least capable of meeting stringent standards.

Finally, to the extent that industry's literal seat at the table is its primary means of influence when it comes to Codex standard-setting, it is not at all clear that we should expect to see much of this influence in the more technical, science-driven areas of Codex's activities. That is because much of the work leading to these standards takes place well before Codex working groups, let alone the full Commission, actually convene, in settings in which industry has little to no physical presence.

6.3 HOW THE STANDARDS ARE MADE

In order to understand the potential avenues of influence that different actors might enjoy under Codex, it is necessary to have a bit more background on how Codex recommendations are developed. Codex publishes a dizzying array of specifications, ranging from the utterly banal, such as what weight denotes the cutoff between gouda and "baby" gouda (2.5 kg, for those interested) to the more consequential, such as the maximum

[18] For example, in the 2018 meeting of the Codex Committee on Pesticide Residues, the German delegation included a representative from chemical giant BASF, in addition to three government representatives. The US delegation similarly included representatives from Monsanto, Luxembourg-Pamol, Inc., Syngenta, and Bayer, as well as from the nonprofit specialty crop group, IR-4.

[19] Rosman (1993).

amounts of chemical contaminants, toxins, and additives permitted to be present in food. The development of all of these standards is the task of a variety of Codex committees, some of which have met only infrequently over the entire history of Codex (such as the Codex Committee on Natural Mineral Waters) and some of which meet as often as annually. These specialized committees, like the Codex Alimentarius Commission itself, reserve voting rights for national and regional members, while allowing nonmembers, such as international organizations and industry associations, to attend in an observational capacity. When it comes to less scientifically demanding work, such as determining what qualifies as an "extra" class rambutan versus merely a class I rambutan, the Codex committees may take it entirely upon themselves, with ample input from interested nations, to develop the appropriate rule, which is then voted on and, if approved, passed along to the full Commission to be voted upon again at the next annual meeting. Thus, in these matters, it seems entirely plausible that powerful nations or members of industry could utilize their voting power (in the case of states) or physical presence (in the case of industry) in order to sway outcomes to their liking.

However, when it comes to more scientifically complex matters related to individual product risks – in other words, the sorts of regulatory arenas that are the focus of this book – the Codex committees are an additional step removed from the start of the process. In fact, the vast majority of these standards are set outside Codex oversight entirely, during meetings of FAO and WHO expert bodies, such as the Joint FAO/WHO Meeting on Pesticide Residues (JMPR), the Joint FAO/WHO Expert Committee on Food Additives (JECFA), and the Joint FAO/WHO Expert Meetings on Microbiological Risk Assessment (JEMRA).

Each of these bodies is comprised of international working groups of scientific experts that meet regularly in order to analyze data and conduct risk assessments for pathogens (in the case of the JEMRA); pesticides (in the case of the JMPR); and naturally occurring toxins, food additives, and veterinary drugs (in the case of the JECFA). These groups then provide recommendations that are taken up by the relevant Codex committee and overwhelmingly adopted, such that out of the nearly 300 residue levels proposed by the 2018 JMPR, fewer than ten were not accepted by the Codex Committee on Pesticide Residues (CCPR), amid requests for additional consideration and/or data. Meanwhile, the full Codex Alimentarius Commission generally implements the recommendations of all of its committees wholesale, meaning that nearly every one of the recommendations provided by the joint FAO/WHO expert groups is adopted shortly after it is put forward, while a tiny handful are either rejected, revised, or simply delayed a year or two until more data can be assembled.

All of this suggests that if we want to understand whether those Codex standards that address product-level risks are susceptible to the sorts of biases that can create trade barriers, we need to be looking less at the decision-making process of the Codex Commission and its relevant subsidiary bodies and more at the process that occurs under the expert committees that create most of the more scientifically demanding (and consequential) standards. Notably, when it comes to some of the sharpest critiques of Codex, particularly those related to direct corporate meddling through industry participation on delegations and as observers, there appears to be very little evidence that such concerns apply to these expert bodies. In fact, lists of participants from the JMPR and JECFA's most recent meetings reveal zero industry insiders,[20] while among the nearly 90 listed experts employed by the JEMRA between 2018 and 2022, a mere four had any sort of industry affiliation.[21] Rather than coming from industry, those attending these expert meetings overwhelmingly come from government agencies or academic research institutions. In addition, participants are required to disclose any conflicts of interest, and scientists who may have an interest in a specific substance or rule are not permitted to participate in its evaluation. In other words, these technical bodies really do seem to be quite removed from the sort of lobbying or meddling that has traditionally been viewed as a central avenue for regulatory capture and the creation of regulatory barriers.

This is not to say that conflicts of interest never arise or that they are always appropriately identified. In an incident that brought a great deal of embarrassment to the JMPR, it was discovered that one of the expert advisors at the 1993 meeting, Dr. Gaston Vettorazzi, had undisclosed ties to the tobacco industry and used his position at the meeting to try to win more lenient evaluations of carcinogenic pesticides favored by tobacco growers. A WHO committee subsequently produced a highly critical investigative report, revealing the tobacco industry's influence at UN organizations, including the JMPR.[22] This helped spur the committee to take a more serious approach to reducing real or perceived conflicts of

[20] JMPR and JECFA provide a full list of participants with their reports. In the handful of cases in which affiliations were not listed, it was either possible to find biographies of the individuals provided through the organizations or to find the individuals' LinkedIn profiles.

[21] Food and Agricultural Organization and World Health Organization (2022).

[22] World Health Organization (2000).

interest going forward.[23] While this has not eliminated occasional accusations of bias,[24] even industry seems to acknowledge that overt attempts to influence these organizations are risky, if not counterproductive. For example, an information document distributed by CropLife International, an industry association that brings together all the largest global pesticide manufacturers, advised its members as follows:

> The panel members [of the JMPR] are under close observation from critical NGOs. It is in the primary interest of CropLife International Members to contribute in an appropriate manner both in correspondence and in direct contact with the panel members in order that their scientific integrity and independence are not compromised.[25]

Of course, even if industry generally avoids conspicuous interference in these expert meetings, industry can continue to have an enormous impact on their recommendations. This is because no matter how objective, independent, and honest the committee experts may be, they remain dependent on industry for information about the products on which they are setting the standards.

This is particularly true for the JMPR and JECFA, which are responsible for studying the risks related to man-made chemical compounds, precisely the sorts of products that this book has shown tend to introduce substantial information dependencies. The easiest way to appreciate the extent of the JMPR and JECFA's dependence is to look at the data sources cited in their published reports. These reports are central to Codex standard-setting because they directly lay out the JMPR and JECFA's recommendations for what Codex standards should be while also providing the scientific basis for those recommendations. Conveniently, each of these reports provides a list of references on which decisions regarding appropriate standards are based. The lists of references reveal, with little ambiguity, that almost all the data used to determine maximum residue levels for food additives, veterinary drugs, and pesticides comes directly from the primary producers of the chemicals under evaluation.

23 Food and Agricultural Organization and World Health Organization (2002), p. 55.

24 A coalition of public interest groups expressed concern in 2016 that JMPR experts' ties to the nonprofit organization International Life Sciences Institute, which had received funds from industry, might lead these experts to take an overly benign view of then-Monsanto's blockbuster pesticide glyphosate, commonly known by it's brand name, Roundup (Gillam [2016]).

25 CropLife International (2017), p. 12.

For example, the most recent JMPR report included a section analyzing the pesticide afidopyropen. The analysis was based on 116 separate studies, all of which were directly conducted or commissioned by the chemical's registrant (in this case, BASF) and all of which remain unavailable for public distribution.[26] Such dependence on manufacturers' privately held data has not been limited to a single substance. In response to an email query regarding the source of data for evaluations, a WHO representative observed:

> Most of the data for an evaluation is indeed submitted by the companies. It is unpublished – but quality assurance is produced under GLP [good laboratory practice] requirements and laboratories and companies are under the oversight of national authorities. Often, a company commissions studies from independent laboratories.

The individual went on to note:

> In addition to the company supplied data, usually a search for data is also carried out in the published scientific literature before an evaluation. However, it is more often than not the case, that only company sponsored (and owned) data will provide a full data set necessary for a thorough evaluation.[27]

The JECFA, for its part, is similarly dependent on registrants for data, even offering what amounts to a disclaimer in its annual reports, which says, "Most of the evaluations and summaries contained in this publication are based on unpublished proprietary data submitted to JECFA for use when making its assessment."[28]

The JMPR's and JECFA's inability to generate risk data, and their resulting dependence on companies for this information, should not be surprising. As laid out in Chapter 2, such dependence is endemic to the national regulation of product risks even in highly developed countries, and international standard-setters are at a significant disadvantage compared to national regulators in wealthy countries when it comes to acquiring resources. The question that is not answered by simply observing that similar dependencies exist is whether these dependencies result in similar biases.

[26] While the vast majority of studies have a BASF study number, suggesting they were conducted by the company itself, a handful of studies were seemingly conducted by outside laboratories. However, even in these cases, the documents are labeled with a BASF registration number, suggesting that the documents came directly from the company and/or were privately commissioned by it.

[27] Both quotes from email communication received May 28, 2019.

[28] Joint FAO/WHO Expert Committee on Food Additives (2019), p. ix.

In order to address this question, it is helpful to compare apples to apples. In other words, it is helpful to look at the specific case of pesticide regulation under Codex. By retaining the same sectoral focus as that in the previous chapter, it becomes possible to draw a direct comparison between international and domestic outcomes.

6.4 PESTICIDES, PRECAUTION, AND THE PERIODIC REVIEW

According to the theoretical predictions laid out in Chapter 3, the inability of regulators to acquire safety information to which producers have privileged access, combined with concerns that inadequate knowledge could lead to significant public harm, can encourage politically accountable policymakers to seek out more stringent regulatory institutions in the form of reevaluations of existing products during which a precautionary standard is applied. It was also theorized that because developed countries ought to prioritize safety concerns relative to costs, as compared to developing countries, and because those producers most likely to gain from precautionary reevaluations are more concentrated in developed markets, we can generally expect this sort of precautionary system to be more popular in wealthier nations. Conversely, those countries that house more generic producers and whose citizens are more dependent on generic products should view precaution more skeptically. In the context of international standard-setting in the realm of agrochemicals – a sector that brings together both significant information asymmetries and legitimate potential for public harm – this suggests that any push for retroactive precaution should most likely be spearheaded by developed countries, whereas much of the resistance to such institutions should come predominantly from developing ones.

As it turns out, the Codex Alimentarius Commission adopted a system of precautionary reassessments of pesticide tolerance levels – or MRLS (maximum residue levels), as the Commission calls them – in 1993, only five years after the United States passed legislation to make its prior attempt at precautionary reevaluations a reality. The initial proposal for a reassessment of pesticide risks can be traced back to a 1982 JMPR report, which recommended implementing a periodical review of agrochemicals' "toxicological aspects."[29] However, the actual development and debate over how such a process should

29 Report referenced by The Codex Committee on Pesticide Residues (1983), p. 6.

be implemented occurred under Codex, with representatives from the Netherlands, Sweden, the United States, France, and Australia expressing encouragement and leading the charge. Not surprisingly, the expressed rationale for such a procedure mirrored the sorts of arguments put forward in support of the United States' reevaluations, with concerns about public risk and inadequate information on existing products front and center. For example, in the opening speech at the Codex Committee on Pesticide Residues' eighteenth meeting, Dr. J. Van Londen, the secretary general of the Committee and the director-general of the Ministry of Welfare, Health and Cultural Affairs of The Netherlands observed the following:

> Since the early sixties ... pesticides have developed as a subject for discussion among ... those who themselves do not use pesticides but make use of the resulting food products ... The bad reputation pesticides obtained in the mind of the general public is, at least partially, due to the discovery of deleterious effects of certain pesticides, not known in the years of the early use. As our knowledge about chemicals and their risks for humans and the environment has increased enormously it should be expected that data on the pros and contras of pesticides are sufficient now to prevent unjustified registration. However, recent discoveries of negative toxicological properties, even of long registered and widely used pesticides, proves that such a situation is not yet reached. They may serve to stimulate the development of a system of periodical review of the toxicological and other data by WHO and FAO.[30]

In the years that followed, with input seeming to come almost exclusively from developed countries and with the initial drafting led by Australia, a periodic review procedure was put in place. The periodic review dictates that each year, the CCPR must produce a list of chemicals from which "MRLs were first estimated more than 10 years ago; or ... for which a periodic review was conducted more than 10 years ago."[31] Data owners (i.e., agrochemical companies) are then notified of the list of candidate chemicals and asked to convey their willingness to provide the necessary information. Lack of willingness to provide the necessary data for an entire pesticide or a given tolerance leads the JMPR to recommend the withdrawal of the relevant tolerance level(s) at the next Codex session. Likewise, should a party commit to provide information but then offer inadequate data, the tolerance levels are only maintained for a maximum of four years, before being removed entirely.

[30] The Codex Committee on Pesticide Residues (1986), p. 65.
[31] Codex Alimentarius Commission (2000), p. 89.

Although the JMPR had been known to reassess various pesticides and/or MRLs on occasion prior to the implementation of the periodic review, the new precautionary rules substantially changed the stakes. This was laid out in a 1992 CCPR report explaining what implementation of the periodic review would mean: "In normal circumstances if no information is supplied the MRL would remain. In the periodic review programme withdrawal of the MRL would be recommended."[32]

The removal of an MRL by Codex has significant trade implications. Because many nations, particularly developing ones, adopt Codex standards automatically, the withdrawal of a Codex MRL means that these countries will also lack a tolerance for the commodity–pesticide combination in question. As a result, because that country will now officially have no registered level at which the pesticide is considered to be safe on the relevant crop, if an import of that crop is found to contain residues of the chemical, it will often be rejected.[33] This, in turn, means that farmers exporting from or to any of the impacted markets will be (rightly) wary of using the pesticide on the crop for which a Codex MRL no longer exists, forcing them to seek out other methods of pest control. More generally, because farmers often find it challenging to keep track of nations' diverging and frequently changing tolerance levels, even those farmers exporting to a market that does not defer to Codex may be wary of using a pesticide that lacks an international MRL.[34] Indeed, according to communications with a regulator at the Chilean Food Safety Agency, the withdrawal of MRLs is significantly more harmful for exporters (particularly in developing countries) than simply a low MRL,[35] because whereas a low MRL implies a pesticide may be used in moderation, a nonexistent MRL suggests that any application could lead to a shipment rejection. Therefore, the withdrawal of a Codex MRL, due to lack of data, has much the same meaning as a national revocation, except in the Codex case, because these standards are adopted by numerous countries at once, the impact can be much more far-reaching.

6.5 WHO'S AFRAID OF THE PERIODIC REVIEW?

While the initial passage of the periodic review was driven by developed nations, the anemic participation of developing countries in Codex meet-

32 The Codex Committee on Pesticide Residues (1992), p. 76.

33 Food and Agricultural Organization (2007).

34 Based on in-person and electronic communications with EPA officials, as well as with a senior manager at BASF.

35 Email communications, August 3, 2016.

ings prior to 1995 means that this can tell us little about the coalitions that have actually supported or opposed this precautionary institution. Therefore, it is far more informative to look at how countries have responded to the periodic review after it was put in place (and after its impacts were broadly understood). When we do this, as the book's theory would predict, a clear divide emerges between developed countries, who seem broadly content with the periodic review, and developing countries, from which numerous complaints about the process have arisen, with comments focusing on the potential for the review to eliminate MRLs for useful chemicals. Complaints from developing countries include a 2013 comment submitted to the CCPR by Brazil, in which the Brazilian delegate noted that the country was extremely worried about the withdrawal of maximum residue levels due to manufacturers' unwillingness to provide the data requested during periodic reviews. The delegate observed that removing the tolerances "of compounds which are still used by countries is very harmful to the international food trade since [it] can raise trade barriers without scientific justification."[36] Likewise, a joint comment submitted by Chile, Brazil, Ecuador, El Salvador, Honduras, Peru, and the Dominican Republic that same year stated, "*La base científica ha sido el pilar fundamental, para las decisiones del Codex, no siendo coherente el hecho que se discontinúe un estándar por el solo hecho del paso del tiempo*,"[37] which roughly translates to, "The scientific basis has been the fundamental pillar for the decisions of Codex, and it is inconsistent to discontinue a standard solely because of the passage of time." Thailand and China have similarly expressed concerns with the periodic review process, arguing that MRLs should "not be deleted without scientific support only as a result of the passing of time."[38]

By contrast, wealthier national members of Codex, including the Netherlands, Australia, and the United States, which helped implement the periodic review in the first place, have continued to support it,[39] and the European Union, during the meeting of the 2015 CCPR, even advocated for more frequent reviews, stating that "the absence of an updated risk assessment for periods exceeding 15 years is a concern."[40]

[36] The Codex Committee on Pesticide Residues (2013), CRD 9.

[37] Ibid., CRD 14

[38] Quote from Thailand (The Codex Committee on Pesticide Residues (2009*a*), CX/PR 09/41/7); China similarly stated "that MRL should not be deleted without any scientific grounds" (Ibid., CRD 17e).

[39] Ibid. p. 4.

[40] CCPR 2015, CRD12.

As for representatives of industry within Codex member states, one can see a clear divide between agrochemical organizations based in the wealthier countries and those located in developing nations, again precisely as the book's theory would suggest. On the developing country side, industry groups such as AgroCare and the Latin American Association of the National Agrochemical Industries (ALINA) – both of which are in the business of manufacturing out-of-patent chemicals – have consistently expressed frustration with and a desire to revise the periodic review. In 2018, AgroCare asserted that "the main reason for withdrawal of MRLs in Codex on [sic] the last years comes from the revocation of active ingredients as a result of nonsupport by the manufacturer." AgroCare went on to conclude "that the approach to review the pesticides active ingredients every 15 years is not reasonable,"[41] arguing that reviews ought to be risk, not time based. Similarly, ALINA has argued that "withdrawal of MRLs should only be science-based" and has suggested extending the time in between reviews to 25 years.[42]

On the other side of this debate, backing and at times even going beyond the positions of the developed countries themselves, has been CropLife, an organization that boasts among its members such innovative powerhouses as Bayer, BASF, and Syngenta, the first two of which are headquartered in Germany and the last of which is based in Switzerland. In total contrast to ALINA and AgroCare, CropLife argued in 2010 "that the criterion to withdraw an MRL *when the compound is not supported* [emphasis added] or manufactured, should be maintained."[43] This statement is remarkable. It shows this organization not merely supporting the periodic review in broad strokes, as a way to ensure the safety of existing chemicals, but directly advocating for the removal of MRLs, not necessarily when the MRLs are unsafe but *whenever producers decline to provide relevant data*. In the case of the United States, discussed in the previous chapter, one could only surmise that innovative companies' support for reevaluating chemicals on a precautionary basis was partially based on the fact that this would result in the removal of tolerances for generic products. However, this quote from CropLife shows these same innovative companies directly throwing their weight behind the specific portion of the precautionary review process that the previous chapter showed has led to systematic bias against generic products at the national level.

41 The Codex Committee on Pesticide Residues (2018), CRD12.
42 The Codex Committee on Pesticide Residues (2009*b*), CX/PR 10/42/12.
43 The Codex Committee on Pesticide Residues (2009*b*), CX/PR 10/42/12.

The coalitions that have arisen both in support of and in opposition to Codex's own version of retroactive precaution, the periodic review, coincide precisely with what we would expect, given who the winners and losers of such a system ought to be. At the same time, the question remains of whether the implementation of the periodic review has led to the same sort of targeted phasing out of more affordable products.

Obviously, some of the complaints that have emerged from developing nations, as well as from ALINA and AgroCare, suggest that a substantial number of standards have been removed as a result of manufacturer nonsupport. And certainly, based on the theory, we would expect that nonsupport to be concentrated among out-of-patent chemicals. Furthermore, considering that almost all of the individual decision-making on MRLs occurs under the auspices of the JMPR, away from the country-level politics of Codex meetings, it seems fairly likely that if MRLs are indeed falling away due to the nonsupport of the innovators and the concomitant inability of generic producers to fill the informational void, those countries most hurt by these dynamics would have little room to stop this. Nevertheless, at the end of the day, this remains an empirical question.

6.6 EMPIRICAL ANALYSIS

In order to assess the underlying determinants of changes to Codex pesticide maximum residue levels over time, this section replicates the analysis that was done for US tolerances in the previous chapter. This entailed recording all MRLs that were in place under Codex in 1996 and then tracking how each of those standards had or had not changed by 2015. Like the US government, Codex publishes its tolerance recommendations annually, following their finalization at the full Codex Alimentarius Commission meeting each June. Historically, these standards were published in hard copy or on CD-ROMs, nearly all of which appear to have been discarded or lost. More recently, tolerances have been reported on the FAO website. After contacting numerous libraries, as well as Codex itself, it was eventually possible to acquire a CD-ROM containing the 1996 Codex tolerance levels. Changes to standards were then tracked and verified using a variety of Codex and JMPR documents to uncover commodity name changes and identify any tolerances that were removed for technical reasons due to revisions to crop classifications or usage. This made it possible to ensure that any MRLs coded as "withdrawn" had not been eliminated due to a nomenclature change or some other technicality.[44]

Following are summary statistics showing how tolerance levels changed under Codex during the period studied (Table 6.1). As in the previous chapter, statistics show both overall changes and changes broken down by commodity type, date of pesticide registration, and the pesticide's toxicity level. The most notable result is the high instance of withdrawals. Whereas in the United States, 28% of tolerances were revoked between 1996 and 2015, the number of withdrawals jumps to 40% under Codex.[45] While the reasons for this are not a central focus of the theory, it could reflect relevant companies' priorities, in the sense that it is possible that certain companies have focused their data provision efforts at the national, rather than international level. In addition to the high number of MRL withdrawals, we also see, much as in the US case, that standards have been fairly fluid over the period under observation, such that only 30% of standards have remained unchanged.

The main question we want to evaluate, though, is whether the patterns of change look similar to those seen at the national level. In particular, we want to know whether, after controlling for the potential risks of the pesticide to which the MRL applies, have standards routinely become stricter or been withdrawn for older, more affordable products, in particular? In order to answer this, a nearly identical model is employed to that used for the United States, with the sole exception that in the Codex case the control for high acreage US crops is omitted due to the fact that Codex standards apply internationally, and different countries have different high acreage crops.

Table 6.2 shows the results. Once again, the analysis uses an ordered logistic regression for which the dependent variable ranges from 1 to 4, depending on whether the tolerance increased, remained the same, became stricter, or was withdrawn between 1996 and 2015 (where higher numbers reflect movement toward stringency). The explanatory variable of interest is again the number of years that have passed since

44 Codex does not use the term "revoked" to describe maximum residue levels that have been deleted. Instead, the terminology is typically that the MRL has been withdrawn.

45 The US data used in the previous chapter did include pesticides that were absent in the Codex sample, due to the fact that the sample included all tolerances on pesticides for which Codex also had a tolerance in *either* 1996 *or* 2015. However, even if we restrict that US sample to only include pesticides for which Codex also had a tolerance in 1996, the percentage of revocations remains the same.

TABLE 6.1. *Summary of Codex MRL changes 1996–2015*

		By Commodity[a]			By Pesticide Registration			By Pesticide Toxicity	
Outcome	All	Produce (%)	Grain (%)	Animal[b] (%)	Pre-1961 (%)	1961–1980 (%)	1981–1996 (%)	High[c] (%)	Low[d] (%)
Withdrawn	40	45	42	13	52	37	34	41	37
Stricter	18	17	19	34	22	16	22	14	19
Same	30	28	20	41	19	36	24	39	23
Less Strict	12	11	19	13	7	11	21	6	20
N	1,360	784	118	196	280	779	301	307	361

[a] Not included are feed, nuts, and miscellaneous crops.
[b] Refers to animal products.
[c] The two most toxic categories.
[d] The two least toxic categories.

TABLE 6.2. *Codex tolerance changes 1996–2015*

	Tolerance Change 1996–2015:		
	1 = Less Strict, 2 = Same, 3 = More Strict, 4 = Withdrawn		
	(1)	(2)	(3)
Pesticide Age	0.036***	0.034**	0.033**
	(0.013)	(0.013)	(0.014)
Toxicity		0.045	0.074
		(0.206)	(0.204)
Toxicity Increased		0.172	0.196
		(0.504)	(0.507)
Carcinogenicity		0.006	−0.007
		(0.123)	(0.124)
Aquatic Chronic		−0.102	−0.108
		(0.111)	(0.111)
Aquatic Acute		0.467	0.478
		(0.662)	(0.659)
Fruit/Veggie			0.393***
			(0.138)
Observations	1,360	1,335	1,335

Note: *p < 0.1; **p < 0.05; ***p < 0.01
Standard errors clustered at pesticide level

the product was first registered in the United States (*Pesticide Age*). The USA is frequently the first national market in which companies register their products, due to the country's massive agricultural production and its history of protecting intellectual property, which differentiates it from some other agricultural behemoths such as China. With companies able to file for patent protection in multiple national markets simultaneously through international patent applications, and with US registration typically following closely on the heels of initial patent filings, time since initial registration in the United States remains a useful proxy for an agrochemical's profitability, as well as the likely existence of a patented alternative, for all of the reasons described in Chapters 4 and 5.

In addition to including a variable for time since registration, the analysis also again controls for a number of relevant confounders, including pesticide toxicity (with higher numbers reflecting higher toxicity), as determined by the WHO in 2009, as well as an indicator for whether the 1996–1997 classification rated the pesticide as less toxic than the 2009 measure. Models 2 and 3 also use the same measure for carcinogenicity and aquatic impact as those used in the US analysis. Although Codex never officially put a rule in place requiring products consumed by children to undergo special consideration, the analysis does again control for whether or not the tolerance applied to a fruit or vegetable, due to the fact that these products are often directly consumed by individuals without additional processing, meaning regulators may be particularly concerned about dietary intake levels for them. Standard errors are again clustered at the pesticide level and robust to heteroskedasticity.

The results show that, just as was true in the US case, the number of years since initial registration remains an important and significant predictor in determining how an MRL was likely to change over the period studied. What this suggests is that even though we might think that Codex would be subject to substantially different political dynamics than domestic regulations, at least to the extent that Codex is directly lobbied by agrochemical companies and also to the extent that the organization takes into account the divergent interests of its members, the financial interests of firms remain a major determinant of its regulatory evolution. Specifically, because the Codex process relies on companies to provide data during periodic reviews, companies' financial decisions about what data to provide or not provide plays a central role in how Codex MRLs evolve. With those companies best positioned to provide the necessary toxicity data during periodic reviews disinclined to defend MRLs on older products that have already lost patent protection, the MRLs for these products are frequently lowered or withdrawn.

Though not included here, the Appendix provides several additional tests mirroring those presented in the previous chapter at the US level. These robustness tests again are included to ensure that the results are not driven by the most dangerous pesticides in the sample or due to changes in pesticide efficacy across time. Importantly, the robustness checks again show that neither of these factors can explain the results in Table 6.2.

The findings suggest that just as in the United States, companies' financial motivations have played a key role in regulatory outcomes under Codex. Yet this still leaves unanswered an important question: To what extent are the trends under Codex more or less pronounced than they are at the national level? In order to help answer this, Table 6.3 shows analysis that allows us to compare the national and international results directly. The analysis was run by first stacking the US and Codex

TABLE 6.3. *Comparing MRL changes under US vs. Codex*

	MRL Change 1996–2015: 1 = Less Strict, 2 = Same, 3 = More Strict, 4 = Withdrawn		
	(1)	(2)	(3)
Pesticide Age	0.038***	0.038**	0.037**
	(0.014)	(0.016)	(0.016)
Pesticide Age*US	−0.0003	−0.002	−0.005
	(0.021)	(0.021)	(0.021)
US	−0.713	−0.570	−0.390
	(0.964)	(1.001)	(1.009)
Toxicity		0.464**	0.483***
		(0.186)	(0.181)
Toxicity Increased		0.299	0.304
		(0.401)	(0.399)
Carcinogenicity		−0.002	−0.005
		(0.116)	(0.115)
Aquatic Chronic		−0.071	−0.070
		(0.113)	(0.108)
Aquatic Acute		0.593	0.599
		(0.579)	(0.563)
Fruit/Veggie			0.383***
			(0.141)
Observations	4,044	3,969	3,969

Note: *p < 0.1; **p < 0.05; ***p < 0.01
Standard errors clustered at pesticide level

datasets.[46] All models include a dichotomous variable equal to 1 if the data came from the United States and 0 if the data came from Codex, as well as an interaction term between this dichotomous variable and *Pesticide Age*. The coefficient on the interaction term can thus tell us whether the number of years since registration has a greater or lesser effect on changes to Codex standards, relative to changes to US standards. The results show that the effect of *Pesticide Age* is not statistically differentiable across the two regulatory bodies, meaning we cannot reject the null hypothesis that this variable has the same effect

[46] For this analysis, the US sample was restricted so that it only included pesticides for which Codex also had a tolerance in 1996 (rather than including any chemicals for which Codex had a tolerance in 1996 or 2015). This was done to ensure greater comparability of the two datasets.

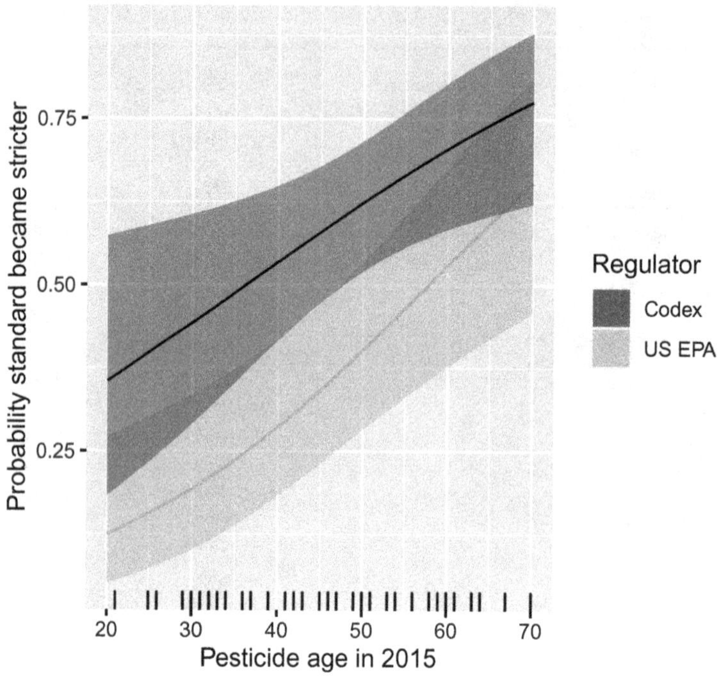

FIGURE 6.1 Comparing predicted probabilities of US and Codex MRL changes

across the US and Codex. This implies that, despite the fact that Codex reflects a far wider array of nations and interests, and despite largely setting standards through the JMPR, a seemingly apolitical, expert body, Codex has apparently done no better at preventing older, more affordable pesticides from receiving increasingly strict standards over time, even after controlling for the actual risk profiles of these products.

The similarity in outcomes across Codex and the United States can also be seen visually, using predicted probability plots. These were generated using the full models run on the separate Codex and US samples (these are models 3 from Tables 6.2 and 5.2, respectively). Figure 6.1 shows these plots. The outcome in the plots is dichotomous, such that the y-axis shows the probability that an MRL in the US or Codex sample either became stricter or was withdrawn/revoked. In light gray, we see the US results, which are the same as those previously displayed in Figure 5.3. Overlaid, in dark gray, are the Codex results. Both the US and Codex predictions use the full set of controls for pesticide characteristics (toxicity, carcinogenicity, and aquatic impact). In addition, both the US and

Codex results control for whether the MRL applied to a fruit or vegetable. The only difference in the relative models is that the US version also controls for whether the MRL applied to a crop that was one of the top three highest acreage crops in the United States while also including an interaction term for this and the age of the pesticide. For a more direct comparison, all the Codex and US controls have been fixed to the same values.[47] The plot shows how closely the slopes of the US and Codex results map one another, demonstrating that the time a pesticide has been on the market and, hence, its level of profitability, has a very similar impact on the probability of both US and Codex standards becoming stricter or being withdrawn/revoked, holding constant the pesticide's risk profile.

Taken together, the findings from this section suggest that moving decisions from the domestic to the international level leads to parallel outcomes, such that in both cases, the resulting standards are biased against more affordable products for reasons that cannot fully be explained by underlying risk. Thus, despite the fact that Codex standards are developed almost entirely by independent scientists, private companies play just as central of a role in influencing these standards as when those charged with developing the rules are bureaucrats, directly answerable to elected officials.

6.7 DISCUSSION

Consumers and generic producers, across countries, inevitably lose out from a system that systematically imposes stricter standards on more affordable, out-of-patent products for reasons that are orthogonal to safety concerns. Yet this harm is not felt equally across countries. Rather, this harm disproportionately falls on developing countries. This is true regardless of the product in question. Not only are innovative producers more concentrated in developed countries, meaning any benefits to the system accrue to wealthier nations, but consumers in developing nations, by definition, tend to be poorer, making the added cost of trading up to more expensive products particularly onerous.

In the case of agrochemicals, which have been the focus of much of the empirical analysis, the disproportionate impact on developing countries is

47 These values are the modes found in the US data for dichotomous variables and the means from the US data for variables with more than two levels.

particularly pronounced. Developing countries tend to be far more reliant on agricultural exports as a percentage of their gross domestic product, and farmers in these countries often face particular hurdles when it comes to acquiring the more expensive alternatives that retain lenient MRLs, as MRLs for more affordable substitutes are withdrawn. Some of these hurdles were highlighted in the course of email communications with an official in Costa Rica's Phytosanitary Department, Servicio Fitosanitario Del Estado. According to that official, "In Costa Rica there are 40,000 hectares planted with pineapple, approximately 70% of that area is cultivated by 5 big companies, the remaining 30% are more than 500 small farmers who don't have the necessary capital to use more expensive pesticides." The individual went on to note:

> Another aspect to consider is that pesticide manufacturers are not interested in the registration and marketing of the newer pesticides because the market in most Latin American countries is very small. Then our farmers still use old pesticides that mostly are no longer used in [the] US or Europe and for which stricter MRLs have been established.[48]

The issues raised by this official regarding Costa Rica apply to other developing countries as well. Not only is it the poorest farmers who are least able to afford expensive substitutes for older pesticides and who are frequently located in the developing world, but even if these farmers could afford such substitutes, the products may not be available to them. In fact, an additional reason, not mentioned by the Costa Rican official, for why some newer products may be hard to find in developing countries relates to the lack of enforcement of intellectual property protections in these jurisdictions. Companies are generally wary of going into markets in which their products might be pirated or reverse-engineered, a particular concern in the case of chemicals and one that thereby limits distribution to less well-regulated markets.[49] Because of this, companies frequently delay selling novel agrochemicals to developing countries until those products are off-or nearly off-patent, at which point these companies' financial interest in retaining lenient standards for such products, nationally or internationally, diminishes substantially or reverses entirely.

Considering the negative impact that the imposition of stricter standards on more affordable products has had on developing countries, we might wonder why actors in these nations have not been more effective at

[48] Electronic communication September 14, 2016.
[49] Phone conversation with official from Bayer AG, June 7, 2016.

the international level either at counteracting the information problems in order to retain tolerances or at pushing back against the periodic review procedure.

On the information side, the struggles faced by both generic producers and developing countries more generally have resulted from similar challenges internationally to those seen domestically. The nature of these challenges has been referenced directly during Codex sessions. For example, during the 2016 meeting of the CCPR in a comment submitted by ALINA, one of the Latin American agrochemical associations mentioned previously, the organization asserted:

> ALINA together with some other developing countries ... alleges that the main reason for withdrawal of MRLs in Codex on [sic] the last years comes from the revocation of active ingredients as a result of the non-support by the manufacter [sic]. This implies severe restrictions being imposed in [sic] a national level of an [sic] useful pesticide. *This situation occurs especially because the developing countries don't have the necessary resources to apply to keep an active ingredient when a manufacter [sic], due to market reasons, choose [sic] to not support the product* [emphasis added].[50]

In other words, much as generic companies in developed markets frequently find themselves unable to address the information gap when larger, innovative companies decide not to provide the required toxicology data during reevaluations, generic companies (and any other interested actors) in developing countries face severe hurdles when it comes to gathering the data needed for periodic reviews. Such hurdles are likely to be particularly exacerbated in the developing country case, not only because the relevant actors in these nations face more severe capital constraints than their counterparts in wealthier countries but also because they typically lack the equivalent level of scientific infrastructure.

It has long been understood that developing countries experience impediments when it comes to enjoying the full advantages of international organizations.[51] The problems developing countries face when it comes to combatting the information problems that lead the periodic review to be so detrimental to their interests are thus yet another way in which developing countries' reduced resources can contribute to international outcomes that do not work in their favor.

50 The Codex Committee on Pesticide Residues (2016), CRD14.

51 For example, it has been shown that because of capacity constraints, developing countries have a lower utilization of dispute settlement mechanisms despite, undoubtedly, facing similar if not higher barriers to trade (e.g., Davis and Bermeo [2009], Busch and Reinhardt [2003], Kim [2008]).

But what about pushing back against the periodic review itself? Given that a change to the periodic review, unlike a change to individual residue levels, would presumably be initiated and decided upon in Codex meetings, this would seem to be a more fruitful avenue through which developing countries might be able to gain leverage. When the periodic review was first put in place in 1993, developing countries not only were not particularly active participants in the Codex process, but they also may not have grasped what the consequences of a periodic review would be for them. Attesting to this latter possibility, a regulatory manager at Associação Brasileira de Defensivos Pós-Patente, a Brazilian association helping companies register out-of-patent pesticides, suggested that, at the time, delegations may have thought it sounded "logical to have a revaluation [sic] on active ingredients according to the most sound science, as many countries and regions do (Europe, for instance)."[52] If this individual's assessment is correct, it is neither surprising that the developed countries had little difficulty instituting the periodic review initially nor that sustained opposition to the periodic review has taken some time to develop.

However, both developing countries' participation in Codex forums and their concern about the periodic review's downstream effects have now increased markedly, and over the past ten years, efforts to reform the procedure have in fact gained momentum. In 2008, Argentina was granted authorization to form a working group, the goal of which was to assess potential changes to the risk analysis principles applied by the Codex Committee on Pesticide Residues and, by extension, the JMPR. A central focus of Argentina's efforts has been on amending the periodic review. Initial proposals by this working group to do away with the periodic review altogether were met with substantial resistance from Europe and other developed nations, along with the WHO. This has led the working group to suggest alternative means of blunting the periodic review's impacts.

In 2011, Brazil proposed that in cases in which chemicals or specific MRLs were not supported by the manufacturer, interested countries could submit their own data that, importantly, would not be held to the same scientific standard that would normally apply. In particular, Brazil suggested that countries could provide information on so-called "good agricultural practices" (or GAP), as well as data on actual residue levels found on crops for which farmers were following these practices. Developing countries could also put together the existing toxicological data for submission to

[52] Email communications, June 11, 2018.

the JMPR while avoiding having to develop new data on this front. Such a proposal has obvious appeal to generic producers and farmers in developing countries because, unlike toxicological data, which is extremely time-consuming and expensive to produce, residue data is comparatively inexpensive to gather.

Unfortunately for Brazil and for others who backed this proposal, it has not made much headway among the broader Codex membership. Tellingly, one of the most vocal opponents of the plan has been CropLife, the same organization that took umbrage in 2010 with the notion that developing nations might be able to retain tolerances without spending millions of dollars on collecting data. In the following year, according to the 2011 CCPR report:

> The Observer from CropLife expressed the view that [Brazil's] recommendations [of retaining tolerances without conducting toxicological assessments] seemed to conflict with JMPR responsibilities as they implied that JMPR would work with reduced data sets for the re-evaluation of MRLs; it was unclear how JMPR could update dietary risk assessment based only on GAP; JMPR can only make an informed decision when they have access to the full data set as currently required and to what extent they need to make use of these data has to be decided on a case-by-case [basis]. The Observer [from CropLife] expressed concern that *these changes may undermine the public confidence in Codex MRL, and generally supported retaining the principle of the current Periodic Review Procedure,* with possible amendments for clarification purposes. [emphasis added] [53]

Croplife's suspect concerns about public confidence aside, resistance to Brazil's proposal among developed nations, which perhaps more genuinely worry about public optics, has seemingly impeded the proposal's progress.

A proposal that seems to be making more headway, however, is one that would allow products not supported by the manufacturer *and* for which there is no evidence of health concerns to retain their MRLs, so long as these products remain in use in member countries. As of this writing, it remains unclear whether this proposal will succeed, as it was still under discussion at the most recent meeting of the CCPR. Thus far, the European Union has expressed its opposition to a blanket policy of this sort,[54] though it has shown some willingness to forego reevaluations of compounds without risk concerns, so long as toxicological data is less

53 The Codex Committee on Pesticide Residues (2011), p. 23.

54 The Codex Committee on Pesticide Residues (2019), CRD16.

than 25 years out of date. Meanwhile, countries like Kenya,[55] Thailand,[56] and Ecuador[57] have offered support for the idea. The final determination will depend on whether the developing nations in favor are able to win over some of their wealthier counterparts, likely over the objections not only of Europe but also of CropLife, whose corporate members have significant lobbying power in both Europe and the United States.

More broadly, the difficulties that developing countries have faced over the years in trying to push back against the periodic review's consequences show that even when those harmed by retroactive precaution are given standing and a voice, they may face an uphill battle. In many ways, the reason for this comes back to the problem of information. Again and again, in the course of debates about what to do regarding the periodic review, it was acknowledged by national representatives and nongovernmental organizations that even if the removal of MRLs for useful pesticides was unfortunate, there was simply no ability for any actor other than the large companies to provide the necessary data to make a safety evaluation, and given the need to ensure standards reflected modern science, this left limited options. This dilemma was explicitly acknowledged by the WHO, whose comments during the 2010 meeting of the CCPR were summarized as follows:

> [The WHO] [c]onsidered that it is of the utmost importance to maintain the periodic review process but admitted that the current system has some problems such as time-frames before CXLs [Codex maximum residue levels] are withdrawn, insufficient data provision by generic pesticide [sic] procedures for compounds no longer supported by the large companies.[58]

With no actor except the large companies often in a position to provide data on risks, and given an inability on the part of regulators, generic companies, or other third parties to evaluate risks themselves, the reality has been that Codex must choose either to maintain existing standards, without knowing whether those standards are still appropriate, or allow the standards to be withdrawn, even though many of the impacted products may be no more dangerous than newer ones for which standards remain.

Fortunately, there does seem to be a rising appreciation among Codex participants, including among developed nations, that the periodic review

55 Ibid., CRD16.

56 Ibid., CRD 20.

57 Ibid., CRD26.

58 The Codex Committee on Pesticide Residues (2009*b*), CX/PR 10/42/12.

can lead to unjustified barriers to agricultural trade. And it is not impossible that the next few years will see a revision to the periodic review process that is more favorable to poorer regions. Nevertheless, even if Codex does decide to revise its periodic review procedure, its broader ability to eliminate arbitrary regulatory barriers while providing more scientifically objective outcomes than national regulators remains in doubt. At the end of the day, Codex will always be beholden to firms for the data necessary to set its standards, and this will almost certainly lead to the privileging of certain products over others in ways that create regulatory impediments, a reality that is likely to hold even if the periodic review is partially reformed. Indeed, the regulatory barriers that have resulted from the periodic review are just one manifestation of the types of barriers that can result from Codex's dependence on firms for information. Other manifestations can be observed in alternative Codex domains, such as in the standard-setting for veterinary drugs, which play a parallel role in the trade of meat to that of pesticides in agriculture.

Companies' selective provision of information in the veterinary drugs case not only has similarly led to the withdrawal of maximum residue levels for less lucrative products (a periodic review problem) but also to the inability to implement MRLs for certain products in the first place. This latter issue was raised during a recent meeting of the Codex Committee on Residues of Veterinary Drugs in Food, when participating delegations "reiterated the importance of developing MRLs in particular for old compounds, which were widely used and for which there was no pharmaceutical sponsor."[59] At this same meeting, a representative from HealthforAnimals, a nonprofit organization representing various industry interests, observed:

> The companies provide nearly 100 percent of the current data. It costs a company large amounts – sometimes over a million dollars [–] to develop a complete data package specific to JECFA. That means that, increasingly, only the most interesting products with promising markets will be put forward and only the largest global companies can afford this process.[60]

As suggested by these quotes, much as with pesticides, difficulties acquiring adequate data for veterinary drugs seem to be concentrated among less lucrative (and frequently out-of-patent) products, again leading developing countries, with less access or ability to afford more

59 Codex Committee on Residues of Veterinary Drugs in Foods (2016), p. 13.

60 Ibid. p. 13.

expensive alternatives, to bear the brunt. Thus, it is not surprising to see Brazil complaining during a 2010 meeting of the Codex Committee on Residues of Veterinary Drugs in Foods about "the difficulties in obtaining standards, especially for those compounds with no patent protection."[61]

The challenges that Codex has encountered when it comes to establishing tolerances for veterinary drugs highlights how, rather than providing more scientifically objective outcomes, international standard-setters may instead introduce even more bias than national regulators. In this case, because Codex and its expert bodies have severely limited resources – which is itself the result of them being international organizations – they have been forced to move much more slowly in evaluating veterinary products than have regulators in developed countries. This, in turn, has meant that by the time these international bodies have gotten around to assessing some of the older drugs, the appetite for providing the data necessary to support them among those companies best positioned to do so has evaporated. Notably, Codex's inability to implement veterinary drug standards in the first place stems from the exact same factors as those that drive the withdrawal of agrochemical standards in the context of the periodic review. These are also the same factors that have been the focus of this book all along: standard-setters' over-dependence on firms for information.

[61] Codex Committee on Residues of Veterinary Drugs in Foods (2010), p. 6.

7

Challenging Barriers

It is often said that we are living in the information age. Never before has it been so easy for the average citizen to download data, access academic studies, or browse international news headlines. Yet even amidst this democratization of knowledge, much of the scientific and technical information most relevant for regulatory policymaking remains privatized. This confers an enormous degree of power into the hands of those who hold an advantage in acquiring the knowledge necessary to set the rules. How these actors use this power is a function of the institutional environment in which they operate and the degree to which they expect other parties to gain access to the information that they hold. This book has explored one of the more surprising and perverse ways in which the holders of private information have sought and succeeded in taking advantage of their information superiority. In doing so, it has revealed how a set of seemingly scientific regulations may in fact result from the strategic wielding and withholding of scientific data.

Specifically, the book has shown that when it comes to the regulation of potentially dangerous products, a small subset of producers frequently hold a near monopoly on relevant technical information. This enables these producers to shape regulatory outcomes in unexpected and problematic ways, by exploiting their information advantages to acquire regulatory rules that curtail the sale of competitively produced, less profitable products while privileging more profitable, higher priced alternatives. In order to accomplish this, producers not only proactively reveal negative information about certain products so as to justify stricter standards on them, but they support broader regulatory institutions that – while ostensibly intended to protect the population through the application of a more precautionary approach to risk – allow producers to use their information advantages in order to shift regulatory outcomes more systematically toward their preferred products.

The result is the creation of arbitrary barriers to domestic competition and international trade that frequently hit developing countries the hardest. Moreover, because international organizations rely on the same powerful firms for information about product risk as domestic regulators, not only will the current method for adjudicating between *legitimate* and *illegitimate* regulatory barriers under international law frequently fall short, but those international standard-setters that have been charged with providing objective standards toward which nations should harmonize will tend to perpetuate and even exacerbate the regulatory biases found at the national level.

The book's findings contribute to the study of a diverse set of important issues spanning international, domestic, and comparative political economy. The remainder of this chapter elucidates each of these contributions in turn and suggests avenues for future inquiry. In addition, the chapter explores the ethical and practical implications of the findings, revisiting the distributive consequences identified and asking how policymakers might seek to redress some of the resulting harms.

7.1 NONTARIFF BARRIERS: REEXAMINING SOURCES AND SOLUTIONS

As tariff barriers to trade have progressively declined around the world, scholars have increasingly turned their attention to nontariff barriers, with regulatory impediments front and center. There are two prevailing explanations for regulatory barriers in the literature. The first is that governments deliberately use regulations as a form of protectionism, whereby they serve as substitutes[1] or complements[2] to tariffs while also allowing governments to obfuscate about their true intentions.[3] The second explanation is that regulatory barriers represent reasonable differences in national risk preferences,[4] such that the barriers they create to trade are an unfortunate side-effect of governments' well-intentioned policies.

[1] Marvel and Ray (1983); Bhagwati (1988); Mansfield and Busch (1995).
[2] Ray (1981).
[3] Kono (2006).
[4] E.g., Sykes (1999); Rodrik (2018).

Although previous work has acknowledged the difficulty of disentangling which of these two motivations is to blame for any given regulatory barrier, it has, nonetheless, generally taken government intent for granted. Governments may be pursuing precaution, protectionism, or some combination of the two, but in either case they are pursuing those interests deliberately. This book has shown that assumptions of government intent may be misleading. Through a deep dive into the origins of a set of nontariff barriers on agriculture that have proven to be among the most commonly cited regulatory impediments since the founding of the WTO, this book has revealed that a primary driver of these barriers has been innovative agrochemical producers' ability to leverage privately-held information about risk to acquire regulations that systematically impose stricter standards on more affordable, out-of-patent pesticide products. While government efforts to reduce risks from agrochemicals opened the door to these dynamics, the specific patterns of regulatory barriers that have emerged can neither be said to result directly from deliberate protectionism nor from deliberate precaution.

This matters because it means, more broadly, that scholars and policymakers may be misinterpreting the sources of regulatory barriers, attributing them to interest group lobbying or government optimization around risk when instead they reflect interest group influence through the provision and withholding of information. Moreover, when it comes to the ability of interest groups to use information as a means of acquiring nontariff barriers, the opportunities extend well beyond the specific case of agrochemicals. As revealed in Chapter 2, particularly when it comes to the regulation of product risk, national regulators are consistently at a substantial information disadvantage relative to those they regulate. This has led to pervasive dependencies on producers to provide nearly all of the information necessary to set appropriate standards and ensure dangerous products are taken off the market. For example, aircraft manufacturers are not only charged with verifying that their craft meet certification requirements, but they play a central role in designing those requirements. Pharmaceutical companies both conduct the clinical studies assessing if their drugs are safe and effective and are responsible for identifying any health risks that arise after the fact. Finally, consumer product producers across the world initiate a substantial portion, if not the majority, of product recalls.

All of this suggests that trade barriers related to the regulation of product risks will frequently reflect not just government intent but the strategic decisions of producers around what information to reveal or withhold.

Whereas scholars of domestic regulation have highlighted the importance of information asymmetries in explaining how firms win preferential outcomes,[5] considerations of information have remained surprisingly absent in the study of regulatory impediments to trade. Given the degree to which information asymmetries define many of the regulatory arenas in which regulatory barriers have proven particularly contentious, a complete theory of these barriers ought to take the role of information more seriously.

Correctly identifying the drivers of regulatory barriers to trade also matters for the ability of the current international trading system to address them. In order to limit the potential for regulations to act as a form of protectionism in disguise, while also circumscribing the ability of governments to put in place regulations that stretch the definition of what is needed to protect the population, the WTO requires that when national regulatory measures are more trade restrictive than the relevant international benchmark, they must be "based on scientific principles and ... not maintained without sufficient scientific evidence."[6] This requirement ought to make it harder for governments to justify regulations that are deliberately set up to favor domestic producers or that clearly go beyond what the *available* science can justify. Yet, when the availability of science itself is biased, and when the regulatory barriers in question result from this, a requirement that regulations be based on science will do little to resolve the problem.

Similar issues arise when it comes to using international delegation as a way of reducing regulatory impediments to trade. Within academic and policy communities, delegation to international standard-setting bodies has often been seen as a way to avoid the prisoner's dilemma of protectionism, by which each country seeks to "beggar-thy-neighbor," protecting domestic producers at the expense of foreign exporters and the broader global economy. The relative remove of international organizations from domestic politics and the need for broader agreement in order to reach decisions has frequently been touted as a way of reducing the influence of the special interest groups that all too often bend domestic regulatory processes to their benefit.[7]

5 See, e.g., Baron and Myerson (1982); Laffont and Tirole (1986); Joskow and Schmalensee (1986); McCarty (2017).

6 World Trade Organization (2020*b*), 2.2.

7 E.g., Kapstein (1989); Nielson and Tierney (2003); Keohane, Macedo and Moravcsik (2009); Mattli and Woods (2009).

While it might make sense that international standards could help reduce the sorts of regulatory biases that stem from deliberate protectionism, there is far less room for optimism that international standards can create more scientifically objective outcomes when the source of bias is an asymmetric information problem between regulators and producers. Beset by free-rider problems and significant underfunding, international organizations have little ability to outperform the information collection efforts of wealthy national bureaucracies. As a result, international standard-setters are also poorly positioned to outperform their domestic counterparts when it comes to ensuring their standards eliminate those arbitrary barriers that result from an inability to overcome the information asymmetries inherent in the regulation of product risk.

The finding that both reliance on science and delegation to international standard-setters may do little to solve some of the major regulatory biases that create impediments to trade suggests a need for more attention to how scientific evidence is incorporated into the WTO process, as well as the factors that lead international standards to reflect certain interests over others. Previous work has shown that "institutional complementarities" between domestic bureaucracies and international standard-setting bodies can help certain nations gain a leg-up in the standard-setting process,[8] and there has been some investigation of the ways in which the participation of industry in standard-setting forums can endow these actors with influence.[9] Nevertheless, scholars should pay closer attention to the intranational information dynamics that, themselves, directly influence outcomes at the international level: Which domestic groups tend to be best positioned to get their information in front of international decision-makers? Whose information wins out when there are multiple information providers with conflicting conclusions? Answering these questions could help shed additional light on the sources of power and bias at the international level.

7.2 REFINING THEORIES OF REGULATION

As for the national level, it has become a truism in the so-called regulatory capture literature that regulations reflect the interests of the regulated.

[8] Mattli and Büthe (2003); Büthe and Mattli (2011).

[9] Underhill and Zhang (2008); Griffith-Jones and Persaud (2008); Lall (2009); Baker (2010); Avery, Drake and Lang (1993); Rosman (1993); Smythe (2009); Sklair (2002); Victor (2002).

Often it is assumed that this outcome is the result of regulated industries' superior capacity to organize, the substantial financial resources they can wield, or their ability to win over those charged with regulating them.[10] At times so automatic is the assumption that industry gets what it wants, that simply showing concordance between industry interests and outcomes has been enough for some to conclude that capture has occurred.[11] While not denying that industry may indeed employ the rather blunt instrument of direct provision of resources in order to "capture" the regulatory process, this book has sought to probe more deeply an underexplored mechanism through which industry can win its preferred outcomes. This is a mechanism that involves firms' ability to exploit information asymmetries, particularly under certain types of precautionary regulatory institutions, in order to shift the market toward their most lucrative products.

Even though economists have long appreciated the importance of information asymmetries to regulatory outcomes, emphasizing, for example, how they allow monopolists to win preferred pricing regulations,[12] information asymmetries between producers and regulators related to product risks have received only limited attention, with scholars generally not moving beyond the simplistic assumption that firms will seek to hide risks so as to retain lenient standards.[13] The theory laid out in Chapter 3 sought to build on these simplistic assumptions, hypothesizing that producers not only might hide negative information about profitable products but also, counterintuitively, might proactively reveal negative information about unprofitable ones. The chapter then went on to consider how regulatory institutions might influence firms' information strategies. This, in turn, was used to explain why we might see the adoption of certain institutions in the first place.

By considering firms' incentives to use regulations against their own products, as well as how information and institutions allow them to do this, the book makes three major contributions to the study of regulation.

First, it sheds light on an important empirical puzzle in comparative political economy: Why do some countries adopt more precautionary regulatory institutions than others? Whereas existing explanations for

10 These various themes can be traced back to some of the earliest theories of regulatory capture, including Bernstein (1955), Huntington (1952), and Stigler (1971).
11 This is a central critique of the capture literature found in Carpenter and Moss (2014).
12 Baron and Myerson (1982); Laffont and Tirole (1986); Joskow and Schmalensee (1986).
13 This is a notable theme in the legal liability literature. See, e.g., Shavell (1984*a*,*b*); Viscusi (1989).

divergence in precaution have predominantly highlighted societal risk preferences,[14] international pressures,[15] or the benefits to those producers that already eschew the affected products,[16] this book has shown how certain types of precautionary institutions – those that apply a precautionary standard retroactively to products already on the market – can amplify producers' information advantages, helping them eliminate some of their own competitively produced, out-of-patent products for which they have a more profitable (i.e., patented) alternative. This helps explain why innovative producers, for whom patents are central to their profitability, would support the implementation of precautionary legislation, even when it threatens the sales of some of their own goods. It also offers new insight into the conditions under which we might expect to see precautionary policies succeed. Specifically, the theory suggests that in countries in which innovative producers have a more dominant presence, support for the types of precautionary institutions that allow these producers to use information to target out-of-patent products for stricter standards is more likely to emerge. Indeed, Chapter 5 revealed that innovative agrochemical producers were instrumental in the implementation of more precautionary regulatory institutions in the United States during the 1980s. At the time, the companies couched their support in high-minded language, saying they had "come to recognize that we are more than simply manufacturers and ... accept our responsibilities to our customers and to the public at large."[17] These unusual displays of civic-mindedness led various members of Congress to express surprise at the apparent eagerness of the companies to take on a greater financial burden in pursuit of the public good. In the context of the theory, however, these companies' support for precaution seems far less surprising: Precaution offered innovative firms an opportunity to increase profits under the guise of protecting the public.

Second, the book's theoretical emphasis allowed it to investigate temporal patterns in regulatory change. Unlike theories of regulatory outcomes, which are supported by a deep and robust literature, theories explaining the timing of regulatory change have tended to receive less sustained study. The most common explanation for shifts in regulatory

14 Vogel (2012).
15 Drezner (2007); Paarlberg (2001).
16 This most frequently comes up in the context of precaution as a nontariff barrier.
17 US Cong. House Subcomm. on Department Operations, Research, and Foreign Agriculture (1986), p. 9.

rules is one that largely sidesteps the interests of the regulated altogether, arguing that these shifts follow from crises, in reaction to sudden and substantial public outcries.[18] Given that regulatory institutions are sticky and path dependent,[19] it is not surprising that scholars have looked to major upheavals to make sense of institutional transitions. Yet these explanations fail to account for why regulatory action often occurs years after public pressure began or long after the science justifying stricter regulations was made clear, at least to some. Why, for example, did it take a decade to ban DDT, the controversial insecticide that was the focus of Rachel Carson's *Silent Spring*? Why did the international community move promptly to take robust action against ozone-depleting CFCs, despite repeated failures to move quickly on other environmental threats?

Public pressure can tell only part of the story. A more complete interpretation requires taking into account the ways in which product profitability changes over time and the fact that producers' incentives to retain lenient standards on their products diminishes once those products lose patent protection. This can explain not only why companies might passively accept more stringent standards – a story that has been told before[20] – but why they might eagerly seek out stricter standards as well, for example, lobbying to ban their own inhalers[21] or suddenly turning against a highly lucrative pain killer.[22] In addition, the book demonstrated the importance of considering the role played by information and institutions. Specifically, it demonstrated the need to incorporate firms' ability to leverage the timing of information revelations to encourage changes to standards at favorable moments, a strategy in which, as Chapter 4 demonstrated, firms have engaged both in the pharmaceutical and agrochemical sectors. In addition, the book showed the relevance of institutions and how these can amplify firms' information strategies, helping them win preferred outcomes not only through acts of information commission but also through acts of omission.

Finally, by considering the interaction of information and institutions, the book was better able to bridge the gap between theories that explain regulation through capture and those that explain it through the public interest. Under theories of regulation that assume influence operates

18 Carpenter and Sin (2007).
19 Pierson (2004).
20 See, e.g., Oye and Maxwell (1994).
21 Baumann (2011).
22 Food and Drug Administration (2013).

through industry lobbying or vote-buying, there is little room for the public to compete. Industry will always be better organized than the people.[23] Moreover, those regulatory capture theories that have historically incorporated a role for information have tended to focus on areas of regulation that have low potential to attract serious public attention, such as the pricing of utilities,[24] again offering little space for considering the role of public pressures. On the flip side, theories of regulation that incorporate the public have looked almost entirely at issues that tend to be lightning rods for public outrage, such as genetically modified organisms or hormones in livestock,[25] often leading scholars to conclude that with enough public mobilization, industry opposition can be overcome.

Yet by evaluating the history of pesticide regulations in the United States, a case in which there was strong public pressure for regulatory improvement, Chapter 5 showed that it was only after the private sector formed a coalition with public interest groups that change occurred. In other words, public and private interests were each necessary but not sufficient requirements for institutional change. This raises questions about the conditions under which public versus private interests play a greater or lesser role in determining outcomes. In attempting to answer this question, the book's theory focused on the degree of information asymmetry between regulators and those they regulate, as well as the institutions under which these actors operated.

In particular, the book found that when it comes to regulating health and safety, it does not appear to be the case that private actors have free rein to demand and receive their preferred regulatory outcomes, against the interests of the public. As was shown in Chapter 4, when confronted with overt attempts by industry to ban out-of-patent pharmaceuticals and pesticides for which no substantial health issues had arisen, regulators were typically unwilling to bend to the most powerful actors' demands in cases in which doing so could lead to backlash from other prominent players or from the public, writ large. Yet the greater the degree of information asymmetry between regulators and those they oversee, and the more responsive regulatory institutions are to acts of information omission as opposed to just commission, the more that regulatory changes will reflect the profit incentives of the regulated over the broader public interest.

[23] Olson (1965).
[24] Joskow and Schmalensee (1986).
[25] Meins (2003); Vogel (2012).

These findings highlight the need for greater attention to the factors that lead regulations to be more or less reflective of private versus public interests. Information and institutions, both separately and in combination, offer a promising avenue for further theorizing, suggesting a number of potential research questions. For example, as the relative concentration of information changes, what strategies do different groups employ in order to get their preferred information in front of relevant policymakers? Are regulations, necessarily, more efficiently updated when there are multiple information sources, or are there mediating factors? In what ways can regulatory institutions incentivize broader participation in the information creation process? And do dynamics in the environmental space, for which the consequences of under-regulation may feel less tangible, look different than in the realm of health and safety?

7.3 NORMATIVE IMPLICATIONS

Beyond the theoretical implications for scholarly work, the book also introduces important ethical considerations. At the most general level, the revelations about the degree to which governments depend on self-interested, private actors to provide much of the scientific information necessary to set regulatory policies raises questions about how we can expect even the most democratic governments to govern objectively. In instances in which governments can supplement or replace proffered private information with their own research or the research of scientists and public interest groups, we may worry less about the ways in which bias will creep into the system. Yet so much of regulatory policymaking and policymaking more generally depends on information provision from a narrow set of actors. Those who stand to lose from the policies preferred by such actors may not be in a position to provide contradicting research, leaving them little room to ensure the political process takes their preferences into account. Such information imbalances have massive implications for who the national and international winners and losers will be.

Nationally, large firms with substantial research and development budgets will be ideally positioned to provide much of the scientific knowledge undergirding government decisions. Internationally, wealthier countries that house these firms will generally be able to contribute more directly to rule-making, resulting in outcomes that reflect their interests over those of their poorer trading partners. Of course, even in the absence of information imbalances, decades of research tells us that the largest, most powerful players usually come out on top. Therefore, in some ways information just provides yet another means by which these actors manage to out-maneuver the rest. Yet, when powerful interest groups win through lobbying or corruption, at least we can identify such influence for what it is and try to combat it through some combination of campaign finance laws,[26] transparency,[27] and democratic incentives.[28] Information dependencies present thornier problems. Not only do governments have little ability to entirely eliminate their dependencies, but the lack of alternative information sources makes it difficult to know if any given political outcome was actually "scientific" or strategic, allowing even the most biased policies to masquerade as impartial.

In addition to the general concerns around issues of fair governance, the findings also introduce specific considerations around intellectual property protections. Patents are considered by many to be a necessary means of encouraging innovation in sectors in which research and development costs are high and in which products can easily be copied or reverse-engineered. Yet patents also produce perverse incentives for those who hold them, encouraging aggressive strategies to thwart generic entry. Patents additionally have a tendency to make life-saving products unavailable to poorer nations and consumers for many years after those products have become available to others.[29]

These are the well-known issues when it comes to patents. Even those that decry these problems may still reason that eventually patents run out, and at least in the end, everyone has access to technologies that are better than they would have been if patents did not exist. The problem is that this logic becomes less convincing if firms are able to use their private information about out-of-patent products to undermine them shortly after developing newer, patented alternatives. Even if, under the most

[26] Mahoney (2007).
[27] Peisakhin and Pinto (2010).
[28] Rose-Ackerman (1999).
[29] One of the most prominent examples of this occurred during the South African AIDS epidemic. In 1998, numerous drug companies sued South Africa to prevent the country from offering generic versions of life-saving HIV drugs, prior to patent expiration. Although the drug companies eventually backed down, allowing the South African government to move forward with circumventing the patents, this did little to address the larger issue of developing countries being unable to afford patented products that could improve the lives of their citizens.

optimistic interpretation, the desire for greater profits encourages additional innovation, the lack of access to that innovation for developing countries and poorer consumers, combined with the regulatory removal of prior innovations for questionable reasons, ought to give us pause.

In particular, Chapters 5 and 6 demonstrated how incentives around patents have combined with information asymmetries and precautionary institutions to contribute to systematically stricter standards, both in developed countries and via international standards, on out-of-patent pesticides, for reasons partially orthogonal to public safety. Because pest control products play a critical role in the agricultural food trade, this has led to substantial barriers to trade for many developing countries, which have frequently decried the stringent standards at international forums. Indeed, the book opened with the description of one such complaint from Argentina, in which the agricultural exporter accused its wealthier trading partners of unfairly imposing barriers to international commerce that were particularly damaging to developing and least developed nations. Some scholars have argued that attempts to eliminate regulatory barriers such as these risk undermining nations' rights to self-determination, as well as the public interest more generally.[30] However, once we understand the underlying causes of these barriers and who they really benefit (and harm), it seems less credible to claim that nothing should be done about them, particularly given the distributive consequences for poorer countries.

But what should be done? Certainly, it would be inadvisable to require nations to conform to the regulatory lowest common denominator. For one thing, nations would never agree to this. As importantly, it would undermine many desirable regulations, not only in the realm of health and safety but also in the realm of the environment, human rights, and labor protections. Likewise, despite this book revealing the hidden downsides of retroactive precaution, eliminating precautionary reevaluations altogether risks sacrificing an important avenue for regulatory updating.

Therefore, rather than gutting regulatory safeguards, the most promising solutions are ones that directly seek to ameliorate the information asymmetry problem while also refining – though not rejecting – retroactive precaution.

30 Rodrik (2018).

7.4 IDENTIFYING POLICY IMPROVEMENTS

7.4.1 Reducing Information Barriers

Asymmetric information is at the heart of the problems identified in this book. Asymmetric information necessitates dependence on producers to provide the knowledge necessary to set the rules. Asymmetric information encourages institutions intended to eliminate dangers posed by producers' unwillingness to reveal the risks they know. And asymmetric information, under these institutions, leads to the systematic regulatory phase-out of more affordable, less profitable products. On the one hand, it would be impossible for governments to entirely eliminate these information asymmetries. On the other, they can take steps both to ameliorate them and to reduce the potential for these asymmetries to work against the public good.

As suggested in Chapter 2, one clear way for governments to ease asymmetries is for them to invest more heavily in the bureaucracy. For example, governments can expand regulators' ability to monitor the market by hiring more agents, and they can improve regulators' levels of expertise through training and higher salaries that attract better talent. Governments can also take steps to encourage and make it easier for third-parties such as independent scientists, individual citizens, and consumer groups to act as supplementary monitors. If Israel's consumer product regulators are to be believed, a robust reporting system about which regular citizens are aware can help regulators reduce their reliance on firms to be the first and last source of information about product risk. Improving alternative information sources may also have the benefit of encouraging producers to be more prompt and forthcoming with their own knowledge, out of recognition that failures to report are likely to be discovered.

Another partial solution to the problems caused by asymmetric information, perhaps counterintuitively given the pessimism expressed in the preceding pages about the ability of international organizations to alleviate regulatory biases, may be increased international cooperation. As suggested by the preceding paragraph, one reason that regulators find themselves at an informational disadvantage relative to those they regulate is insufficient resources. Even within the best-funded bureaucracies, no regulators have the necessary resources to actively monitor every product variation on the market. Yet, the more that national regulatory agencies are able to divide the work across countries, rather than engaging in redundant oversight and evaluations, the more resources each agency will have to dedicate to oversight of the products in its particular domain and the less leeway producers will have to engage in the information suppression or avoidance behaviors that make retroactive precaution so attractive.

Nations have indeed already recognized the benefits of this sort of division of labor, at times pursuing more cooperative regulatory efforts through what are known as mutual recognition agreements. Under these agreements, products recognized as safe by one government are considered safe by the other. Combined with requirements to share with other governments any new information about uncovered risks or benefits, these agreements can help reduce unnecessary redundancies. Yet, to date, these agreements only cover a small subset of regulated industries, and as typically bilateral agreements, they are severely limited in scope. By increasing the number and coverage of these agreements and moving toward more multilateral forums, governments would be in a better position to study existing products themselves, thereby (somewhat) reducing dependence on firms.

The above solutions could help mitigate some of the information asymmetries in sectors for which risks are more easily or cheaply identified and perhaps even, to some degree, in more technologically complex areas. However, these solutions are still unlikely to uncover certain types of dangers or obviate the need for reevaluations for the sorts of products for which risks are prohibitively expensive for third-parties to study and difficult to tie back to their source. For these products, reevaluations on a precautionary basis may still offer the best means of ensuring that risks do not go unidentified, raising the question of how policymakers might ensure that precaution does not beget protectionism.

7.4.2 Improving Precaution

When it comes to reducing the biases from retroactive precaution, mutual recognition agreements might again offer a partial solution, helping with the specific problem of innovative producers seeking to withhold information in order to push out-of-patent products off the market. One of the central impediments for generic producers in combatting the unwillingness of innovators to provide data on out-of-patent products during precautionary reevaluations is the cost of doing so. This cost is substantially increased by the fact that different national markets require different data packages in order to retain a product during reevaluations. By harmonizing data requirements across borders, governments could make it easier for generic producers to fill the informational void, and so long as the data requirements were sufficiently rigorous, governments could do this without sacrificing the quality of the reevaluations and without increasing the possibility that dangerous products could slip through.

In addition to expanding mutual recognition agreements, more could also be done at the international standard-setting level to prevent retroactive precaution from creating biases that disproportionately harm developing countries. For example, in order to prevent precautionary reevaluations from undermining products that play an important role in the exports of developing countries, international organizations could create a funding pool specifically dedicated to fielding the necessary studies on these products, even in the absence of a commitment from the primary developer. While such a system could potentially result in moral hazard, encouraging producers to refuse to invest in studying products they otherwise would, so long as there was a high bar to pulling on the dedicated funds, such that only a small number of products met the relevant criteria and perhaps even then only with the acquiescence of a majority of the relevant international organization's voting members, moral hazard could be mitigated.

Another partial solution at the international level is one already under discussion in the Codex forum. In particular, Codex members have been debating instituting more accommodating reevaluation rules for out-of-patent argrochemicals for which no health concerns have arisen and that are still in heavy use by developing nations. This could help reduce the number of unnecessary standard removals, without substantially increasing risks. At the same time, any solution involving retaining international standards for out-of-patent but safe products will only be as effective as those standards are influential, and while previous work has shown that developed nations are influenced by Codex recommendations,[31] many attractive markets with precautionary institutions, including the USA and Europe, still have their own procedures in place mandating stricter standards in the absence of firm-provided data. It is, therefore, unclear whether governments in these markets would be willing to follow the international standard-setters' lead in maintaining lenient standards for which adequate data supporting those standards was lacking. This suggests that solutions implemented at the international level would need to be combined with efforts to encourage greater harmonization with international standards.

[31] Perlman (2020*a*).

Of course, none of the proffered policy suggestions are silver bullets. Even to the extent that some might help reduce the specific impediments resulting from precautionary institutions and producers' incentives to skew the market toward their most lucrative products, it is unrealistic to expect that governments or international standard-setting bodies can ever fully eliminate the biases stemming from industry's superior ability to acquire safety information about their products. Nonetheless, policy solutions require that we first understand the problem. This book has taken a step in that direction, revealing a previously underexplored and poorly understood source of regulatory barriers to domestic competition and international trade.

7.5 CONCLUSION

Governance can only be as good as the information upon which it is based. Across every policy domain, from public health to the environment to immigration and trade, information is the sine qua non. We often want to know the conditions under which scientific information, in particular, is successfully incorporated into policy. What, for example, allows groups of experts to gain influence?[32] Why, when faced with evidence of environmental harm, do some governments quickly join international agreements, while others are laggards?[33] When will politicians or the population at large internalize and act on the clear threat of climate change?[34] Those asking these questions tend to treat the availability of scientific information as objective and exogenously determined. The problem is not acquiring the information – it is convincing relevant actors to use it.

This book has pushed us to take more seriously the endogenous and at times biased nature of the science available to policymakers. In doing so, it has revealed how challenging it is for even well-meaning policymakers to arrive at any sort of objective outcome. Although political scientists and pundits frequently highlight the role that lobbying or corruption can play in contributing to suboptimal policies, in the absence of such crass strategies, industry can still exert enormous influence through the avenue of information. What makes this method of influence particularly troubling is that it may be nearly impossible to identify it for what it is. Even those directly disadvantaged by private actors' strategic leverag-

32 Haas (1992).

33 Sprinz and Vaahtoranta (1994).

34 See, e.g., Hazlett and Mildenberger (2020); Hart and Nisbet (2012); Deryugina (2013); Bergquist and Warshaw (2019); Hai and Perlman (2022).

ing of scientific information may mistakenly attribute the resulting bias to lobbying or deliberate protectionism. Thus, when Argentina raised a trade concern in 2007 about the overly stringent pesticide standards of its trading partners – the example with which this book opened – some of the developing countries that supported Argentina's complaint suggested that the harmful standards might "present disguised barriers to trade,"[35] with the implication that governments had instituted these policies as a deliberate way to disadvantage foreign agricultural exporters, in favor of domestic growers. Not expressly considered was that these policies might instead reflect agrochemical producers' wielding of scientific information.

The centrality of information to policymaking and the pervasiveness of information asymmetries highlight the value of dedicating greater attention to information dynamics, particularly for scholars of international political economy, for whom information has often taken a back seat to lobbying.[36] Recent work in international environmental politics has made progress in this domain, showing the importance of considering how the strategic use of scientific information by scientists, governments, and non-governmental organizations can shape the policy debate in important and unexpected ways.[37] Continued theorizing on the provision of scientific and technical information might similarly offer new insights not only to the study of regulatory barriers to trade – which has been a focus of this book – but also to the study of other types of trade barriers, including anti-dumping policies and tariffs.

Beyond international political economy, there remains a need for scholars to investigate more deeply the political and institutional determinants of what science is available to be incorporated into policy. Long a focus of qualitative research in the field of science and technology studies,[38] questions about how scientific evidence emerges and how it is deployed have largely escaped quantitative empirical analysis. This offers an opportunity to approach these questions in new ways, building off existing qualitative studies to identify how the source of scientific information might lead to systematic patterns of bias in policy outcomes. Such work could not only enrich our understanding of what it means for policies to be based on science, but it might also reveal the many unexplored ways in which science is shaped by politics.

35 World Trade Organization (2020*b*), G/SPS/R/45, para. 13.

36 One exception to this can be found in the literature on how international organizations communicate to national governments. See, e.g., Johns (2007); Carnegie and Carson (2019, 2020); Fang and Stone (2012).

37 See, e.g., Oreskes and Conway (2011); Hai (2022); Miyano (2022).

38 See, e.g., Jasanoff (1987*b*, 1998).

Statistical Appendix

A.1 ROBUSTNESS CHECKS FOR CHAPTER 5

A.1.1 Regulatory Change Using EU Carcinogenicity Measure

Below I use the EU classification for carcinogenicity instead of the US classification when testing the impact of pesticide age on regulatory change in the United States. The EU classification is available at https://echa.europa.eu/regulations/clp/cl-inventory. It has only a two point scale indicating whether a product is considered carcinogenic (1) or not (0). We can see that using the EU measure does not have a significant impact on the coefficient of interest.

TABLE A.1. *US tolerance changes using EU's carcinogenicity measure*

	Tolerance Change 1996–2015: 1 = Less Strict, 2 = Same, 3 = More Strict, 4 = Revoked		
	(1)	(2)	(3)
Pesticide Age	0.049***	0.050***	0.044***
	(0.012)	(0.014)	(0.015)
Toxicity		0.658***	0.671***
		(0.191)	(0.189)
Toxicity Increased		0.281	0.289
		(0.384)	(0.389)
EU Carcinogenicity		0.396	0.381
		(0.403)	(0.400)
Aquatic Chronic		0.113	0.115
		(0.134)	(0.131)
Aquatic Acute		0.448	0.457
		(0.478)	(0.474)
Fruit/Veggie			0.358*
			(0.192)
Primary Acreage			−1.264
			(0.770)
Pesticide Age*Primary Acreage			0.024
			(0.016)
Observations	3,683	3,459	3,459

Note: *p < 0.1; **p < 0.05; ***p < 0.01
Standard errors clustered at pesticide level

A.1.2 Robustness Check with Higher Order Clustering

Prior to the passage of the Food Quality Protection Act in 1996, the EPA did not consider the cumulative effects of different pesticides. However, this has increasingly become a concern for regulators. The EPA has now done several cumulative risk assessments in which it evaluates the cumulative toxicity of pesticides with similar mechanisms of toxicity.[1] Because this could lead to nonindependence, I have re-run the baseline regulatory change model clustering the standard errors according to the five toxicity groups that the EPA has identified as posing cumulative concern. Where a pesticide does not fall into one of these groups, I kept the clustering at the pesticide level, giving a total of between 68 and 54 clusters across the three models. Results are robust to this specification.

[1] Environmental Protection Agency (2018)

TABLE A.2. *US tolerance changes with higher order clustering*

	Tolerance Change 1996–2015: 1 = Less Strict, 2 = Same, 3 = More Strict, 4 = Revoked		
	(1)	(2)	(3)
Pesticide Age	0.049***	0.048***	0.043***
	(0.012)	(0.013)	(0.014)
Toxicity		0.647***	0.666***
		(0.250)	(0.243)
Toxicity Increased		0.243	0.254
		(0.346)	(0.348)
Carcinogenicity		0.082	0.091
		(0.157)	(0.157)
Aquatic Chronic		0.082	0.090
		(0.127)	(0.123)
Aquatic Acute		0.495	0.490
		(0.591)	(0.580)
Fruit/Veggie			0.367
			(0.253)
Primary Acreage			−1.373*
			(0.760)
Pesticide Age*Primary Acreage			0.026*
			(0.014)
Observations	3,683	3,459	3,459

Note: *p < 0.1; **p < 0.05; ***p < 0.01
Standard errors clustered at toxicity level

A.1.3 Pesticide Age Buckets (Test 1)

Given the sharp change in companies' profits following patent expiration, and given that companies may try to develop alternatives to correspond with patent expiration, the effect of pesticide age may look more like a step function than a continuous linear function, with the most recent products far less likely to see their tolerances decreased or revoked than older alternatives. In order to account for this, I placed pesticides into two age groups. The reference age group includes pesticides that were registered within ten years of the start of the dataset, as these are the ones most likely to enjoy market protections over the period studied. The other group includes pesticides registered earlier. As expected, we see that the older pesticides are much more likely to have their tolerances become stricter or be revoked, with the coefficient significant at the 1% level across all specifications.

TABLE A.3. *US tolerance changes with age dummy*

	Tolerance Change 1996–2015: 1 = Less Strict, 2 = Same, 3 = More Strict, 4 = Revoked		
	(1)	(2)	(3)
Older Pesticides	1.460***	1.468***	1.351***
	(0.316)	(0.395)	(0.407)
Toxicity		0.600***	0.624***
		(0.203)	(0.200)
Toxicity Increased		−0.008	0.038
		(0.353)	(0.351)
Carcinogenicity		0.020	0.032
		(0.151)	(0.153)
Aquatic Chronic		−0.021	−0.001
		(0.138)	(0.132)
Aquatic Acute		0.895*	0.846*
		(0.457)	(0.453)
Fruit/Veggie			0.470**
			(0.184)
Primary Acreage			−0.184
			(0.231)
Observations	3,683	3,459	3,459

Note: *p < 0.1; **p < 0.05; ***p < 0.01
Standard errors clustered at pesticide level

A.1.4 Pesticide Age Buckets (Test 2)

We may be worried that the previous result, which placed pesticides in only two categories, was driven by the oldest pesticides in the sample, thereby ensuring that the newer and older pesticides would look different. This next test, therefore, groups pesticides into three buckets by age, such that the youngest, reference group is the same, the middle group only extends to pesticides registered during or after 1970, and the oldest pesticides (those registered before 1970) get their own group. Notably, there remains a statistically significant difference at the 1% level across all models between both older groups and the youngest group, again suggesting that those pesticides without market protection are far more likely to receive stricter tolerances, regardless of whether those pesticides are extremely old or just slightly older than those most likely to have market protections.

TABLE A.4. *US tolerance changes with three age buckets*

	Tolerance Change 1996–2015: 1 = Less Strict, 2 = Same, 3 = More Strict, 4 = Revoked		
	(1)	(2)	(3)
Older Pesticides	0.975***	1.206***	1.142***
	(0.355)	(0.396)	(0.400)
Oldest Pesticides	1.823***	1.716***	1.575***
	(0.385)	(0.494)	(0.521)
Toxicity		0.612***	0.633***
		(0.204)	(0.202)
Toxicity Increased		0.184	0.194
		(0.404)	(0.406)
Carcinogenicity		0.034	0.043
		(0.148)	(0.151)
Aquatic Chronic		0.014	0.026
		(0.149)	(0.142)
Aquatic Acute		0.706	0.690
		(0.524)	(0.512)
Fruit/Veggie			0.418**
			(0.199)
Primary Acreage			−0.216
			(0.229)
Observations	3,683	3,459	3,459

Note: *p < 0.1; **p < 0.05; ***p < 0.01
Standard errors clustered at pesticide level

A.2 ROBUSTNESS CHECKS FOR CHAPTER 6

A.2.1 Eliminating the Most Dangerous Pesticides

We might worry that the results are driven by something to do with the dangers of the older pesticides that has not been adequately captured by the controls. I therefore dropped all pesticides that had had tolerances revoked in the USA for reasons related to safety or the environment. I use those revoked in the USA for these reasons because Codex does not provide as extensive notes explaining revocations, meaning that using Codex explanations could result in too conservative of a culling. Even using this more aggressive culling strategy, we see that the results hold.

TABLE A.5. *Codex tolerance changes dropping most dangerous pesticides*

	Tolerance Change 1996–2015: 1 = Less Strict, 2 = Same, 3 = More Strict, 4 = Withdrawn		
	(1)	(2)	(3)
Pesticide Age	0.037***	0.037**	0.037**
	(0.014)	(0.015)	(0.015)
Toxicity		0.162	0.178
		(0.242)	(0.241)
Toxicity Increased		0.169	0.190
		(0.528)	(0.531)
Carcinogenicity		0.068	0.056
		(0.131)	(0.132)
Aquatic Chronic		−0.040	−0.047
		(0.126)	(0.126)
Aquatic Acute		0.332	0.348
		(0.710)	(0.705)
Fruit/Veggie			0.303**
			(0.151)
Observations	1,155	1,130	1,130

Note: $^{*}p < 0.1$; $^{**}p < 0.05$; $^{***}p < 0.01$
Standard errors clustered at pesticide level

A.2.2 Is This about Efficacy?

In order to evaluate whether the Codex results are driven by reduced efficacy of pesticides over time, I drop the revoked category and just look at tolerances that were made stricter, less strict, or remained the same. If pesticides become less effective over time, farmers would presumably either stop using them altogether or need to use more of them (leading to an increased tolerance). This suggests that if we drop the revoked category, and changes are the result of efficacy, the sign of the coefficient for *Pesticide Age* should reverse. Instead, we find that the coefficient for *Pesticide Age* retains its sign and significance, while losing some of its magnitude.

TABLE A.6. *Codex tolerance changes dropping withdrawn*

	Tolerance Change 1996–2015:		
	1 = Less Strict, 2 = Same, 3 = More Strict		
	(1)	(2)	(3)
Pesticide Age	0.031***	0.028***	0.028***
	(0.009)	(0.010)	(0.010)
Toxicity		0.154	0.161
		(0.110)	(0.113)
Toxicity Increased		0.133	0.140
		(0.238)	(0.240)
Carcinogenicity		0.068	0.065
		(0.081)	(0.084)
Aquatic Chronic		−0.197**	−0.199**
		(0.100)	(0.100)
Aquatic Acute		0.520*	0.530*
		(0.299)	(0.302)
Fruit/Veggie			0.079
			(0.219)
Observations	822	806	806

Note: *p < 0.1; **p < 0.05; ***p < 0.01
Standard errors clustered at pesticide level

Bibliography

111th Congress. 2010, February 4. "Current Science on Public Exposures to Toxic Chemicals." www.hsdl.org/?view&did=29623.

Ahmad, Syed Rizwanuddin. 2003. "Adverse drug event monitoring at the Food and Drug Administration." *Journal of General Internal Medicine* 18(1): 57–60.

American Chemistry Council. 2015. "ACC Welcomes Frank R. Lautenberg Chemical Safety for the 21st Century Act." www.americanchemistry.com/Media/PressReleasesTranscripts/ACC-news-releases/ACC-Welcomes-Frank-R-Lautenberg-Chemical-Safety-for-the-21st-Century-Act.html.

Ansell, Christopher and David Vogel. 2006. The contested governance of European food safety regulation. In *What's the Beef? The Contested Governance of European Food Safety*, ed. Christopher Ansell and David Vogel. MIT Press, pp. 3–32.

Applegate, John S. 1991. "The perils of unreasonable risk: Information, regulatory policy, and toxic substances control." *Columbia Law Review* 91(2): 261–333.

2008. "Bridging the data gap: Balancing the supply and demand for chemical information." *Texas Law Review* 86(7):1365–1407.

Australian Government Productivity Commission. 2006. "Review of the Australian Consumer Product Safety System." *Productivity Commission Report*. www.pc.gov.au/inquiries/completed/consumer-product-safety/report/productsafety.pdf.

Avery, Natalie, Martine Drake and Tim Lang. 1993. *Cracking the Codex: An Analysis of Who Sets World Food Standards*. National Food Alliance London.

Bagley, Nicholas. 2010. "Agency hygiene." *Texas Law Review* 89(1):1–14.

Bagwell, Kyle and Robert W Staiger. 2011. "What do trade negotiators negotiate about? Empirical evidence from the World Trade Organization." *American Economic Review* 101(4):1238–1273.

Baker, Andrew. 2010. "Restraining regulatory capture? Anglo-America, crisis politics and trajectories of change in global financial governance." *International Affairs* 86(3):647–663.

Barboza, David. 2001. "The Power of Roundup; A Weed Killer Is a Block for Monsanto to Build On." *The New York Times*.

Baron, David P. 1985. "Regulation of prices and pollution under incomplete information." *Journal of Public Economics* 28(2):211–231.

Baron, David P and David Besanko. 1984. "Regulation, asymmetric information, and auditing." *The RAND Journal of Economics* 15(4):447–470.

Baron, David P and Roger B Myerson. 1982. "Regulating a monopolist with unknown costs." *Econometrica: Journal of the Econometric Society* 50(4):911–930.

Baumann, Nick. 2011. "Why You're Paying More to Breathe." *Mother Jones* July/August.

Bedford Laboratories. 2008. "Citizen Petition, Referencing Discontinued Brevibloc Injection." www.regulations.gov/document?D=FDA-2008-P-0284-0001.

Bergquist, Parrish and Christopher Warshaw. 2019. "Does global warming increase public concern about climate change?" *The Journal of Politics* 81(2):686–691.

Bernard, Andrew B, Jonathan Eaton, J Bradford Jensen and Samuel Kortum. 2003. "Plants and productivity in international trade." *American Economic Review* 93(4):1268–1290.

Bernauer, Thomas and Erika Meins. 2003. "Technological revolution meets policy and the market: Explaining cross-national differences in agricultural biotechnology regulation." *European Journal of Political Research* 42(5):643–683.

Bernauer, Thomas and Ladina Caduff. 2004. "In whose interest? Pressure group politics, economic competition and environmental regulation." *Journal of Public Policy* 24(1):99–126.

Bernstein, Marver H. 1955. *Regulating Business by Independent Commission*. Princeton University Press.

Besanko, David. 1987. "Performance versus design standards in the regulation of pollution." *Journal of Public Economics* 34(1):19–44.

Bhagwati, Jagdish N. 1988. *Protectionism*. MIT press.

Bosso, Christopher. 1987. *Pesticides and Politics: The Life Cycle of a Public Issue*. University of Pittsburgh Press.

Braden, John B and Kathleen Segerson. 1993. Information problems in the design of nonpoint-source pollution policy. In *Theory, Modeling and Experience in the Management of Nonpoint-Source Pollution*, ed. Clifford S Russell and Jason F Shogren. Springer, pp. 1–36.

Busch, Marc and Eric Reinhardt. 2003. "Developing countries and GATT/WTO dispute settlement." *Journal of World Trade* 37(4):719–735.

Büthe, Tim. 2009. The politics of food safety in the age of global trade: The Codex Alimentarius Commission in the SPS-agreement of the WTO. In *Import Safety: Regulatory Governance in the Global Economy*, ed. Cary Coglianese, Adam Finkel and David Zaring. University of Pennsylvania Press, pp. 88–109.

Büthe, Tim and Walter Mattli. 2011. *The New Global Rulers*. Princeton University Press.

Buzby, Jean C and Donna Roberts. 2011. "Food trade and food safety violations: What can we learn from import refusal data?" *American Journal of Agricultural Economics* 93(2):560–565.

Carnegie, Allison and Austin Carson. 2019. "The disclosure dilemma: Nuclear intelligence and international organizations." *American Journal of Political Science* 63(2):269–285.

2020. *Secrets in Global Governance: Disclosure Dilemmas and the Challenge of International Cooperation*. Cambridge University Press.

Carpenter, Daniel. 2014. *Reputation and Power*. Princeton University Press.

Carpenter, Daniel and David A Moss. 2014. ""Introduction." In *Preventing Regulatory Capture: Special Interest Influence and How to Limit it*, ed. Daniel Carpenter and David A Moss." Cambridge University Press, pp. 1–22.

Carpenter, Daniel and Gisela Sin. 2007. "Policy tragedy and the emergence of regulation: The Food, Drug, and Cosmetic act of 1938." *Studies in American Political Development* 21(2):149–180.

Carpenter, Daniel P. 2002. "Groups, the media, agency waiting costs, and FDA drug approval." *American Journal of Political Science* 46(3):490–505.

2004. "Protection without capture: Product approval by a politically responsive, learning regulator." *American Political Science Review* 98(4):613–631.

Chen, Chunlai, Jun Yang and Christopher Findlay. 2008. "Measuring the effect of food safety standards on China's agricultural exports." *Review of World Economics* 144(1):83–106.

Clarke, Andrea, Jonathan J Deeks and Saad AW Shakir. 2006. "An assessment of the publicly disseminated evidence of safety used in decisions to withdraw medicinal products from the UK and US markets." *Drug Safety* 29(2): 175–181.

Codex Alimentarius Commission. 2000. "Codex Alimentarius: Pesticide Residues in Food, Methods of Analysis and Sampling." Volume 2A, Series 1.

2016. "About Codex." www.fao.org/fao-who-\codexalimentarius/codex-home/en/.

2019. "Codex Budgetary and Financial Matters: Progress Report 2018–19." www.fao.org/fao-who-codexalimentarius/meetings/detail/en/?meeting=CAC&session=42.

The Codex Committee on Pesticide Residues. 1983. "Report of the Fifteenth Meeting of the Codex Committee on Pesticide Residues."

1986. "Report of the Eighteenth Meeting of the Codex Committee on Pesticide Residues."

1992. "Report of the Forty-Third Session of the Codex Committee on Pesticide Residues."

2009*a*. "Related Documents." www.fao.org/fao-who-codexalimentarius/meetings/detail?meeting=CCPR&session=41.

2009*b*. "Related Documents." www.fao.org/fao-who-codexalimentarius/meetings/detail?meeting=CCPR&session=42.

2011. "Report of the Twenty-Fourth Session of the Codex Committee on Pesticide Residues."

2013. "Related Documents." www.fao.org/fao-who-codexalimentarius/meetings/detail?meeting=CCPR&session=45.

2016. "Related Documents." www.fao.org/fao-who-codexalimentarius/meetings/detail?meeting=CCPR&session=48.

2018. "Related Documents." www.fao.org/fao-who-codexalimentarius/meetings/detail/en/?meeting=CCPR&session=50.

2019. "Related Documents." www.fao.org/fao-who-codexalimentarius/meetings/detail/en/?meeting=CCPR&session=51.

Codex Committee on Residues of Veterinary Drugs in Foods. 2010. "Report of the Nineteenth Session of the Codex Committee on Residues of Veterinary Drugs in Food."

2016. "Report of the Twenty-Third Session of the Codex Committee on Residues of Veterinary Drugs in Food."

Coglianese, Cary and Gary E Marchant. 2003. "Shifting sands: The limits of science in setting risk standards." *University of Pennsylvania Law Review* 152(4):1255–1360.

Coglianese, Cary, Richard Zeckhauser and Edward Parson. 2004. "Seeking truth for power: Informational strategy and regulatory policymaking." *University of Minnesota Law Review* 89(2):277–341.

Collins, Craig. 2010. *Toxic Loopholes: Failures and Future Prospects for Environmental Law*. Cambridge University Press.

Cook, Anna. 1998. *How Increased Competition from Generic Drugs Has Affected Prices and Returns in the Pharmaceutical Industry*. US Government Printing Office.

CropLife International. 2017. "Working with the JMPR and CCPR: A manual for the agrochemical industry." croplife.org/wp-content/uploads/2018/03/Working-with-the-JMPR-and-CCPR-A-Manual-for-the-Agrochemical-Industry.pdf.

Cropper, Maureen L, William N Evans, Stephen J Berardi, Maria M Ducla-Soares and Paul R Portney. 1992. "The determinants of pesticide regulation: A statistical analysis of EPA decision making." *Journal of Political Economy* 100(1):175–197.

Dal Bó, Ernesto. 2006. "Regulatory capture: A review." *Oxford Review of Economic Policy* 22(2):203–225.

Davis, Christina L and Sarah Blodgett Bermeo. 2009. "Who files? Developing country participation in GATT/WTO adjudication." *The Journal of Politics* 71(3):1033–1049.

Dedieu, François. 2021. "Organized denial at work: The difficult search for consistencies in French pesticide regulation." *Regulation & Governance*. 16(3): 951–973.

Deryugina, Tatyana. 2013. "How do people update? The effects of local weather fluctuations on beliefs about global warming." *Climatic Change* 118(2): 397–416.

DiMasi, Joseph A, Henry G Grabowski and Ronald W Hansen. 2016. "Innovation in the pharmaceutical industry: new estimates of R&D costs." *Journal of Health Economics* 47:20–33.

Downer, John. 2010. "Trust and technology: The social foundations of aviation regulation." *The British Journal of Sociology* 61(1):83–106.

Drezner, Daniel W. 2004. "The global governance of the internet: Bringing the state back in." *Political Science Quarterly* 119(3):477–498.

2007. *All Politics Is Global*: Explaining International Regulatory Regimes. Princeton University Press.

DuPont. 1981. "Comments on the Advance Notice of Proposed Rulemaking: Ozone - Depleting Chlorofluorocarbons: Proposed Production Restriction by the Environmental Protection Agency – Volume I." https://nepis.epa.gov/.

Economist, The. 2019. "Regulatory capture may be responsible for Boeing's recent problems." 2019, March 23. https://www.economist.com/business/2019/03/23/regulatory-capture-may-be-responsible-for-boeings-recent-problems. Last checked October 26, 2022.

Eid, Noran and Cyrus Lotfipour. 2009. "REACH Update: Strategic Risks and Opportunities." www.msci.com/documents/10199/16e1af6a-98b5-4ad0-b645-ea84e5260332.

Environmental Protection Agency. 2017. "Food and Pesticides." www.epa.gov/safepestcontrol/food-and-pesticides.

2018. "Chemicals Evaluated for Carcinogenic Potential Annual Cancer Report 2018." http://npic.orst.edu/chemicalsevaluated.pdf.

2018. "Cumulative Assessment of Risk From Pesticides." www.epa.gov/pesticide-science-and-assessing-pesticide-risks/cumulative-assessment-risk-pesticides."

European Chemicals Agency. 2018. "C&L Inventory." https://echa.europa.eu/information-on-chemicals/cl-inventory-database.

European Union Commission. 2001. "Directive 2001/83/EC."

2001. "White Paper: Strategy for a Future Chemical Policy."

Fagerstone, Kathleen A, Roger W Bullard and Craig A Ramey. 1990. "Politics and economics of maintaining pesticide registrations." *Proceedings of the Vertebrate Pest Conference* 14:8–11.

Fang, Songying and Randall W Stone. 2012. "International organizations as policy advisors." *International Organization* 66(4):537–569.

Federal Register. 1997, July 25. "Notice of Filing of Pesticide Petitions."

2003, June 6. "Determination That Brimonidine Tartrate Ophthalmic Solution 0.2% Was Not Withdrawn From Sale for Reasons of Safety or Effectiveness."

2005, October 13. "Establishment of Organization Designation Authorization Program."

2008, September 9. "Determination That Tequin Was Withdrawn for Reasons of Safety or Effectiveness."

2013, June 11. "Determination That SUBOXONE (Buprenorphine Hydrochloride and Naloxone Hydrochloride) Sublingual Tablets, 2 Milligrams/0.5 Milligrams and 8 Milligrams/2 Milligrams, Were Not Withdrawn From Sale for Reasons of Safety or Effectiveness."

Food and Agricultural Organization. 2007. "Helping Farmers Export 'Forgotten' Crops." www.fao.org/Newsroom/en/news/2007/1000718/index.html.

Food and Agricultural Organization and World Health Organization. 1962. "Report of the Joint FAO/WHO Conference on Food Standards."

2002. "Review of the Working Procedures of the Joint FAO/WHO Meeting of Pesticide Residues (JMPR)." www.fao.org/3/cb5126en/cb5126en.pdf.

2022. "Joint FAO/WHO Expert Meetings on Microbiological Risk Assessment (JEMRA) Roster of Experts." www.fao.org/fileadmin/userupload/agns/pdf/jemra/ExpertsRosterJEMRAMay2018.pdf.

Food and Drug Administration. 2009. "Report to Congress: Encouraging Early Submission of Citizen Petitions and Petitions for Stay of Action."

2013. "FDA Actions on OxyContin Products, 4/16/2013 FDA Actions on OxyContin Products, 4/16/2013 FDA Actions on OxyContin Products." www.fda.gov/Drugs/DrugSafety/InformationbyDrugClass/ucm347857.htm.

Frankel, Todd C. 2019. "Fisher-Price invented a popular baby sleeper without medical safety tests and kept selling it, even as babies died." *Washington Post*.

Gates, Dominic. 2019. "Flawed analysis, failed oversight: How Boeing, FAA certified the suspect 737 MAX flight control system." *The Seattle Times*.

Germain, D Saint. 2019. "The Boeing debacle is the latest example of regulatory capture." *Medium*.

Gillam, Carey. 2016. "Conflict of interest concerns cloud glyphosate review." *U.S. Right to Know*.

Glaberson, William. 1988. "Behind Du Pont's shift on loss of ozone layer." *New York Times*.

Gormley Jr, William T. 1979. "A test of the revolving door hypothesis at the FCC." *American Journal of Political Science* 23(4):665–683.

Government Accountability Office. 1993. "Aircraft Certification: New FAA Approach Needed to Meet Challenges of Advanced Technology." www.gao.gov/assets/160/153711.pdf.

2004. "Aviation Safety: FAA Needs to Strengthen the Management of Its Designee Program." www.gao.gov/assets/250/244458.pdf.

2010. "Biomonitoring: EPA Could Make Better Use of Biomonitoring Data. Testimony before the Subcommittee on Superfund, Toxics, and Environmental Health." www.gao.gov/assets/gao-10-419t.pdf.

2014. "Consumer Product Safety Commission: Challenges and Options for Responding to New and Emerging Risks." www.gao.gov/assets/670/666488.pdf.

Grabowski, Henry, Genia Long and Richard Mortimer. 2014. "Recent trends in brand-name and generic drug competition." *Journal of Medical Economics* 17(3):207–214.

Gray, Wayne B and John T Scholz. 1989. "A behavioral approach to compliance: OSHA enforcement's impact on workplace accidents." National Bureau of Economic Research, Inc, NBER Working Papers.

Grey, Felix. 2018. "Corporate lobbying for environmental protection." *Journal of Environmental Economics and Management* 90:23–40.

Griffith-Jones, Stephany and Avinash Persaud. 2008. "The pro-cyclical impact of Basle II on emerging markets and its political economy." in *Capital Market Liberalization and Development*, ed. José Antonio Ocampo and Joseph E. Stiglitz. Oford University Press. pp. 262–287.

Grossman, Gene M and Elhanan Helpman. 1994. "Protection for sale." The American Economic Review 84(4):833–850.

Gulotty, Robert. 2020. *Narrowing the Channel: The Politics of Regulatory Protection in International Trade*. University of Chicago Press.

Gupta, Himanshu, Suresh Kumar, Saroj Kumar Roy and RS Gaud. 2010. "Patent protection strategies." *Journal of Pharmacy and Bioallied Sciences* 2(1):2–7.

Haas, Peter M. 1992. "Introduction: Epistemic communities and international policy coordination." *International Organization* 46(1):1–35.

Hai, Zuhad. 2022. "Scientific Consensus and International Climate Cooperation." www.internationalpoliticaleconomysociety.org/sites/default/files/paper-uploads/2021-10-21-00_24_43-zuhadhai@stanford.edu.pdf.

Hai, Zuhad and Rebecca Perlman. 2022. "Extreme weather events and the politics of climate change attribution." *Science Advances* 8(36): eabo2190.

Hart, P Sol and Erik C Nisbet. 2012. "Boomerang effects in science communication: How motivated reasoning and identity cues amplify opinion polarization about climate mitigation policies." *Communication Research* 39(6):701–723.

Hazell, Lorna and Saad AW Shakir. 2006. "Under-reporting of adverse drug reactions." *Drug Safety* 29(5):385–396.

Hazlett, Chad and Matto Mildenberger. 2020. "Wildfire exposure increases pro-environment voting within democratic but not republican areas." *American Political Science Review* 114(4):1359–1365.

Hird, John A. 1993. "Environmental policy and equity: The case of Superfund." *Journal of Policy Analysis and Management* 12(2):323–343.

Huntington, Samuel P. 1952. "The marasmus of the ICC: The commission, the railroads, and the public interest." *Yale Law Journal* 61(4):467–509.

Inglehart, Ronald. 2000. "Globalization and postmodern values." *Washington Quarterly* 23(1):215–228.

International Organization for Standardization. 2018. "All about ISO." www.iso.org/about-us.html.

Jamasmie, Cecilia. 2015. "Total, Shell exit coal mining." *Mining.com*. www.mining.com/total-shell-exit-coal-mining/.

James, Barry. 1999. "Belgium Is Castigated as Dioxin Scare Spreads." *The New York Times*.

Jasanoff, Sheila. 1987*a*. "Cultural aspects of risk assessment in Britain and the United States." In *The Social and Cultural Construction of Risk*: Essays on Risk Selection and Perception, ed. Branden B. Johnson and Vincent T. Covello D. Reidel Publishing Company, pp. 359–397.

1987*b*. "Contested boundaries in policy-relevant science." *Social Studies of Science* 17(2):195–230.

1998. *The Fifth Branch: Science Advisers as Policymakers*. Harvard University Press.

2006. "Transparency in public science purposes, reasons, limits." *Law & Contemporary Problems* 69(3):21–45.

Johns, Leslie. 2007. "A servant of two masters: Communication and the selection of international bureaucrats." *International Organization* 61(2):245–275.

Johnson, Renée and Charles Hanrahan. 2010. *The US-EU beef hormone dispute*. Congressional Research Service.

Joint FAO/WHO Expert Committee on Food Additives. 2019. "Evaluation of certain veterinary drug residues in food." www.who.int/foodsafety/publications/jecfa-reports/en/.

Joskow, Paul L and Richard Schmalensee. 1986. "Incentive regulation for electric utilities." *Yale Journal on Regulation* 4(1):1–49.

Kahn, Joseph. 2007. "China Quick to Execute Drug Official." *The New York Times*.

Kapstein, Ethan B. 1989. "Resolving the regulator's dilemma: International coordination of banking regulations." *International Organization* 43(2):323–347.

Karagueuzian, Hrayr S, Celia White, James Sayre and Amos Norman. 2011. "Cigarette smoke radioactivity and lung cancer risk." *Nicotine and Tobacco Research* 14(1):79–90.

Karlas, Jan and Michal Parízek. 2020. "Supply of policy information in the World Trade Organization: Cross-national compliance with one-time and regular notification obligations, 1995–2014." *World Trade Review* 19(1):30–50.

Katz, Benjamin D. 2019. "EU Signals Caution on Max Return with No Rubber Stamp of FAA." *Bloomberg*.

Kennard, Amanda. 2020. "The enemy of my enemy: When firms support climate change regulation." *International Organization* 74(2):187–221.

Kent, Sarah and Inti Landauro. 2015. "Oil Industry Takes Aim at Coal, Pushes Gas Ahead of Climate-Change Talks." *The Wall Street Journal*.

Keohane, Robert O, Stephen Macedo and Andrew Moravcsik. 2009. "Democracy-enhancing multilateralism." *International Organization* 63(1):1–31.

Kim, In Song. 2017. "Political cleavages within industry: Firm-level lobbying for trade liberalization." *American Political Science Review* 111(1):1–20.

Kim, Moonhawk. 2008. "Costly procedures: Divergent effects of legalization in the GATT/WTO dispute settlement procedures." *International Studies Quarterly* 52(3):657–686.

Kip, Viscusi W and Richard Zeckhauser. 1979. "Optimal standards with incomplete enforcement." *Public Policy* 27(4):437–456.

Kitroeff, Natalie and David Gelles. 2019. "Before Deadly Crash Boeing Pushed for Law that Undercut Oversight." *The New York Times*.

Kono, Daniel Y. 2006. "Optimal obfuscation: Democracy and trade policy transparency." *American Political Science Review* 100(3):369–384.

Koster, Maria C, Bart Teeuw and Iain Cockburn. 2000. "Compliance in European pharmacovigilance: How compliant is compliant?" *Pharmacoepidemiology and Drug Safety* 9(6):473–478.

Krasner, Stephen D. 1991. "Global communications and national power: Life on the Pareto frontier." *World Politics* 43(3):336–366.

Kun, Yang and Liu Cunxi. 2011. "Comparison on the ways of airworthiness management of civil aircraft design organization." *Procedia Engineering* 17:388–395.

Kwak, James. 2014. "Cultural capture and the financial crisis." In *Preventing Regulatory Capture: Special Interest Influence and How to Limit It*, eds. Daniel Carpenter and David A. Moss. Cambridge University Press, pp. 79–81.

Laffont, Jean-Jacques and Jean Tirole. 1986. "Using cost observation to regulate firms." *Journal of Political Economy* 94(3, Part 1):614–641.

1991. "The politics of government decision-making: A theory of regulatory capture." *The Quarterly Journal of Economics* 106(4):1089–1127.

1993. *A Theory of Incentives in Procurement and Regulation.* MIT press.

Lall, Ranjit. 2009. Why Basel II failed and why any Basel III is doomed. *Technical report GEG working paper.*

Lemmens, Trudo and Shannon Gibson. 2012. "The Case for Improved Post-Market Surveillance of Pharmaceuticals." *Available at SSRN 2341992.*

Levin, Richard C, Alvin K Klevorick, Richard R Nelson, Sidney G Winter, Richard Gilbert and Zvi Griliches. 1987. "Appropriating the returns from industrial research and development." *Brookings Papers on Economic Activity* 18(3):783–831.

Libgober, Brian. 2020*a*. "Meetings, comments, and the distributive politics of rulemaking." *Quarterly Journal of Political Science* 15(4):449–481.

2020*b*. "Strategic proposals, endogenous comments, and bias in rulemaking." *The Journal of Politics* 82(2):642–656.

Lyndon, Mary L. 1989. "Information economics and chemical toxicity: Designing laws to produce and use data." *Michigan Law Review* 87(7):1795–1861.

Maggi, Giovanni and Andres Rodriguez-Clare. 2007. "A political-economy theory of trade agreements." *American Economic Review* 97(4):1374–1406.

Mahoney, Christine. 2007. "Lobbying success in the United States and the European Union." *Journal of Public Policy* 27(1):35–56.

Malhotra, Neil, Benoît Monin and Michael Tomz. 2019. "Does private regulation preempt public regulation?" *American Political Science Review* 113(1): 19–37.

Mansfield, Edward D and Marc L Busch. 1995. "The political economy of nontariff barriers: a cross-national analysis." *International Organization* 49(4):723–749.

Marvel, Howard P and Edward J Ray. 1983. "The Kennedy round: Evidence on the regulation of international trade in the United States." *The American Economic Review* 73(1):190–197.

Mattli, Walter and Ngaire Woods. 2009. *The Politics of Global Regulation.* Princeton University Press.

Mattli, Walter and Tim Büthe. 2003. "Setting international standards: Technological rationality or primacy of power?" *World Politics* 56(1):1–42.

McCarty, Nolan. 2017. "The regulation and self-regulation of a complex industry." *The Journal of Politics* 79(4):1220–1236.

McCubbins, Mathew D and Thomas Schwartz. 1984. "Congressional oversight overlooked: Police patrols versus fire alarms." *American Journal of Political Science* 28(4):165–179.

McFadden, Daniel. 1975. "The revealed preferences of a government bureaucracy: Theory." *The Bell Journal of Economics* 6(2):401–416.

McGreal, Chris. 2016. "Reckitt Benckiser sued by 35 US states for 'profiteering' from opioid treatment." *The Guardian*. www.theguardian.com/business/2016/oct/21/reckitt-benckiser-drug-company-sued-suboxone-profiteering-opiod-addiction.

Meins, Erica. 2003. *Politics and Public Outrage: Explaining Transatlantic and Intra-European Diversity of Regulations on Food Irradiation and Genetically Modified Food*. Lit Verlag.

Melitz, Marc J. 2003. "The impact of trade on intra-industry reallocations and aggregate industry productivity." *Econometrica* 71(6):1695–1725.

Miyano, Sayumi. 2022. "Regime Complexity and Overlapping Information: The Case of Energy Projections." *Working paper presented at PEIO*.

Moe, Terry M. 1989. "The politics of bureaucratic structure." In *Can the Government Govern*? ed. John E. Chubb and Paul E. Peterson. The Brookings Institution, pp. 267–329.

Moehlecke, Carolina. 2020. "The chilling effect of international investment disputes: Limited challenges to state sovereignty." *International Studies Quarterly* 64(1):1–12.

Monsanto. 2016. "Annual Report: A Limitless Perspective." https://monsanto.com/app/uploads/2017/05/2016monsantoannualreport.pdf.

Moore, Thomas J, Curt D Furberg, Donald R Mattison and Michael R Cohen. 2016. "Completeness of serious adverse drug event reports received by the US Food and Drug Administration in 2014." *Pharmacoepidemiology and Drug Safety* 25(6):713–718.

National Research Council. 1986. "The airliner cabin environment: air quality and safety."

Neslen, Arthur. 2017. "Monsanto sold banned chemicals for years despite known health risks, archives reveal." *The Guardian*. www.theguardian.com/environment/2017/aug/09/monsanto-continued-selling-pcbs-for-years-despite-knowing-health-risks-archives-reveal.

New York Department of Environmental Conservation. 2015. "Active Ingredient Data Package Metalaxyl & Mefenoxam." www.dec.ny.gov/docs/materials mineralspdf/mefenoxamdata.pdf.

Nielson, Daniel L and Michael J Tierney. 2003. "Delegation to international organizations: Agency theory and World Bank environmental reform." *International Organization* 57(2):241–276.

Niles, Mark C. 2002. "On the hijacking of agencies (and airplanes): The Federal Aviation Administration, agency capture, and airline security." *American University Journal of Gender Social Policy and Law* 10(2): 381–442.

Nita, Mihaela and Dieter Scholz. 2009. "The process chain to a certified cabin design and conversion." https://reposit.haw-hamburg.de/handle/20.500.12738/3206?mode=full.

Olson, Mancur. 1965. *The logic of Collective Action*. Harvard University Press.

Oreskes, Naomi and Erik M Conway. 2011. *Merchants of Doubt: How a Handful of scientists Obscured the Truth on Issues from Tobacco Smoke to Global Warming*. Bloomsbury Publishing USA.

Osgood, Iain. 2016. "Differentiated products, divided industries: Firm preferences over trade liberalization." *Economics & Politics* 28(2):161–180.

Oye, Kenneth A and James H Maxwell. 1994. "Self-interest and environmental management." *Journal of Theoretical Politics* 6(4):593–624.

Paarlberg, Robert L. 2001. *The Politics of Precaution: Genetically Modified Crops in Developing Countries*. International Food Policy Research Institute.

Paulsrud, Bruce E. 1998. "Fungicide Registration Dilemma." *Illinois Pesticide Review*.

Peisakhin, Leonid and Paul Pinto. 2010. "Is transparency an effective anti-corruption strategy? Evidence from a field experiment in India." *Regulation & Governance* 4(3):261–280.

Pelaez, Victor, Letícia Rodrigues da Silva and Eduardo Borges Araujo. 2013. "Regulation of pesticides: A comparative analysis." *Science and Public Policy* 40(5):644–656.

Peltzman, Sam. 1976. "Toward a more general theory of regulation." *The Journal of Law and Economics* 19(2):211–240.

Perlman, Rebecca L. 2020*a*. "The domestic impact of international standards." *International Studies Quarterly* 64(3):600–608.

2020*b*. "For safety or profit? How science serves the strategic interests of private actors." *American Journal of Political Science* 64(2):293–308.

Pierson, Paul. 2004. *Politics in Time: History, Institutions, and Social Analysis*. Princeton University Press.

Posner, Richard A. 1974. "Theories of economic regulation." *The Bell Journal of Economics and Management Science* 5(2):335–358.

Ray, Edward John. 1981. "The determinants of tariff and nontariff trade restrictions in the United States." *Journal of Political Economy* 89(1):105–121.

Rich, Nathaniel. 2016. "The Lawyer Who Became DuPont's Worst Nightmare." *The New York Times*.

Rodrik, Dani. 2018. "What do trade agreements really do?" *Journal of Economic Perspectives* 32(2):73–90.

Rose-Ackerman, Susan. 1999. "Political corruption and democracy." *Connecticut Journal of International Law* 14(2):363–378.

Rosman, Lewis. 1993. "Public participation in international pesticide regulation: when the Codex Commission decides, who will listen?" *Virginia Environmental Law Journal* 12(2):329–365.

Saffer, Henry, Daniel Dench, Michael Grossman and Dhaval Dave. 2020. "E-cigarettes and adult smoking: Evidence from Minnesota." *Journal of Risk and Uncertainty* 60(3):207–228.

Sato, Suguru. 2018. "Japan Revising Domestic Pesticide Registration System." *USDA Foreign Agricultural Service, Tokyo*.

Schierow, Linda-Jo. 2008. "The toxic substances control act (TSCA): implementation and new challenges." Congressional Research Service. www.acs.org/content/dam/acsorg/policy/acsonthehill/briefings/toxicitytesting/crs-rl34118.pdf.

Schlossberg, Tatiana. 2016. "How Bad Is Your Air-Conditioner for the Planet?" *The New York Times*.

Schmutzler, Armin. 1996. "Pollution control with imperfectly observable emissions." *Environmental and Resource Economics* 7(3):251–262.

Shapira, Roy and Luigi Zingales. 2017. "Is pollution value-maximizing? The DuPont case." Technical report National Bureau of Economic Research.

Shavell, Steven. 1984*a*. "Liability for harm versus regulation of safety." *The Journal of Legal Studies* 13(2):357–374.

1984*b*. "A model of the optimal use of liability and safety regulation." *The Rand Journal of Economics* 15(2):271–280.

Siramshetty, Vishal B., Janette Nickel, Christian Omieczynski, Bjoern-Oliver Gohlke, Malgorzata N. Drwal, and Robert Preissner. 2016. "WITHDRAWN–a resource for withdrawn and discontinued drugs." *Nucleic Acids Research* 44(D1): D1080–D1086.

Sklair, Leslie. 2002. "The transnational capitalist class and global politics: Deconstructing the corporate-state connection." *International Political Science Review* 23(2):159–174.

Smythe, Elizabeth. 2009. "In whose interests? Transparency and accountability in the global governance of food: Agribusiness, the Codex Alimentarius, and the World Trade Organization." In *Corporate Power in Global Agrifood Governance*, ed. Jennifer Clapp and Doris Fuchs. MIT Press, pp. 93–124.

Sprinz, Detlef and Tapani Vaahtoranta. 1994. "The interest-based explanation of international environmental policy." *International Organization* 48(1): 77–105.

Standeven, Matthew. 2012. "The inherent uncertainty of risk assessment: How pesticide residue tolerances fall short on safety." *Journal of Health Care Law and Policy* 15(1):227–248.

Stigler, George J. 1971. "The theory of economic regulation." *The Bell Journal of Economics and Management Science* 2(1):3–21.

Stone, Randall W. 2004. "The political economy of IMF lending in Africa." *American Political Science Review* 98(4):577–591.

2008. "The scope of IMF conditionality." *International Organization* 62(4):589–620.

Sykes, Alan O. 1999. "The (limited) role of regulatory harmonization in international goods and services markets." *Journal of International Economic Law* 2(1):49–70.

Tawasha, Mary Ann. 1998. "Pesticide Supplier Sues Novartis, US EPA." *ICIS*. www.icis.com/resources/news/1998/03/18/55782/pesticide-supplier-sues-novartis-us-epa/.

Thomas, Lacy Glenn. 1988. "Revealed bureaucratic preference: Priorities of the consumer product safety commission." *The Rand Journal of Economics* 19(1):102–113.

Tirole, Jean. 1986. "Hierarchies and bureaucracies: On the role of collusion in organizations." *Journal of Law, Economics, and Organizations* 2(2): 181–214.

Trefis Team and Great Speculations. 2020. "How Airbus Has Grown Over The Years To Dethrone Boeing As The Largest Commercial Aircraft Maker." *Forbes*.

Underhill, Geoffrey RD and Xiaoke Zhang. 2008. "Setting the rules: Private power, political underpinnings, and legitimacy in global monetary and financial governance." *International Affairs* 84(3):535–554.

US Cong. House Comm. on Agriculture. 1971. "Federal Pesticide Control Act of 1971. Hearings Feb 22, 23, 24, March 1, 2, 3, 8, 9, 10, 15, 16, 17, 18, 22, 23, 24, 25."

US Cong. House Subcomm. on Department Operations, Research, and Foreign Agriculture. 1986. "Reauthorization of the Federal Insecticide, Fungicide, and Rodenticide Act. Hearings."

US Cong. House Subcomm. on Department Operations, Research, and Foreign Agriculture of the Committee on Agriculture. 1988. "Pesticide Food Safety Act of 1988."

US Cong. House Subcomm. on Environment and the Economy. 2015. "H.R. ______, The TSCA Modernization Act of 2015."

US Cong. Senate Comm. on Agriculture, Nutrition, and Forestry. 1986. "To Amend the Federal Insecticide, Fungicide, and Rodenticide Act. Hearings April 22 and 30."

US Cong. Senate Comm. on Agriculture, Nutrition, and Forestry. 1987. "Federal Insecticide, Fungicide, and Rodenticide Act. Hearings."

US Department of Agriculture. 2020. "FY 2020 Budget Summary." www.usda.gov/sites/default/files/documents/fy2020-budget-summary.pdf.

Vargesson, Neil. 2015. "Thalidomide-induced teratogenesis: History and mechanisms." *Birth Defects Research Part C: Embryo Today: Reviews* 105(2): 140–156.

Veggeland, Frode and Svein Ole Borgen. 2005. "Negotiating international food standards: The world trade organization's impact on the codex alimentarius commission." *Governance* 18(4):675–708.

Victor, David G. 2002. "WTO efforts to manage differences in national sanitary and phytosanitary policies." In *Dynamics of Regulatory Change: How Globalization Affects National Regulatory Policies*, ed. David Vogel and Robert A Kagan. University of California Press, pp. 227–268.

Viscusi, W Kip. 1989. "Toward a diminished role for tort liability: social insurance, government regulation, and contemporary risks to health and safety." *Yale Journal on Regulation* 6(1):65–107.

Vogel, David. 2012. *The Politics of Precaution*: Regulating Health, Safety, and Environmental Risks in Europe and the United States. Princeton University Press.

Vreeland, James Raymond and Axel Dreher. 2014. *The Political Economy of the United Nations Security Council: Money and Influence*. Cambridge University Press.

Wagner, Wendy E. 1995. "The science charade in toxic risk regulation." *Columbia Law Review* 95(7):1613–1723.

2003. "Commons ignorance: The failure of environmental law to produce needed information on health and the environment." *Duke Law Journal* 53(6):1619–1745.

Watkins, Karen. 2002. "Company Sues EPA Over Pesticide: Syngenta seeks to block registration of racemic metolachlor." *CENEAR* 80(11):10.

Wilson, James Q. 2019. *Bureaucracy: What Government Agencies Do and Why They Do It.* Hachette UK.

Wilson, John S and Tsunehiro Otsuki. 2004. "To spray or not to spray: Pesticides, banana exports, and food safety." *Food Policy* 29(2):131–146.

Wood, Donna J. 1985. "The strategic use of public policy: Business support for the 1906 Food and Drug Act." *Business History Review* 59(3):403–432.

World Health Organization. 1997. "The WHO Recommended Classification of Pesticides by Hazard." *International Programme on Chemical Safety.*

2000. "Tobacco company strategies to undermine tobacco control activities at the World Health Organization: Report of the committee of experts on tobacco industry documents."

2009. "The WHO Recommended Classification of Pesticides by Hazard." *International Programme on Chemical Safety.*

World Organization for Animal Health (OIE). 2021. "What we do." www.oie.int/en/what-we-do/.

World Trade Organization. 1995*a*. "Agreement on Technical Barriers to Trade."

1995*b*. "The WTO Agreement on the Application of Sanitary and Phytosanitary Measures (SPS Agreement)."

2015. "International Trade Statistics." www.wto.org/english/rese/statise/its2015e/its2015e.pdf.

2020*a*. "Chronological list of disputes cases." www.wto.org/english/tratope/dispue/dispustatuse.htm.

2020*b*. "Sanitary and Phytosanitary Information Management System." http://spsims.wto.org/.

Wouters, Olivier J, Martin McKee and Jeroen Luyten. 2020. "Estimated research and development investment needed to bring a new medicine to market, 2009–2018." *JAMA* 323(9):844–853.

Index

Printed in the USA
CPSIA information can be obtained
at www.ICGtesting.com
LVHW040735170124
769162LV00004B/16

9 781009 291927